Penguin Education
Whose City?
R. E. Pahl

R. E. Pahl was educated at St Catharine's College,
Cambridge, and the London School of Economics. He is
now a professor of sociology at the University of Kent at
Canterbury and is the author of a number of books and
articles on urban sociology. He was an assessor to the
Panel of Inquiry into the Greater London Development
Plan and has contributed to seminars and conferences in
most Eastern and Western European countries and in
Australia and Canada.

R. E. Pahl

Whose City?

And further essays
on urban society

 Penguin Books

Penguin Books Ltd,
Harmondsworth, Middlesex, England
Penguin Books Inc.,
7110 Ambassador Road, Baltimore, Maryland 21207, USA
Penguin Books Australia Ltd,
Ringwood, Victoria, Australia
Penguin Books Canada Ltd,
41 Steelcase Road West, Markham, Ontario, Canada
Penguin Books (NZ) Ltd,
182–190 Wairau Road, Auckland 10, New Zealand

First published by Longman 1970
Published by Penguin Books 1975
Copyright © R. E. Pahl, 1965, 1966, 1967, 1968, 1969, 1970,
1971, 1974, 1975
'Private residential expansion in Kent' copyright
© Edward Craven, 1969

Made and printed in Great Britain by
Hazell Watson & Viney Ltd,
Aylesbury, Bucks
Set in Monotype Times

For Jan

Contents

List of diagrams

Sources of the papers

Chapter 14 Prepared for the Anglo-German Conference on Urban Change held at the Centre for Environmental Studies, April 1973. Published in the conference report, *Management of Urban Change in Britain and Germany*, edited by Richard Rose, Sage, 1974

Acknowledgements

We are grateful to the following for permission to reproduce copyright material: W. Heffer & Sons Ltd for 'Newcomers in Town and Country' by R. E. Pahl from *East Anglian Studies*, edited by L. M. Munby; IPC Magazines Ltd for 'Whose City?' by R. E. Pahl, from *New Society*, 23 January 1969; the Town Planning Institute for 'Residential expansion: The role of the private developer in the South-East' by R. E. Pahl and Edward Craven from the *Journal of the Town Planning Institute*, April 1967; Architecture and Planning Publications Ltd for 'The social objectives of village planning' by R. E. Pahl from *Official Architecture and Planning*; European Society for Rural Sociology for 'Class and community in English commuter villages' by R. E. Pahl from *Sociologia Ruralis*, 1965; the proprietors of *Urban Studies* and author for 'Private residential expansion in Kent' by Edward Craven from *Urban Studies*, February 1969; Cambridge University Press for 'Poverty and the urban system' by R. E. Pahl from *Spatial Policy Problems of the British Economy*, edited by Michael Chisholm and Gerald Manners; Sage Publications Ltd for 'Social processes and urban change' by R. E. Pahl from *Management of Urban Change in Britain and Germany*, edited by Richard Rose.

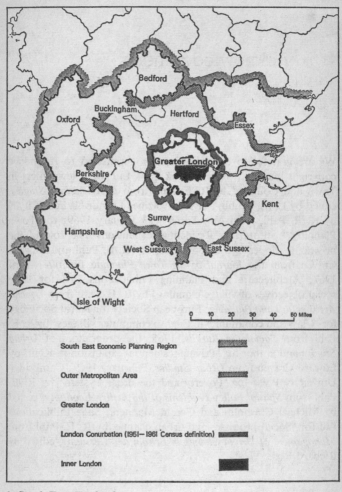

1. South-East England.

Introduction to the second edition

The opportunity presented by my publishers to bring out a new edition of my essays enables me to replace material which has become more dated and less relevant with four more recent essays. These now appear as Chapters 8, 12, 13 and 14; I have also rewritten the Epilogue. Similarly, the Introduction to the first edition no longer reflects my present interests and concerns and does not justify inclusion here.

During the five years which have elapsed since I wrote the first introduction, some of the rhetorical questions which I posed have been answered. These have been the years of 'asset-stripping', of rapid inflation, of the shift of major institutional investors and merchant banks into land and property, of dramatic increases in the price of housing and the rates of interest, of empty Centre Point in London, and of widespread discussion of these and other matters in the mass media. One does not have to be very astute now in order to answer the question 'Whose City?': quite evidently the capitalists own British cities and up to 1973 they grew fat on their rents and the revaluations of their portfolios. From the Church Commissioners to the trade unions, property and property bonds provided one of the few ways of ensuring that the capital to pay parsons or to provide pensions for workers did not melt away. The more dependent on property such investors become, the more they have a vested interest in the very inflation that ensures the continuing increase in property values. The ambiguities and contradictions of finance capitalism are evident to all those who are buying their homes, trying to save, or having their rent raised to what is called a 'fair rent level'. Even the most unresearched television documentary on

this subject included some startling statistics on, say, the proportion of the cost of local authority housing that had to be paid back
as interest on borrowed money, or the substantial capital gains that
were made from land and property in a very short time. In a
curious way the traditional picture of the dynamic central
business district of a city, once seen as symbolic of a modern,
successful society, was taken to be a symbol of the 'unacceptable
face of capitalism', in the phrase of a Conservative prime minister.
This change in meaning from 'success' to 'failure' of the same
symbol was astonishing. Admittedly the 'casual empiricism'
which prompts such statements may have led me astray: it is very
difficult to make firm scholarly statements about the change in
national mood between 1969 and 1974. However, I doubt if many
would dispute that the nakedness and transparency of capitalist
enterprise in land and property had alarmed Conservatives and
roused radicals.

Similarly, the question 'Is the mobile society a myth?' has also
been answered. With petrol rationing in many West European
countries and with frequent industrial action disrupting the
railways, those who can walk or cycle to work do not have to be
persuaded of their advantage. The excellent PEP Broadsheet on
Personal Mobility and Transport Policy provides the detailed
documentation to show how clearly the mobile society is not
only a myth but a dangerous one. The more it was believed that
people were 'mobile', the more most people suffered. As the
PEP study reminds us, 'less than one third of the adult population
have the optional use of a car'.[1] My polemic on the myth of a
mobile society in the earlier edition has little justification to be
published in the mid 1970s.

Finally, it has also passed into the conventional wisdom in
planning circles that land-use allocations do affect real incomes
and that planning is a political exercise in determining the
allocation of who gets the 'urban goodies'.[2] At a time when
planning officers may be getting a little disillusioned about their
capacity to be effective under the new planning legislation, it is
no doubt agreeable to them to be reassured that their decisions
have important effects. So perhaps the urban sociologist can bow
out, now that geographers, economists, social administrators and

other executives of the urban research industry are busily devising appropriate ways of measuring the redistribution of real income in urban areas through the provision of various facilities and resources. True, there are a multitude of detailed studies still to be done to show that more sensitivity and more resources would enable a 'better' and more humane service to be given in particular contexts. Also, the same lessons must be passed on to each new generation of students and so the continued repetition of arguments and the replication of studies is still needed. Judging from the work of such sociologists as Sean Damer, Jon Davies, Norman Dennis, John Lambert, Peter Norman and John Rex, to take the first half-dozen names that come to mind, it is more likely to be the sociologists who show 'who gets the goodies' and 'who decides who gets the goodies'. However, one should also acknowledge the work of the geographer, David Harvey, whose attempt to generate a paradigmatic shift in urban analysis will probably succeed after some years of conceptual confusion and unproductive debate.[3]

However, if all student planners learn in their first few weeks that 'urban' problems are a product of the capitalist mode of production, that most people have severe limitations on their personal mobility and that, whilst planners could have the power to reallocate real income, it is unlikely that, on balance, they have been able to effect any marked redistribution towards the poor – and, indeed, may have been responsible for the reverse – then their disillusion and cynicism may be great. It is unlikely that sociologists will be thanked for making that clear. The growth of some sociological awareness in the planning profession may indeed make it *more* difficult to plan. Once, for example, it appeared that everyone 'knew' about the problems associated with social polarization and social mix. Then some careful analysis was done and no one was sure any more.[4]

Those in central and local government who sponsor research may well be feeling cheated and irritated. They were urged to find out more about the urban system before they fiddled about with it and perhaps created undesirable and unintended consequences. So funds were made available to set up the Centre for Environmental Studies (CES) to produce large, government-sponsored regional planning studies and to support the Greater London Development Plan (GLDP) Inquiry for two years, as well as to support a host of other research projects in government departments, universities and research institutes. Yet when the CES helped to map the limits of our knowledge and the Report of the Panel of Inquiry into the GLDP helped to show the limits of planners' powers, no one responsible for determining policy was made particularly happy.

Government departments are loath to acknowledge that the positivist assumptions of social science research must be questioned. It is one thing to sponsor a research programme into a specific social problem area which is particularly intractable; it is quite another to acknowledge that the problem area is a product of a situation where the majority feel moderately well-off and do not feel much concern to redistribute their modest level of affluence to the poor. Government departments *have* to assume that solutions can be found within the economic and political system broadly as it is. The simple facts of our geographical situation impose constraints which cannot be ignored. Densely populated islands, heavily dependent on external sources of food, finance and energy cannot afford a 'socialist revolution' *and* very soon afterwards create good cities for the people. From what I have seen and read, other parts of the world and other political systems are not noticeably more successful than we are in creating humane cities. Problems still seem to exist in Stockholm, Paris and Havana; whether these are more or less serious than ours is extremely difficult to determine. For example, it might be more difficult to achieve *equality* in access to urban resources and facilities than to achieve an efficient use of limited resources and facilities. The demand for both justice and efficiency may be too much.

Living in a capitalist society, which is linked with other capitalist societies in the European Economic Community, we are obliged to consider not only what is desirable but also what is possible by way of planned intervention into various markets and systems of allocation. Redistribution is more expensive if it has to be pursued against the self-interest of the majority. Leadership groups are unlikely to give up voluntarily their power and advantage, although small concessions may be made. And even with the possibility of an agreed and voluntary incomes policy, there would still be conflicts and new lines of inequality as the relative positions of occupational groups fluctuated through the operation of manifest or latent market mechanisms. Positivistic research in the social sciences is essentially a means of providing 'facts' for interest groups. The government or the local authority sponsor research to justify the policies which they later pursue; minority groups use other 'research' to justify their opposition to given policies. It was evident to me, as an assessor to the Panel of Inquiry into the Greater London Development Plan, that experts could readily be hired to support almost any position with appropriate research and documentation.

Research for policy-making and practical action is inevitably conducted in a political context. If research is to be 'useful' it must relate to the art of the possible. 'Pure' research on, say, territorial justice, which involves the abolition of central places or postulates a complete knowledge of subjective needs by those allocating resources is unlikely to have practical policy implications or even to lead to a 'revolution'.

'Revolutions' are essentially about the redistribution of power and advantage and the creation of new values and forms of consciousness. They may be industrial, technological or political; they may be gradual or they may be very sudden. They certainly do not always produce the results early enthusiasts may have expected. Certainly, to achieve many of the goals of those who usher in the new order, a more altruistic or socially responsive human nature must be postulated: without this there is likely to be replacement of one sort of system of inequality by another. Maintaining commitment and revolutionary fervour is easier said than done.[5]

This all leads to the dilemma felt by those who work within the present system and who seek rapid social and economic change based on a radical redistribution of resources. Research and policy-making within the framework of the *status quo* is unsatisfactory – providing new ways of wiping up the drips from a leaky tap. However, the introduction of a new system of plumbing is likely to produce different sorts of defects and different taps: *and there will still be taps*.

It seems to me that we have now reached a stage where the

type of plumbing system is seen by many to be the question at issue. Students appear less ready to rest content with ways of turning taps and stopping leaks. The reason for the apparent failure of our planners and researchers is that *they so often appear to have assumed an independent urban system*, which could be managed, researched and altered. However, it is no longer possible to consider 'urban' problems and 'urban' studies separately from the political economy of the society as a whole.

Thus, it will no longer do for student planners to learn a little 'urban sociology' or 'urban economics' as specialist tools with which they can the better manipulate an independent and controllable 'urban system'. Rather they should, perhaps, be given some understanding of the nature of British capitalism and how it is changing. They will need conceptual tools with which they can rigorously analyse the political economy of the advanced societies. I am, of course, using the term 'planner' in a somewhat broader sense than simply town-planner. Rather, I am referring to all those to whom I have referred in one of my earlier essays as the 'social gatekeepers who help to distribute and control urban resources'.[6] If such planners see the broader context within which their more limited intervention takes place they may at least be prepared to live with their ambiguous position more readily. Clearly many will find this unsatisfactory.

I recognize that over the years I have shifted positions: to begin with I was anxious to emphasize the constraints which exist in localities, particularly as these impinge on disadvantaged groups and categories. This led to the familiar trap of seeming to knock the middle dog whilst championing the underdog, for which I was chided quite sternly by Professor Broady.[7] (It so happened that I also wrote about the middle dogs at about the same time but then appeared to be sympathetic towards them too which, in turn, provoked the scorn and disapproval of Professor Frankenberg.[8] I am now completing some research on the top dogs . . .[9]) However, I would not now want to emphasize locality-based constraints quite so strongly. I am more impressed by the way broader flows of investment and other matters at a national and international level do so much to make our cities what they are. Indeed, as I argue in Chapter 13, I see a danger in limiting the attention of 'urban' sociology and in risking falling into the managerialist heresy. It is not without significance that my main research in the period since I wrote the introduction to the first edition of *Whose City?* has been on managers and directors in British industry. This has perhaps helped me to see more clearly matters which a narrower focus on 'urban' questions blurs.

Courses for planners in the future might include rather less on the micro-analysis of urban renewal and local patterns of social relationships and rather more on rents, incomes, interest rates and labour markets. When *the constraints on planners* are given as much weight as the constraints on the poor, there may be more pressure for change put on the main leadership groups. So long as planners were led to believe that they had the power to affect people's life chances in a fundamental way, so long would they not wish to make radical changes in their training and position in society, confident that they had the wisdom and humanity to plan well. However, once planners – again defined in the broadest sense – start suspecting that they are the bailiffs and estate managers of capitalism, with very little power to affect in a fundamental way job markets, housing markets and incomes, then they may begin to explore policies and programmes of a more radical nature. By this I mean taking initiatives in exploring the possibilities for, and constraints against, creating more territorial and social justice. I fear that if planners do not grasp these larger questions they will find themselves reduced to being mere technicians, tidying up the urban scene and approving the changes in land use that bring profit to others. Only by making it quite clear what they cannot do and why they cannot do it will the planning profession as a whole regain the credibility it has lost. Until such time as the community gets its fair proportion of the land value which the community itself has created, urban planning will remain an ineffectual means for creating a fairer society. And, further, until land-use allocations are coupled with real controls over the nature and scale of local employment markets, the territorial distribution of the forces of production will remain unplanned, generating new and unintended inequalities. The purpose of planning is to create a more convenient, humane and satisfactory environment in a context which is moving towards greater social and territorial justice.

If, however, that purpose is effectively frustrated by the workings of finance capitalism, which shifts resources through land and property markets solely to get the maximum return on investment rather than for any social benefit, then planners will be frustrated. This is not necessarily an unusual situation in our society. All those who do their jobs less well than they would like to, because of the system within which they work, and who understand that this is so, are likely to be dissatisfied. Yet the more such professions recruit social science graduates, with their aspirations for achieving change, the less easy it is for such professions to keep them in their role as technicians serving the interests of finance capitalism. Of course it will be in the self-interest of such professions to make pompous statements of their importance within the *status quo* in order to maintain their market position in relation to other groups. Yet, quite evidently, the control of the value and use of urban land is far too valuable an asset in advanced urbanized societies to be left totally in the hands of a professional group. Inevitably urban land, as a scarce resource, will be owned and controlled by a private or state monopoly. I would think it unlikely that large financial enterprises can continue to accumulate vast capital gains in the way they have done in recent years: the state is sure to take over the ownership and control of urban land eventually for the same reason that it owns the coal industry or the Bank of England. Under such circumstances there would be a renewed focus on the twin concepts of allocation and accessibility. The mechanisms of distribution might become more opaque and hidden markets would gain greater salience. This retreat from allocation according to overt market mechanisms is likely to be paralleled by a greater public concern with matters of *distribution*, which is clearly taking the place of growth as a common focus of political concern. The problem is increasingly a matter of 'how much of the cake and for whom?' rather than a matter of measures to increase the size of the cake. The smaller the cake, the more important do matters of distribution become. And similarly the more that the part of the cake which is allocated under the terms of a voluntary or statutory incomes policy cannot be altered, so other sources of indirect wages increase in importance. If the wages of a machine-tool operator or a plasterer are similar wherever he works, but if nevertheless the real conditions of life vary substantially for himself, his wife and his children, depending on the part of the country in which he lives, then he will either move to a better area (change his accessibility) or improve his own area's system of allocation so that it compares more favourably with elsewhere. And even then, as I argue in Chapter 14 below, territorial inequality will continue to be inevitable.

This inevitability of territorial inequality forces us back to pragmatism and ameliorism. Given functional differentiation and specialization in work, centralization and the friction of space must produce differential access to urban resources and facilities leading to territorial inequality. The role of the state is, of course, crucial: universalistic provision of a public good in the name of equality will not be equitable given the uneven distribution of that society on the ground. The spatial component of reward-distributing systems poses severe political problems and may give rise to internal conflict and tension in societies committed to greater equality.

I now see an important area of study concerned with space as both a cause and also a reflection, both of patterns of *allocation* of given services and facilities, and also of patterns of *access* to these same services and facilities. These patterns or 'structures' of allocation and accessibility will take different forms depending on the particular social structure or political arrangements of the society in question. Clearly, the meaning and importance of space will vary greatly, depending on the empirical context: in the case of a society's policy towards personal mobility and public transport, space would be central; for the policy on family allowances, spatial arrangements may have very little significance. The process of location may be related to the social structure in different ways. Not all 'allocative structures' or reward-distributing systems have spatial elements in them and access cannot always be improved by physical mobility. The *degree* to which space is important in a given distributive system is a matter for empirical investigation. Different societies may have different solutions to similar problems of distribution. In later chapters of this book I tend to use the word 'city' as shorthand for 'a given context or configuration of reward-distributing systems which have space as a significant component'. Thus housing and transportation are elements in my view of a city, family allowances and pension schemes are not. An *urban* resource or facility must have a spatial component.

There are few guidelines for those who believe in radical strategies for social change with regard to the future spatial form of a society. The concern by Marx and Engels to break down the distinctions between town and country cannot be achieved in practice so long as the different settlement forms exist. Capitalism may one day give way to 'socialism' in an advanced industrial society but the city as a spatial and social form will no doubt continue. In these circumstances it would then be clearer that urban processes are not *all* created by economic processes: the relative autonomy of spatial forms and their effect on distributive systems would be made more explicit. There does not appear to be a socialist spatial form which may be contrasted with a capitalist spatial form in ideal-typical terms. Rather, there are forms which make it more or less easy to make indirect wages redistributive. Hence my view that urban social theory, at its present stage of development, provides no choice in terms of policy and practice: there is no alternative to ameliorism in spatial redistributive systems. Even if all those who turn the taps of urban resources were concerned to redistribute with the goal of achieving a more equal society, they could not all be certain that their *collective* activities would achieve that end. Those who argue otherwise must have a faith in the perfectibility of societal planning and in the possibility of infinite knowledge and social consensus. In the same way that productive enterprises under socialism would presumably still have the goal of producing goods at the smallest unit cost, so socialist cities might develop some concept of 'optimal access'. Yet it is this concept which I find hard to grasp in physical terms.[10] Certainly, I would think that the imposition by the state of common standards is not possible in a society where people have different incomes: the most that could be hoped for would be the imposition of certain minimal standards of provision. The setting of such standards is highly complex and contentious. There would probably be conflict between those responsible for different sectors or types of provision, each wanting to raise its own 'minimum standards' even higher, at the expense of someone else's minimum level. There may even be reluctance from certain categories of the population to conform to the nationally determined minimum standard. What are the limits of state intervention in compulsorily insisting that its citizens have minimum levels of education, housing and so forth? Should there be compulsory physical exercise in the interests of preventive medicine? Can different cities be allowed to have different levels of access for given facilities? How much local autonomy is permissible in the interests of equality? The tension between the centre and the periphery, which exists in all societies, can become particularly acute under socialism. Centralization is necessary for equality; decentralization is necessary for self-management. This clash of principles may be reflected if not reinforced by spatial forms. It is not clear whether self-management involves the right to refuse to have certain standards imposed by the centre. Do people have the right to lower standards than the national minimum if they want them? In a specific area such as land-use planning, can the same planning rationally operate whether or not there is a land market? How are the 'best sites' to be allocated?

The combined experience of learning a great deal about planning in London and also knowing something of the problems and experience of the command economies of Eastern Europe has helped to make me cautious and more prepared to live with ambiguity. The resolution of conflicts between basic principles, such as that between efficiency and territorial justice, are bound to be messy. The description and analysis of hidden mechanisms of redistribution in putative non-market situations is bound to cause distress and confusion to powerful policy-makers. The sociologists' lot is likely to be increasingly an unhappy one with increasing state control of markets. The more coordinated and central planning is expanded, the greater the opportunity for larger errors and the greater the disinclination to have such errors pointed out by sociologists. The command economies' and peoples' republics' use of sociologists to analyse the unintended consequences of and popular responses to political actions is not encouraging. If urban sociologists are prepared to continue to show that cities and equality are incompatible they must be prepared to be unpopular. Any young recruit to the urban research industry would do better to do his training in law or economics if he wants to be popular. Accounting would probably be an even better bet. All of which makes me personally believe that the need for sociology as a means of demystifying the urban social processes of allocation and accessibility has never been greater.

REFERENCES

1 Hillman, M., with Henderson, I., and Whalley, A., *Personal Mobility and Transport Policy*, PEP Broadsheet 542, 1973.

2 See Donnison, D., and others, 'Observations on the Greater London Development Plan', *Problems of an Urban Society*, Vol. III, Ch. 3, Cullingworth, J. B. (ed.), Allen & Unwin, 1973.

3 Harvey, D., *Social Justice and the City*, Arnold, 1973.

4 Harris, M., 'Some aspects of social polarization', *London: Urban Patterns, Problems and Policies*, Donnison, D., and Eversley, D., (eds.), Heinemann, 1973.

5 Kanter, R. M., *Commitment and Community*, Oxford University Press, 1973; Whyte, M. K., 'Bureaucracy and modernization in China: The Maoist critique', *American Sociological Review*, 1973, 149–63.

6 In my essay 'Urban social theory and research' in *Environment and Planning*, 1, 1969, 146. Reprinted below as Chapter 10.

7 Broady, M., unpublished paper presented to the conference of the British Sociological Association, Teachers' Section, at Leeds, September 1972.

8 Frankenberg, R., 'An awful warning to managerial socialists', review of *Managers and their Wives* (Pahl, J. M. and R. E., Allen Lane The Penguin Press, 1971) in *Morning Star*, September 1971.

9 See the preliminary statement on 'Economic Élites: Theory and

practice' by Pahl, R. E., and Winkler, J. T., in *Élites and Power*, Stanworth, P., and Giddens, A. (eds.), Cambridge University Press, 1974. A more detailed account will be given in the authors' forthcoming book.

10 See below in Chapter 14, pp. 296-9.

Part 1 Newcomers in town and country

Introduction

The essays in this part are largely based on empirical research done in Hertfordshire between 1960 and 1965. They reflect a concern with the social effects of growth and expansion in 'rural' pressure areas adjoining a major metropolis. Chapter 1 is concerned with change within the village, as the result of the arrival of a new professional–managerial element without the 'buffer' of intermediate strata between them and the existing, mainly working-class, village population. Some of the implications of this and other work on Hertfordshire villages are brought together in Chapter 2, having in mind the particular concerns of those responsible for planning villages. Chapter 3 provides three vignettes of different social situations, based on material gathered through adult classes in the places concerned. Much of the material was gathered by the students themselves and suffers certain limitations on that account. However, given the remarkable dearth of information on the social categories which appear in this essay, it seems that even a short step from casual empiricism is worth making and recording. Finally, in this part, Chapter 4 is more broadly based; here I attempt to sketch some of the sociological consequences of a dispersed settlement pattern and I discuss the point that the significance of the settlement pattern will vary not only for different social groups within a society but also between societies. The emphasis is, however, on locality-based constraints and the arguments have relevance in contexts where planners are concerned about the dangers of under-urbanization and over-urbanization. I suspect that my discussion of the impact of economic growth and change on locality-based patterns of social relationships will continue to have relevance in specific locations such as those parts of Scotland and the east coast of England affected by newcomers connected with North Sea oil.

Chapter 1 Class and community in English commuter villages

Sociologists and planners have recently been warned by Constandse that the mentally urbanized, but physically rural, parts of the countryside may not receive the investigation, within the necessarily distinctive theoretical framework, which they merit.[1] Certainly in Britain there has been some danger that concentration on the specifically *rural* village will lead to the neglect of the rapidly changing villages within easy commuting distance of urban employment. Postwar socio-anthropological studies such as those by Rees[2] and Williams[3] had a strong bias towards the analysis of the traditional aspects of community life. Even in the latter author's more recent study it appeared 'essential that the community should be *rural*, that is based on an agricultural economy'.[4] Hence the *urban* nature of rural areas, particularly in parts of South-East England, the West Midlands and Cheshire, has been inadequately covered and the published literature is slight. Workers in rural demography, such as Saville[5] and Vince,[6] have urged that more field surveys should be undertaken in areas which have an increasing tertiary or adventitious population, but we have had to be content with studies from what the planners would call 'non-pressure areas'.

A further line of approach to the study of changing rural areas, typified by the work of Dickinson[7] and Bracey,[8] stressed the 'service factor' and attempted to apportion rural communities to their respective urban hinterlands. However, a description of where individuals of a given community might go for certain services and functions does not do much to provide insight into the nature and social structure of that community. It may also be supposed that 'urban influences' decline from the centre to the edges of a town's hinterland; this gradient hypothesis has been adduced by Martin[9] in the USA. It would be dangerous to accept this theory too readily for England.

Perhaps the most useful theoretical approach to urbanized rural areas has been developed in America in the literature concerned with what we may loosely call the rural–urban fringe. Much of this work has been brought together by Wissink,[10] who, although a social geographer, nevertheless adopts a particularly sociological viewpoint. With the city as the agent of change he sees the rural–urban fringe as an area of consistent heterogeneity with no gradient of density of development.

The landscape may be completely rural and yet there may be a wide variety of changing community structures which it is still too early to classify. The *meaningful* location of such communities is changing, so that the attitude to the crossing of space is changing within the different social groups who live there. This move from functional to more sociological criteria in determining urban influences or degree of urbanization means that a village may be best understood as 'a state of mind'. As 'rural' people acquire an urban outlook and 'urban' people try to escape from the physical urban world into an arcadian vision of a 'rural' area, then perhaps, in a culturally urbanized nation, those who are truly village people are those who have defined themselves in their own minds as villagers and act as they suppose villagers should act.

For the past few years I have been analysing the rural areas of Hertfordshire, a county to the north of the Greater London conurbation, but lying entirely within the metropolitan region. This larger region has been described in a recent government report as follows:

It contains 70 per cent of the population of the South East of England and has had 75 per cent of the employment increase over the last seven years. $4\frac{1}{4}$ million people live in the outer metropolitan region (that is to say, the metropolitan region less the conurbation). This is a crucial part of the South East. It contains a good deal of the area's growing industries and population. It also contains nearly all of the existing metropolitan green-belt extensions proposed by the planning authorities, as well as the first generation of new towns for London. It is in this ring that most London commuters will have to look for homes.[11]

It is not possible here to go into the full implications of the South-East Study for the villages of the area, but experience in Hertfordshire provides some guide for the future. The population of the county as a whole increased by 222,126 or 36·6 per cent, from 1951 to 1961 and nearly a third of this increase took place in areas administratively designated Rural Districts. This overall view masks depopulation at one extreme and the construction of a New Town in part of one Rural District at the other. Not only has population increased, but so has employment in the towns, particularly in the factories manufacturing engineering and electrical goods and vehicles. There have consistently been more jobs on offer than workers unemployed, even though the number employed in agriculture declined by some 5,000, well above the national average proportion, during the decade. Hence the rural areas have become more dormitory in character. Labour has been drawn out of the villages, often collected by the private bus of the firm, and at the same time a new mobile population has been attracted into the villages. This latter group may be either 'pushed' into remoter rural areas, owing to the difficulty of finding a house at a suitable price in or near a town, or 'pulled' by the superior status value of rural living. This is an over-simplified account to which we shall return later.

CASE STUDIES IN HERTFORDSHIRE

Within this context of rural areas in the process of planned and unplanned change a more detailed survey was undertaken. A number of considerations were involved in the choice of villages. It was important to avoid areas which were immediately contiguous to urban areas and were thus simply extensions of the urban area, yet it was necessary to choose an area where the speed of change had been rapid enough for the effects to be apparent and significant and where the processes of current changes could be observed. Hence an area with a high proportion of recent immigrants was required. Further, it was hoped that it would be possible to assess the importance of accessibility to main lines of communication as a factor inducing change.

Finally, it was hoped to include within the sample sufficient postwar local authority and privately built houses in order to give balanced proportions of newcomers of different social groups.

A full analysis of rural Hertfordshire and a detailed discussion on the choice of parishes has been made elsewhere.[12] Two neighbouring parishes, one with a postwar estate of 75 local authority houses out of 268 dwellings, and the other with 100 postwar privately built houses out of a total of 342 dwellings, both lying within the triangle formed by a garden city, a New Town and the county town, were eventually selected. Since these two parishes were under such very great pressure to change, a third, seemingly more rural, village was selected as a sort of control, in which there had been negligible postwar development. The initial assumption, therefore, was that the mobile newcomers would be the agents of change in the more-enclosed, traditionalist, hierarchical rural society. It might be possible to measure the differences between the more-established village people, who have now become commuters to jobs in the expanding industries of the surrounding towns, and the newcomer commuters, who use the village simply as a suburb in the country some minutes' driving time from their place of work, and to compare their places in the village social structure. The change in their 'state of mind' was therefore assumed to take place from contacts with the outside world – the shops and factories of the nearby towns. It should be stressed that all the area discussed here is in protected 'green-belt' land and physically it is a fairly prosperous mixed-farming area.

Some attempt to compare and contrast these three villages is made below in chapter 3 (pp. 78–82). The social history of the previous fifty years together with, in the case of two of the villages, the attitudes and policy of the squire, are more important factors in accounting for many of the villages' present characteristics than simply accessibility to nearby towns. The essential theme to be presented here is that it is *class*, rather than *commuting* characteristics alone, which is the most important factor in promoting change in the social structure of villages in the rural–urban fringe of metropolitan regions.

THE PROCESS OF POLARIZATION

In order to bring out more clearly the social characteristics of the two adjoining parishes in central Hertfordshire, their populations were combined. A 50 per cent sample survey of the households, using a comprehensive questionnaire, was carried out in the spring of 1961 and the head of each household was classified according to a scale derived from the Registrar General's *Classification of Occupations 1960*. Agricultural workers were classified separately. It was found that the other socio-economic groups tended to polarize between the non-agricultural manual workers on the one hand and the professional and intermediate non-manual workers on the other. There were proportionately fewer of the occupational groups between these extremes, since to *buy* a house in the country, added to the extra expense of rural living, is an economic burden only the relatively affluent can afford. On the other hand, the local working class are subsidized in their continued residence in the rural area through the provision of rented local authority housing, for which local people have priority. Small local tradesmen were classified with the non-manual class and thus it was relatively easy to apportion all heads of households into groups which, for convenience, have been termed middle and working class. The following table (I) shows

TABLE I Social class and commuting characteristics of the population of two adjoining parishes in central Hertfordshire

Head of Household	Place of Work	Total	Percentage of Sample
Middle class	London	38	14
	Near-by town	59	22
	In parish or adjacent rural parish	20	8
Working class	Near-by town	56	21
	In parish or adjacent rural parish	34	13
Agricultural worker	In parish	28	11
No information, retired etc.		29	11
		264	100

clearly the importance of commuting in both classes, but particularly in the middle class, which, if one excluded local tradesmen, would be composed almost entirely of commuters. It should be remembered that both parishes are over twenty miles from the centre of London.

The influence of the middle class is a relatively recent phenomenon, 81 per cent having arrived in the period 1945–61, compared with 29 per cent among the working class. As would be expected it is the middle-class commuters who are overwhelmingly newcomers. In the working class, however, the chief earners are more likely to have been born in the parish or at least to have been established in the parish before 1945 whether they commute or not, as the following table shows.

TABLE II   Proportion of working-class chief earners who moved into the parishes before and after 1945

Working-Class Chief Earner	Percentage 'Established'	'Newcomer'	Total Nos (100 per cent)
Commuter	75	25	56
Non-commuter	65	35	34

It is also significant that nearly a half of the agricultural workers are also newcomers. The total of 147 newcomer households arriving since 1946 is made up as follows.

TABLE III   Characteristics of all chief earners who have moved into the parishes since 1945

Period of Arrival in Parish	Total = 100 per cent	Percentage Middle-Class Chief Earner Commuter	Non-commuter	Percentage Working-Class Chief Earner Commuter	Non-commuter	Agricultural Workers, No Information etc.
1946–56	80	55	6	11	9	19
1957–61	67	62	6	7	7	18
	147					

In the previous five years, then, at least two thirds of the sixty-seven incoming families have been middle class and most of the chief earners have been commuters. Surprisingly perhaps, the most stable group is the non-agricultural working class, many of whom started their lives in agriculture and, while taking up more-highly-paid employment in the towns, have continued to live in the villages.

Of crucial importance when considering the links with the outside world is the degree to which households have their own form of private transport. About a half of all working-class families has neither a car nor a motor-cycle and this situation did not seem to be related to the commuting characteristics of the chief earner. However, most middle-class families had at least one car and over a quarter had two. The proportion of working-class families with one car was about the same as the proportion of middle-class families with two. Over 90 per cent of the middle-class commuters leave for work each morning by car; those travelling to near-by towns generally go all the way by car, but half of the London commuters only use the car to get to the station. The working-class commuters are much more dependent on the inadequate bus service or pedal cycles, yet the battered second-hand car is becoming an increasingly common sight, parked on the verges by the local authority estate or at infrequently used entrances to fields.

It might be expected that there would be some relation between the town used for shopping and similar services and the place of work, irrespective of class. This was not found to be so. The shopping places for various commodities were analysed and the differences between the working-class commuters and non-commuters appeared slight, while agricultural workers and their wives appeared the least mobile. The middle-class wives ranged widely, unlike the working-class wives who almost without exception could not drive themselves and were limited to the towns served by the local bus. There was some indication that those working-class families which did not have the economic burden of commuting or running a car were able, on occasions, to make the special effort to travel up to London for shopping or entertainment. However, this could also be seen as the result of a more determined demand for novelty and change by those in the more restricted circumstances.

Thus in their relations with the outside world the middle-class and working-class villagers moved in separate worlds. This may simply be a reflection of the basic economic differential between the two broad groups but the purpose of the survey was to analyse *all* social and economic links with the outside world and it did appear that the two broad groups had different social and cultural norms.

The world of the working class was as enclosed and traditional as in any village in the more remote rural areas. The village social structure has remained remarkably unaffected by the development of working-class commuting; other independent research substantiates this point.[13] The policy of building subsidized, rented housing for the working class in the villages has ensured the continuity of kinship links and social networks. Parents and siblings were frequently visited but formal entertaining was slight. It is considered to be an unwarranted intrusion of a family's privacy for casual friends to enter working-class homes, whereas for the middle class such visits enabled them to display the items characteristic of 'gracious living' of which they were most proud.

Of course, as a high proportion of the middle-class group has recently moved from a previous address within easy motoring distance, it is inevitable that old social links should be maintained, and the motor-car enables them to keep up this characteristic of regional living. Some of the problems of the migratory élite have recently been adumbrated[14] and it seems remarkable that such people should still consider themselves to be true villagers. Their whole outlook is urban and cosmopolitan. Most go on holiday every year and are then likely to leave South-East England for Scotland or the West Country, with a substantial minority travelling abroad. The London commuters, who appeared to be the most affluent, had the most mobile pattern in all the linkages with the outside world. One woman stated the middle-class view with clarity – 'One of the things that makes the difference between – if you like to call them – middle-class people and working people – is the lack of transport, very often you simply must have a second car in the household if you really intend to take advantage of living here the way you'd wish to.'

If, then, the two broad groups live in such different worlds, it is clearly of great interest to analyse the interaction of the two worlds in the local setting. The established working-class villagers clearly look to the local area as their home and most of their friends and relatives live locally. However, the vision of the middle-class newcomers may be quite different. They may have defined the situation to themselves in ways different from reality. The rustic pastorale, which often passes as rural reality in many novels and magazine articles, is a peculiarly English myth. The proliferation of growth industries in the inner country ring of the London metropolitan region, with a high management to workers ratio, has led to a considerable middle-class demand for a house in a village. There is a reluctance to live cheek by jowl with colleagues and subordinates, and, since it was the policy of the neighbouring new town to allocate houses in blocks to the employees of individual companies, there was certainly some danger of this being inevitable. Hence the development of 'pressure villages' within easy commuting distance of these towns, where land zoned for building by the County Council is immediately bought at inflated prices by speculators. Landlords allow cottages to fall empty so that the plot of land on which they stand may be sold and a new house built.

THE CASE OF 'DORMERSDELL'

One of the adjoining parishes, which we may call 'Dormersdell', had a population of nearly 1,200 in 1961 and has a concentration of middle-class housing in an area of poor-quality woodland about a mile from the local authority housing around the school at the centre of the village. A description of the interaction of the middle-class world – euphemistically described as 'The Wood' by 'The Village' – and the working-class world will be used to substantiate the hypothesis that the introduction of a new class element has a more fundamental impact on the village social structure than simply the commuting to nearby towns by the established villagers.

TABLE IV   Class of heads of households in areas of 'Dormersdell'

'Dormersdell'	Middle Class	Working Class	Agricultural Workers	No Information	100 per cent
'The Wood'	92	1	1	5	65
'The Village'	39	45	13	4	77

Because of the peculiar geographical circumstances of 'Dormersdell', it is possible to discern a certain ecological segregation of the population according to socio-economic status. The preceding table shows the social composition of the two areas – the one centred round the old village centre and the other based on the area of woodland with the lanes leading to it. The geographical and social divisions were mutually reinforcing.

Social class differences in 'Dormersdell' did not have to be approached in any delicate or circuitous manner. The village schoolmaster said bluntly, 'We're a split society.' 'I expect you've heard of the difficulties between here and the village,' said the wife of a technologist. '"The Wood" people are energetic and run things and the village people complain; but they do nothing by themselves, so what is one to do?' Even the Women's Institute has two groups; one was described as, 'In the daytime for commuters' widows – lots of cars and posh hats' and the other in the evening for the village, although there was some indication that this, too, was taken over by what were termed the '£1,000–£2,000 people'. (Those whose husbands earned more than £2,000 went to the daytime session.) It was easy to understand how the take-over took place. As one village woman said, 'Nobody spoke to the villagers if they went and when there was a special lecture only people from "The Wood" were invited.' Because the Women's Institute has been taken over by the middle class, the Young Wives' Club of the Church is almost entirely composed of council-house tenants, thus confirming the division between the two worlds.

Not all middle-class respondents used the euphemisms of 'The Wood' and 'The Village':

> It's a split between classes: the working class are more class conscious because of an inferiority complex . . . but anyway the old community has been killed by commuting.

This is a debatable analysis of the problem to which we shall return. The working-class people often make light of the two worlds, referring to the 'rich man and Lazarus', or, less clearly, 'Sodom and Gomorrah', in a detached sort of way. Some 'Wood' people felt a responsibility towards the village and deplored the fact, as one woman put it:

> There isn't quite as much linkage between the two sections as many of us would wish . . . it is difficult to get real cooperation from the village in many of the things that are done in this district.

Others, however, perhaps too readily, accepted the divisions in society. One man was warned before he moved in that 'You have to decide on which side you are batting – "The Wood" or "The Village".'

A village woman, who is a domestic cleaner in 'The Wood', saw things differently:

> When I first came here I was the *only* stranger and it took fifteen years before I was considered to belong. Now so many strangers move in and out every week there's no real feeling of belonging left. It's not just 'The Wood' who change, but also the farm workers stay for only a few weeks or months. Perhaps that's why there's so much less independent life. We used to do our own entertainment until 'The Wood' took over the Village Hall ten years ago. There used to be dances every week and now they're only occasional. The badminton is only for 'The Wood' people. They tend to be snobbish when they've no reason to be – you know people when you work in their houses. There used to be fewer people here but you saw more of them. Now even in the pubs you must leave before the evening customers.

All this is rather enigmatic and sometimes overstated, but it does reflect views which were often encountered.

It is important to understand more clearly how the people of 'The Wood' see themselves. A 30-year-old mechanical engineer who had just moved in summed up his first impressions as follows:

It's a self-contained community; the wives form their own coffee groups, wine-making groups and so on. It's only thirty-five minutes by train from London, yet it's quite secluded. We have the best of all worlds.

The 35-year-old-wife of a technical manager said:

We wanted to get out into the country and we were obliged to go to the other side of the green belt. We much prefer it here to Southgate – there's more space for the children and it's much easier to get to know people. There's more individuality here; it's easier to be what you are and you don't have to pretend to be anything else. It's easy to be left in peace if you want to.

Another woman who had been in 'The Wood' for about ten years has found,

That this little community to me is a shining example of how people can live together amicably, in friendship, ... I've never known a quarrel between any of these people (if one wishes to be primitive).

The wife of a research worker who had moved into 'The Wood' in 1958 said:

Sensible people rarely come in unannounced but there's a lot of social mixing. The wives all go out for coffee in the mornings. It's marvellous here – in the New Town the people are lonely, but when we went on holiday the neighbours came in and dusted and made us a pie for when we came home.

The 59-year-old wife of a sales representative had been in 'The Wood' since 1946 but had not wearied of the social round: 'There's lots of cocktail parties and dinner parties. We're always giving little dinner parties.'
Another woman, who arrived about the same time, felt much the same:

It's one of the most delightful places in the world. People of the same sort are all around, all very friendly: it's quite exceptional – people of the same education and income, who come out here for the same reason. It's near to London but a lot goes on here and it's well supported.

The idyll painted by these people appeared to be largely true, although many needed the second car in the household in order not to feel too isolated.

Probing into the isolation of commuters' wives was difficult and it was hard to get beyond the flood of *gemütlichkeit*.

There is something in common here and it isn't really money. It's the same outlook on life – there's a feeling that your neighbours are there to be done good to – that you're there to be a neighbour if you're wanted. If you have a car, you fill it up, so that you go and pick all the children up or you could take everybody to the W I meeting or whatever it is.

There were some exceptions to this typical middle-class pattern, but they were hard to find. The 37-year-old wife of an assistant accountant frankly admitted, 'We don't mix very much; we're living here by the skin of our teeth and could not keep up with the entertaining that mixing would involve.' Another woman had made 'no particular friends since coming here: it's rather cliquey but the people are quite pleasant, mostly conservative – of course we're socialist here'.

Many middle-class people move out to a village in order to be a member of a 'real community', which, in practice, means 'joining things'. It might be thought, however, that the length of the journey to work would make it difficult for commuters to get home in time to participate in local organizations in the evening and that the women might be housebound on account of their children during the day. Discussion has often centred on the *lack* of participation in local activities by middle-class commuters, while it has long been widely known that it is not part of the working-class culture to join formal social organizations. The working-class men may be members of the local darts team or football club but their wives would not be expected to join a dramatic society or discussion group. The growth of social activities centred on the factory would seem to be a further factor militating against the development of activities centred on the village.

In fact 'Dormersdell' is renowned for the wealth of activities which flourish there. Middle-class commuters' wives not only join more activities than any other group, but take a dominant part in running them. Working-class people do not participate in such activities, apart from a few wives of working-class commuters. Commuting does not appear to be a disincentive for some of the middle-class men to take part in local organizations, and the proportion of active participants who work in London is about the same as of those who work locally in near-by towns. They are also likely to act as honorary officers in organizations, both in and outside the village. This is further evidence of the urban, mobile and outward-looking, middle-class living in a wider, regional sphere of action, though no doubt men would not be so likely to maintain links with these other organizations unless they had office-holding responsibilities in them.

Although it first appeared that middle-class people are well integrated into village social organizations and indeed appear to run most of them, this is in fact rather a false picture of middle-class dominance, although one the working class seem happy to hold. Certain organizations *are* run by and for the middle class but there are other activities, such as the Football Club or Greenleaves Club for old-age pensioners, with predominantly working-class membership. Perhaps the only Club where 'The Village' and 'The Wood' meet on anything like equal terms is the Village Horticultural Society, where the officers and committee members are widely representative. This is likely to be a field where the working-class villagers excel, and, since it is increasingly a middle-class status symbol to produce home-grown vegetables, 'The Wood' has much to learn. The Church also provides some common meeting ground for the two worlds. Here the respectable, conservative working class are matched with a similar proportion of middle-class people.

By and large the working class are not *deprived* of any activity by the middle-class immigrants, despite many activities taking place in which they are not represented: they just do not *want* to join things. Because of this lack of contact each group accuses the other unfairly. On the one hand, 'The Wood' claims that the village will not do anything for itself; on the other hand, the village accuses 'The Wood' of having organizations run by and for themselves and thus, curiously, of dominating the village.

Generally the ordinary villagers were not effusive about

'Dormersdell'. 'It's quite nice in summer but a bit dreary in winter' summed up many people's feelings. One of the advantages of the place frequently mentioned was that it was not 'nosey'. – 'I see my mother and father regularly but not many other people.' – 'I never go inside other people's houses – except my children's' – 'I keep myself to myself; there's no one else I really bother with.'

In one part of the village where the houses are more mixed up one middle-class woman was able to say – 'It's ideal – a truly rural area near to shops,' whereas her neighbour, a tractor driver's wife, said, 'We like the country but the shops seem so far away, which makes shopping so expensive.' Indeed, if one wanted to draw further comments from working-class respondents, the inadequacy of the bus service would be a certain talking point. Clearly working-class respondents were much less articulate in describing what they felt about 'Dormersdell'. It was simply where they had always lived and where many of their relatives lived. This is not to say that the working-class world was simpler to understand than that of the middle class.

The whole working-class situation was a highly complex structure of definite roles, relationships and behaviour, far too delicate to be able to generalize easily from it about the 'working-class world'. The broad distinctions *between* the middle and working class were so enormous that quite crude methods could be used to portray them. But *within* the classes much greater study in depth is required than was possible with a sample of this size. Not only has there been little contact between the worlds but the main way of breaking down these barriers – by the children of the two groups going to the same schools – seems less likely to take place. A discussion of the effects of social class on parental aspirations for their childrens' education and the differences in type of education received by the children of the two classes has been made elsewhere.[15] It is enough to say that there are few signs that the barriers between the two worlds are likely to become less marked for many years.

The changeover from the hierarchical social structure, which was functionally suited to the old village 'community', to what now appears to be a polarized two-class division may be the chief cause of working-class people's resentment. The more traditional working-class element is resentful, partly because it has lost its clear position in the hierarchy and the reflected status of the gentry for whom it worked, and partly because it now finds itself lumped with what it would feel to be the less respectable working class. This traditional group would like to be given respect and position in society, but gets neither. The non-traditional working class sees the segregated middle-class world as a symptom of the inequalities in society, and condemns all middle-class people as snobs and *nouveaux riches* without basing this on individual knowledge and experiences.

The middle-class people come into rural areas in search of a meaningful community and by their presence help to destroy whatever community was there. That is not to say that the middle-class people change or influence the working class. *They simply make them aware of national class divisions, thus polarizing the local society*. Part of the basis of the local village community was the sharing of the deprivations due to the isolation of country life and the sharing of the limited world of the families within the village. The middle-class people try to get the 'cosiness' of village life, without suffering any of the deprivations, and while maintaining a whole range of contacts with the outside world by means of the greater mobility afforded by their private transport.

Both the middle- and working-class groups view each other with only partial understanding with, perhaps, the only real personal relationships developing between the middle-class wife and her working-class domestic cleaner. Clearly it would be a delusion to imagine that this sort of interaction can provide a genuine friendship on a basis of equality.

The case of 'Dormersdell' typifies the sort of situation which is likely to arise when a large group of professional and managerial people comes to live in a rural parish. But this is admittedly a rather extreme situation and one that is not likely to be repeated in all villages around the rapidly industrializing towns in South-East England. County Councils adopt some sort of a policy through their Planning Departments, which is concerned to inhibit the growth of most villages in their respective areas. This is only partially successful, as Mandelker[16] and others have point-

ed out, but certainly without such restrictive policies many
villages would have become overwhelmed by speculative building.

SOME FUTURE LINES OF RESEARCH

Given that the demand by mainly, at the moment, middle-class
people to live in villages is greater than the amount of accommodation available, a number of problems in 'rural' sociology
are likely to be increasingly important in the years ahead. A
suitable way to conclude this chapter might, therefore, be to
indicate certain lines of research which are likely to be both
interesting and useful.

The social delineation of middle-class immigrants to rural areas

Much more needs to be known about the reasons different
groups *within* the middle class give for their move or desire to
move into rural areas. Aspirations should be analysed in relation
to actual experience and an attempt made to judge the degree of
adjustment to a rural environment by different middle-class
groups. This could be related to previous places of residence and,
possibly, childhood experiences. It would also be interesting to
know if it is the socially mobile or established middle class which
is most likely to move into the country.

The social interaction of middle-class groups with each other
in rural areas

There is a tendency in England at the moment for people to move
to estates which are dominated by people of similar socio-
economic status. However, within a village it is possible for there
to be a wide variety of house types of different values so that a
broader spectrum of the middle class may be in a relatively close
physical relationship. It would be interesting to know whether
normative and relational aspects of inter-class relationships, as
defined by Goldthorpe and Lockwood,[17] become less important

in the smaller scale of a rural community. Would one, for example, expect there to be normal social interaction between a managing director of a large company and a bank clerk or primary-school teacher and also between their wives? There was some indication that in 'Dormersdell' the husband's occupation was not known to their neighbours and, when the place of work may be anywhere within a large region, it is possible, without any great duplicity, to keep such information concealed. This sort of urban anonymity in a rural situation is unique to the urbanized villages. It may be more difficult to maintain rigid status categories when the numbers involved are small.

The social interaction of middle and working class in rural areas

The polarization described in the case of 'Dormersdell' is not so likely to take place when fewer middle-class people of high status are involved, in which case they may be grafted on to a hierarchical structure. Similarly, if the middle-class element is composed of marginal middle-class white-collar workers, who have simply moved to rural areas in search of cheap housing, then their effect on the village may be so slight as to be barely noticeable. More needs to be known about the expectations of community life which different middle-class groups may have before moving to a village and the effect 'communities in the mind' may have on the actual interactions between the new middle-class and the established working-class villagers. It may be that certain immigrant groups are more easily socially integrated than others (cf. Vidich and Bensman[18]).

Change within the rural working class

Further analysis is needed on the relative importance of *physical* contact with the world outside the village through commuting, the spread of private motor transport and so on, and *social* contact within the village with groups of different status, as forces making for change in the social norms and outlook of the rural working class. The relative importance of conservatism/individualism and radicalism/collectivism might also provide a guide to changing self-images and life-styles associated with urbanization. Attempts should be made to distinguish between those general changes affecting rural life and culture and the particular changes which occur, which may be due to the introduction of industry, commuting to urban employment or the immigration of new social elements. The effects of such changes on kinship linkages and demographic structure could be analysed, and finally the impact of economic changes in agriculture could be related to changes in status and life styles.

The physical planning of rural communities

In view of the points already raised more needs to be known about the social implications of new housing in regard to its amount and positioning. It would seem that at 'Dormersdell' the spatial pattern helped to heighten the polarization of the community's social structure, and the creation of an estate at the edge of a village may inevitably have this result. There are indications that social tension is less likely in an entirely new village, creating its own communal life within itself, or where a few new houses are simply interspersed with older houses within the village. The actual size of the community, which many people claim should not exceed 1,250–1,500 inhabitants, may not be so important.

In fine, it should be emphasized that the work outlined here has been a preliminary study in a field which has to date been little explored. The large-scale movement of middle-class commuters into rural England is essentially a phenomenon of the last fifteen years and it is likely that more rigorous documentation of the situation and conceptualization of the problem will now begin to appear. In particular, it will become clearer to what extent the problems and tensions are due to the novelty of the situation, so that, with time, maybe a new form of rural community will emerge, being quite distinct from a piece of suburbia or exurbia in the countryside. There appears to be no doubt, however, that, in an increasingly leisure-oriented society, space has become a status symbol, so that with increasing affluence the proportion of the population which wants, and can afford, to live in the country will grow. This being so the changing social structure of commuter villages will continue to provide social laboratories in which broader, national changes can be observed in detail.[19]

REFERENCES

1 Constandse, A. K., 'Planning in agricultural regions', *Sociologia Ruralis*, Vol. 11, No. 1/2, 1962, 79–104.
2 Rees, A. D., *Life in a Welsh Countryside*, University of Wales Press, 1950.
3 Williams, W. M., *The Sociology of an English Village: Gosforth*, Routledge & Kegan Paul, 1956.
4 Williams, W. M., *A West Country Village: Ashworthy*, Routledge & Kegan Paul, 1963.
5 Saville, J., *Rural Depopulation in England and Wales 1851–1951*, Routledge & Kegan Paul, 1957.
6 Vince, S. W. E., 'Reflections on the Structure and Distribution of Rural Population in England and Wales 1921–1931'. *Transactions and Papers of the Institute of British Geographers*, No. 18, 1952, 53–76.
7 Dickinson, R. E., *City, Region and Regionalism*, Routledge & Kegan Paul, 1947.
8 Bracey, H. E., *Social Provision in Rural Wiltshire*, Methuen, 1952.
9 Martin, W. T., 'Ecological change in satellite rural areas', *American Sociological Review*, 22, 1957, 175–85.
10 Wissink, G. A., *American Cities in Perspective, With Special Reference to the Development of their Fringe Areas*, Van Gorcum, 1962.
11 Ministry of Housing and Local Government, *The South East Study*, HMSO, 1964.
12 Pahl, R. E., 'Urban influences on rural areas within the London Metropolitan Region: Case studies of three Hertfordshire parishes', Unpublished Ph.D. Thesis, University of London, 1963.
13 Pons, V. G., 'The social structure of a Hertfordshire parish', Unpublished Ph.D. Thesis, University of London, 1955.
14 Musgrove, F., *The Migratory Elite*, Heinemann, 1963.
15 Pahl, R. E., 'Education and social class in commuter villages', *Sociological Review*, 11, 2 (new series), 1963, 241–6.

16 Mandelker, D., *Green Belts and Urban Growth*, Madison, Wisconsin, 1962.
17 Goldthorpe, J. H., and Lockwood, D., 'Affluence and the British class structure', *Sociological Review*, 11, 2 (new series), 1963, 133–63.
18 Vidich, A. J., and Bensman, J., *Small Town in Mass Society: Class, Power amd Religion in a Rural Community*, Doubleday Anchor Books, 1960.
19 Since this chapter was written there have been further studies concerned with some of the issues I have raised in the last section. See, for example, the study of Ringmer in Sussex – Ambrose, P., *The Quiet Revolution: Social Change in a Sussex Village 1871–1971*, Chatto & Windus, 1974, and the references cited therein.

Chapter 2 The social objectives of village planning

There now appears to be widespread agreement that the indiscriminate addition of private housing development to villages is unsatisfactory. The lead given by Kent County Council in attempting to prevent piecemeal development by acquiring consolidated parcels of land and making such blocks available to private builders, while maintaining some overall planning control, will surely be followed by other planning authorities in the pressure areas around the main conurbations.

If, then, the small settlement in the fields, which, for want of a better word, I shall call a village, is to play a positive role in meeting the housing demands of a city region, it is important that architects and planners should approach it free from 'vague, romantic flub-dub' as *The Economist* once described *The Scott Report*. Furthermore, when *new* villages are planned it is important that sentimental, outmoded notions of 'community' do not cloud a realistic assessment of the quality of the social life which may be created. A number of important points are worth emphasizing:

(a) In Hampshire the Mass Observation survey[1] underlined the conclusions of previous surveys in Hertfordshire, Kent and elsewhere, namely that there is no typical pattern of village life; that there is a marked difference between occupational groups in place of work, pattern of joining and taking office in clubs, and reasons for coming to the village; and that these and other differences between social groups are greater than differences between villages.

(b) Despite the evidence of increasing personal mobility in rural areas there is also disquieting evidence of rural poverty and isolation. Even in the more prosperous villages of the South-East there is what I would call 'masked depopulation': that is to say the immigration of middle-class commuters conceals the emigration of young manual workers. It is easy when discussing results in terms of percentages to ignore the smaller proportions. For example, in the Hampshire study, 48 per cent of the skilled and 31 per cent of the unskilled could drive a car and *of these* only 39 per cent of the former and 22 per cent of the latter were actually car owners. Similarly two fifths of the village population do *not* leave the village at least once a week to shop. The relative deprivation of the old and poor is perhaps more acute in the countryside. Even middle-class people who retire into a village may find the lack of public transport a problem, when they are too old or unable to drive a car.

(c) The question whether a village is 'a stable tangible community', as posed by the Hampshire county planning officer, is perhaps raised more frequently than it is honestly answered. Sociologists have shown that in some parts of various cities there are 'urban villages' where a variety of local job opportunities and long-established kinship networks have helped to create a pattern of social relationships which may be nearer to the middle-class image of a village than rural retreats for commuters.

SOCIAL GROUPS IN THE COUNTRYSIDE

With these points in mind I would like to isolate and portray the various social elements which make up that curious phenomenon – the village in the South-East. This is not based on any actual village but arises out of an analysis of field studies and surveys undertaken in south-east England in the 1960s by a number of research workers and planning departments. I hope to make explicit what is implicit in their work.

Large property owners

Many of the country houses of the traditional English landed society are still occupied by capitalist farmers, often owning huge acreages. Links may be stronger with London than any local social element. In a study of the Berkshire villages of Ardington and Lockinge,[2] where one property owner is virtually the only ratepayer, his influence predominates. The social situation is benevolently feudal: a Conservative association is active only at general elections and villagers are either uninterested,reluctant,or afraid to discuss politics. More generally the large landowner's role in the village is more symbolic: he is elected vice-president of as many organizations as he can decently be expected to give donations to. Even where the local farmer is of more modest means and status, his social contacts are more likely to be with other farmers in the area than those living in the local village.

Salaried immigrants with some capital

Those living in a period property full of beams, latches, central heating and assorted reproduction ironmongery from the little shop off the Tottenham Court Road certainly help to maintain something of our rural domestic architecture. They are joined by those who specifically seek a style of life associated with space and seclusion: both such groups of people are attracted to a particular *house or plot* rather than the village as a social entity. They have the means to afford the equipment, such as gardeners, motor mowers and cars which are essential in the pursuit of such a style of life. They are not particularly interested in living in a new village.

'Spiralists'

Sociologists have used the terms 'cosmopolitans', 'non-traditionalists' or 'spiralists' to describe employees in large-scale organizations who are obliged to change their place of residence as they move through and up the status hierarchies of these organizations. Local government officers, managers in industry and even university teachers are increasingly obliged to move their families a number of times in the course of their careers. There are indications from some research I am starting that it is not uncommon for an industrial manager to have moved nine or ten times by the age of 40. Such people, or more especially their wives, may feel that they can integrate themselves more readily into a small-scale community. They may thus decide to look for a house in a village with a vague, and probably not consciously formulated, notion of the quality of social life which they expect to find there. These people are nevertheless consciously seeking a particular *place* (and a self-defined type of social life to go with it) rather than a particular house or plot.

Those with limited income and little capital

These are the reluctant commuters forced out from the towns, not because they want to live in a village, but simply because at this point in their family-building cycle they cannot find a house at a price they can afford elsewhere. With the wives tied to the home by young children and the husbands away with the only car, these little village estates can present a number of social problems. It is important that the architect-planner should not get so concerned with supplying 'community facilities' that he forgets that the housing needs of this group might be better catered for in the towns. Very often the main concern of such people, as their children get older, is to move closer to a centre with a good grammar school. I am quite certain that one of the most crucial determinants of housing demand will be the future pattern of schools. Education and housing policy must be very closely tied together and in the present period of discussion about patterns and types of comprehensive education it is important that physical planning remains sensitive to housing demands which may follow from the reorganization of education.

The retired

Of varied financial backgrounds, this group moves for a variety of reasons, some of which are often based on the same myths of 'friendly village life' too readily accepted by many planners. Having retired from their life-long occupations and moved away from relatives and friends, increasingly less active and less able to drive a car, many of this group find themselves lonely, bored and isolated and it is small consolation that this exile was self-imposed.

Council house tenants

The size of the council estate relates to the needs of an agricultural population of between twenty and forty years ago rather than to the needs of rural manual workers in the last quarter of the twentieth century. Very rarely, for example, are these estates adequately provided with garages and there are generally but two house-types to meet all needs: the standard three-bedroomed house and the old people's bungalow. Assuming that the RDC as a housing authority will have disappeared within twenty years, it is extremely important that a new policy for publicly built housing to rent is evolved so that in a new, regional, local government structure the needs of manual and junior non-manual workers are met. I think it right to assume that houses in the countryside will not be limited to the middle class and that there will be a continuing demand for houses to rent. One should question the rationale of providing council housing in villages with no local employment; particularly as very few of the amenities provided in urban estates, such as play facilities for children, are considered necessary in the country. Just because the urban middle class think that the countryside is a park is no reason for assuming that it is so.

Tied cottages and other tenants

It is easy to forget the rural poor: the combination of low average wages, isolation and poor housing conditions must compare very unfavourably with what is seen in the homes of the immigrant commuters. Those in tied cottages are at the mercy of their landlords, who may be doing a reasonable job in modernizing their properties, but who very often prefer to wait until tenants die off before knocking cottages together to make better accommodation for a smaller labour force. Landlords are quick to point out how low are the rents they receive, but neglect to mention the relatively low wages and the fact that in effect those in tied cottages have no one to whom they may appeal. Too often the RDC is in the hands of the largest landowners and most powerful people in the area. One of the most useful amenities for the rural poor and elderly would be a telephone, which could do much to overcome their isolation from their offspring working away in the towns. Yet most landlords would judge one to be crazy for suggesting they might take some responsibility for installing one.

Local tradesmen and owners of small businesses

This is an essential element in the population and has no specific housing problem but is added for completeness.

RURAL REALITY

These eight groups provide a preliminary framework for further analysis. I very much hope that if planning consultants or local authorities are considering further research on 'villages' they will concentrate on the specific problems and housing needs of particular social groups. To consider 'the village' as a sort of average of all such groups is extremely misleading and possibly accounts for much of the confusion in rural planning. *There is no village population as such; rather there are specific populations which for various, but identifiable, reasons find themselves in a village.* Some *choose* to move out of the town to live in the village, some have property in the country but choose to spend more time living in the city. Others are obliged or forced to live in the country but have their employment in the towns. In those regions where certain types of employment have expanded more rapidly than the availability of housing, reluctant commuters have been pushed into the villages to find houses at a reasonable price. Hence much of the expansion of residential development in rural parts of city regions may be related more to the distorted nature of the housing market than to any more specific urge on the part of new home owners to move to 'villages'.

EVIDENCE FROM SURVEYS

Unfortunately this kind of assertion is not easily documented with hard empirical data. Evidence from the surveys certainly suggests that more junior non-manual workers are attracted by the house rather than by more general environmental considerations. As long as the land market remains as it is, distorted by planning restrictions which create a shortage of land within town map areas, then the result may be misinterpreted as a desire by people to live in villages. For the same reason market research on consumer preferences is unlikely to be particularly helpful to the builder. People's subjective assessment of their environmental situation may differ from what may objectively be the case: for example when I interviewed two women in adjoining houses on an estate built at the edge of a small town of 14,000, one woman said how nice it was to be able to live in a town, whereas her neighbour remarked how nice it was to live out in the country. Where they *think* they live is in some ways more important to people than where they actually live.

Many of the small towns of 7,000 or 8,000 inhabitants are still self-consciously called villages by those who prefer this definition of the situation. Many middle-class people create for themselves a village-in-the-mind and no matter what the physical situation, it is in this that they live.

COMMUNITY AND ASSOCIATION

Creating a new town involves planners and architects in hard-headed thinking about the relationships between homes, work, shops and traffic. Certain technical problems have to be solved if the town is to be a success in twenty or thirty years' time. However, when faced with the problem of creating a new village the same hard-headed professionals may sink back into the language of nineteenth-century philanthropists, who hoped to create their own brand of the good life through planned communities. It almost seems as if to such people the quality of 'the social life' is the only thing that distinguishes a village from a suburb in the country. John Rae provided an example of this way of thinking when he claimed that 'The balance between local life and commuter life is one that needs accurate measurement and can be regulated by planning policy.'[3]

The implications of this statement are enormous: two types of social life, however difficult to assess, have to be 'balanced'. The local member of the National Union of Agricultural Workers hopes that his union will achieve a 33⅓ per cent wage increase to give him £14 a week and likes beer, football and darts. Two hundred yards down the road the member of the Institute of Practitioners in Advertising is worried about the public image of his profession and likes wine, travelling and golf. There might be a link between the two if the farmworker's wife comes into the IPA man's house to clean and serve at dinner parties. The IPA man and his wife pride themselves on their radical views, pay the woman well, and retell snippets of working-class culture that the clever wife picks up over mid-morning tea ('My dear, it's just like the Archers the way these people complicate their lives . . . one can hardly believe this all goes on within thirty miles of London').

The developer or architect may be understandably irritated by my example, as perhaps he feels that the creation of a new village is a magnificent opportunity for social engineering; forming a sense of enclosure (a link with the time when the beasts were herded together on the village green at night). In a skilful intermingling of houses of different sizes (and prices) he would recreate the intimate variation in scale which is a characteristic of 'the village', it perhaps has a tower block or community centre as a modern counterpart to the medieval wool Church as its focus. And this would surely make the agricultural worker on £11 a week as much part of the community as the commuter in the dower house on £250 a month. Even if they don't invite each other into their homes, they're sure to meet over a pint in the pub or possibly play cricket together. And if this is not the case, he would argue, it is the business of the sociologist to provide the architect with the principles for making a community. Maybe if the tenants for the overspill element were sufficiently carefully selected, or if there were a collective responsibility for the village green, all would be well.

When one compares this kind of vague hypothesis with the sort of survey work carried out for establishing New Towns, one can seen why consultants refer to the rural areas within the area of their regional survey with some embarrassment.

It is for the sociologist to try to provide data on how existing small communities work, rather than attempting to 'make people happy'.

WHAT MAKES A COMMUNITY?

A community may arise out of a common disaster or common restrictions on freedom and is not, according to the value judgements I would wish to make, part of 'the good life'.

(a) A communal or collective consciousness may arise out of common deprivation.

(b) Where the whole village or parish is owned by one man a feudal-type pattern of functional interdependence emerges among the now increasingly elderly agricultural workers. This situation of consensus without change does produce a certain funereal harmony.

(c) The social relationships in a feudal community were involuntary, making for some feeling of identity with a particular place.

(d) All the evidence suggests that people are 'happiest', that is most at ease, when they associate with those of similar social status.

When I was interviewing in one of the villages I studied, a lorry swerved on to the pavement one sunny afternoon, killing two young mothers as they stood chatting by their prams. For a few weeks afterwards that village was, in a sense, a community, united despite differences of class and status. The limit of the power of this 'community' was reached when a notice urging traffic to be cautious was placed at either end of the village. Should one be surprised that the village so soon reverted to the 'normal' situation of a collection of social groups with separate and distinctive life-chances and styles of life?

CONFLICT

Different groups are knit into a cohesive structure through conflict and indeed the degree of conflict in any social system may be a measure of its cohesion. This may appear paradoxical and certainly it is important to distinguish between different types of conflict. As long as the social conflicts which concern goals, values or interests do not contradict the basic assumptions upon which the relationships are founded, then the conflict is likely to be cohesive rather than disruptive. The familiar example of the Residents' Association, formed in the early days of an estate to fight, say, the developers about the drains, landscaping or garage roofs, which collapses when the battles are won, comes readily to mind. Without the common cause, collective action and responsibility disappears.

It has also been shown by sociologists that conflict within a community will not be disruptive if people feel they can identify themselves with the community and they are more likely to achieve such identification through the membership of voluntary associations. Thus, it is argued, the more voluntary associations there are in a place the more likely will people identify themselves with that place, but also the more likely will conflicts emerge. This is a very important point: high organizational density tends to draw the community into conflict, but it also acts to regulate the controversy and contain it.

VOLUNTARY ASSOCIATIONS

Spiralists and other middle-class newcomers, who come into a village expecting a social life characteristic of a village, help to create such a social life amongst themselves by 'joining things'. Hence any developer concerned with the quality of the social life in a new village is, in effect, concerned with the voluntary associations which may develop. The criticism that architects and planners have no right or responsibility to arrange the good life for others may fall down when it is remembered that for *a particular group* – the spiralists – the village is defined in terms of the quality of its social life. However, part of the definition of the situation is a pattern of interaction (in a manner not precisely formulated) with *other* status groups. Hence the developer's obsessive concern for what he believes to be a beneficial 'mixture of social classes'. Certainly, in comparison with the single status-group segregated suburb, the village may provide a valuable lesson in social consciousness for the middle class. At least the minimal face-to-face contact of domestic cleaner and her mistress provides some understanding of the fundamental differences of life-chances in our society. Yet however salutary this may be for the middle class, it is difficult for the working class to be anything but patronized.

COMMUNITY INVOLVEMENT

The idea that it is good for people to be mixed-up socially has received well-deserved criticism over the years. Nevertheless, the idea that conflicts should be encouraged to develop the feeling of belonging to a particular *place* has received less attention.[4]

A small-scale settlement in a rural setting is an attractive proposition, both for the developer who considers himself more than a provider of little boxes and for the spiralist who defines part of the good life for his wife and family in this sort of setting. There seems little doubt that managerial and professional mobility will continue and also that architects will continue to search for the physical basis for a 'better' quality of life. If the architecture of harmony has not been very successful it will be at least interesting to see something of the architecture of conflict! I do not mean to be unnecessarily obscure. Let us assume a new 'village' of 3,000 people divided between local authority housing to rent and privately built houses for sale to spiralists. Let there be an arrangement whereby the comprehensive primary school has a managing committee elected proportionately from the two types of housing and let the new equivalent of a parish council, similarly elected, have some power over local planning decisions. It is not difficult to imagine that different interest groups would emerge to do battle in the local arena: being 'involved in local community life' might then mean something.

RURAL AND URBAN VILLAGES

Expressing community involvement as a local power struggle might seem distasteful to those who see 'community life' as a succession of 'coffee mornings' for the wives. Those who see Consumer Associations and the Campaign for the Advancement of State Education as new forms of collective action, bringing together both the middle-class element, which is prepared to use collective means for individualist ends and the more affluent, family-centred manual worker prepared to act in the same way, could perhaps relate this to the other demand to live in a small community. Others may regret any tendency for the 'socially responsible' middle class, who may be prepared to stimulate and lead a new collectivism, to withdraw into a rustic arcadia. Such people are desperately needed in the cities. As some are discovering in Islington and elsewhere, cities have both period houses for conversion and opportunities for collective action based on the conflicts essential to a feeling of identification with a place. Indeed my own prejudice would be to urge the developer to turn his attention to *urban* rather than rural villages. Only those with the necessary capital or confidence can stop or fight planning blight in potentially attractive parts of our cities.

CONCLUSIONS

To the working class, life in the village means family life and possibly life at work; to the middle-class spiralists, life in the village means life in the voluntary associations. Future research on 'the village' should be concentrated on the life-styles of the distinctive groups along the lines I have suggested. Furthermore, if the assumption is that, though the town may be a technological thing, the village is a *social* thing, then it is important that research is directed into the function of social conflict, particularly as this is revealed in voluntary associations or in relation to the local schools. A certain middle-class demand for a greater social consciousness through social interaction with other status groups in a village can only be met, without patronizing the manual workers, in a situation of conflict reflecting the realities of our society.

Architects and planners, who admit to having social objectives when considering a new village, may, nevertheless, find this emphasis on conflict unpalatable. In which case they should perhaps remember my group two, who will continue to demand half- or three-quarter-acre plots tucked away in pleasant scrub woodland. They want the trees and they want the space; they are even prepared to use *au pairs* rather than rely on local labour to clean the house (the garden can after all remain wild). Such people do not need or want a local community and there is much to be said for planting patches of wilderness on low-quality land throughout the South East for the next generation of affluent pioneers. They are prepared to pay for a new rural vernacular architecture; they like light and shade and natural wood. But they are not concerned with 'village life' as others may be.

If architect-planners want to concern themselves with new small-scale settlements for spiralists in rural parts of city-regions, then they would do well to investigate the needs of this specific group more closely. Building the good life for a broader cross-section of the population is a much more dubious proposition.

REFERENCES

1 *Village Life in Hampshire*. A report by Mass Observation Ltd and Hampshire County Planning Department, Winchester, 1966.
2 Havinden, M. A., *Estate Villages*, Lund Humphries, 1966.

3 Rae, J., 'Town and Country Interaction', *Official Architecture and Planning*, July 1966, 1010.
4 Popplestone, G., 'Conflict and Mediating Roles in Expanding Settlements', *Sociological Review*, N.S. 15(3) 1967, 339–55.

Chapter 3   Newcomers in town and country

In the late 1940s Hertfordshire was referred to by its planners as 'a county of small towns set in a rural background on London's fringe'. Yet Hertfordshire had been changing since the beginning of the century. Letchworth and Welwyn Garden Cities brought in many new people and the Watford area was an important centre of light industry: indeed, in February 1930 Watford was practically the only town in Britain with no unemployment. The population of the county had more than doubled between 1901 and 1951, a rate five times that of the country as a whole. The momentum was building up: the New Towns Act of 1946 and the Town and Country Planning Act of 1947 were the instruments which were to do so much to change the character of the county. Situated in the important growth zone between London and the Midlands the county could not escape. At first there were signs that this new wave of change would be welcomed. In 1947 an editorial in the *Hertfordshire Mercury* entitled 'The Old Order Changeth' argued:

We have lived far too long on tradition and custom without questioning even social justice and we have carved our communities into cliques and coteries ... [but] ... the self-centred community today simply will not fit into the larger frame of human endeavour.

However, as the months went by a more cautious note appeared as the paper realized that 'the threat of Herfordshire becoming urbanized is real in the minds of old residents'. The storm over the designation of Stevenage New Town led to a prolonged lawsuit which was eventually decided in the House of Lords. Yet few newcomers were able to come until the early

1950s. Various economic difficulties held up large-scale developments, apart from the essential London County Council overspill estates at Borehamwood and Oxhey.

The new Hertfordshire was typically exemplified by the four New Towns, which grew and expanded in the 1950s. Among the lawns and flower beds of the industrial sites were neat little factories producing nice clean things like pens or guided missiles. New shopping centres with new supermarkets were surrounded by acres of car parks filled with new cars. Talk was about money and children. Everybody had lots of children. Schools and libraries were the centres of a booming growth industry. Between 1951 and 1961 Hertfordshire's rate of population growth was greater than that of any other county in the country. Nearly a quarter of a million newcomers, mostly married couples building up their families, came in during the ten-year period.

It is understandable that within this situation people coming to adult education classes should wish to make conscious the processes of which they formed a part. In this essay I have chosen to describe the investigations which the situations of three classes suggested. In a New Town class newly arrived wives were interested in friends and neighbours and bringing up children; in a village there was the problem of integrating the established villagers with the new commuters; finally, in a new estate at the edge of a small market town the new suburban situation created a self-conscious appraisal of the wives' situations within their families.

NEWCOMERS IN A NEW TOWN: THE ENERGETIC LAITY OF THE WELFARE STATE'S PRIESTHOOD

A group of young wives in a New Town felt that they would like to focus the discussions they had been having together informally. Thus early in 1964 a short series of classes on 'Growing Up in a New Town' was held in the afternoons and was later repeated in the evenings, with some husbands coming as well. I had the impression that this group was particularly lively, yet introspective, and I felt that here was an opportunity to gather more

detailed information from the group, with the intention of analysing it in a future class. I accordingly devised a short questionnaire,
asking for basic information about the socio-economic structure
of the household, the wife's attitude to paid employment since
marriage (together with her husband's reaction to his wife taking
a job); there were also questions about children (play facilities,
baby-sitting problems and so on) and finally questions about
friends and neighbours.

In no sense is this a sample with the slightest statistical validity.
It was self-selected and exceptional (in that most people do not
attend WEA classes) and the class was focused directly on itself.
They were all newcomers in a New Town with young children.
Being in this situation they were self-consciously interested in
their own problems. Hence I think they enjoyed filling in the
questionnaire; they knew why I was asking the questions and they
wanted to help. All this introduces considerable bias: they thought
they knew what I expected and what other people thought about
the various issues. Nevertheless it would be foolish to dismiss
these twenty-eight families as being of no interest. I believe that
they are representative of a more articulate element which may be
characteristic of the New Towns. The fathers of the husbands
were more likely to be junior non-manual workers or skilled
manual workers whereas the husbands themselves were overwhelmingly white-collar workers (see Table I). Ten out of
twenty-eight were teachers or concerned with education and only
three were manual workers. Their wives had been secretaries,
teachers or nurses, and although fewer wives than husbands had
had further education, more wives had stayed at school until 16
or older. They all wanted their children to stay on at school as
long as possible, many mentioning University, even though they
themselves had not been there.

The wives were almost too neatly type-cast as readers of the
Guardian women's page. 'Full-time housewife' sounded degrad-
ing to them but they enjoyed their young children and were acutely
aware of their responsibilities. 'The garden has sand, a swing and
in warm weather a plastic pool, however they prefer the street for
skates, pram, pedal car and group play.' Most husbands reflected
Guardian women's-page views about a part-time job for their

TABLE I Occupations of a Group of People in New Town (mostly members of WEA classes)

Husband's job	Wife's job before marriage/now	Husband's father's occupation	Wife's father's occupation
Tutor-Librarian Coll. of Further Ed.	Librarian	Coal miner	'clerical work'
Grammar school teacher	Educational psychologist	Headmaster	Insurance agent
Printers' cutter and warehouseman	Cashier in butcher's shop	Machine setter	Labourer
Plastics injection moulder	Assistant librarian	Electrician	Carpenter
Assistant foreman inspector	Dental nurse	Storekeeper	GPO Engineering executive
Community centre warden	Invoice clerk	Joiner	Farmer
Draughtsman	Cashier	Pub manager	Clerk of works
Electronic design engineer	Teacher	Film technician	Sales representative
Fork lift driver	Children's nurse	?	?
Secondary modern teacher	Grammar school teacher	Accountant and company secretary	Sub-postmaster/retailer
Cost accountant	Nursery nurse	Clerk in civil service	Toolmaker
Mechanical inspector	Nurse	Petrol pump attendant and fishing boat owner	Butcher
Chartered surveyor	?	Building contractors' general foreman	Clerk
Pharmacist	Student	Foundry worker	School attendance officer
Works study	Window dresser	Detail fitter	Shop manager

Husband's job	Wife's job before marriage/now	Husband's father's occupation	Wife's father's occupation
Geologist	Social worker	Engineer	Headmaster
Toolmaker	Commercial driver	Hairdresser	Confectioner
Schoolmaster	Actress	Diplomat	Managing director of firm importing and exporting scientific equipment
Quantity surveyor	Secretary	Quantity surveyor	Parks superintendent
J.I.S. headmaster	Secretary	Signalman	Coachdriver/proprietor
Student Ruskin Coll. (formerly electronics technician)	Nurse	Seaman	Seaman
Teacher College of Further Education	Exec. officer civil service	?	Book publisher's agent
Lecturer Technical College	Local govt. officer	Burner and riveter in shipyard	Printers' warehouseman
Community centre warden	Now clerk accounts BR	Clerical in bookshop	Master dyer and cleaner
Architect	Secretary	Insurance agent	Train driver

wives when the children are at school. They felt that the occupation 'housewife' was dull and soul-destroying and they wanted their wives to be 'stretched', to receive 'mental stimulation' so that they did not get discontented. They were very conscious of their spouses' lively minds, which must not be allowed to stagnate. 'Although she loves being with the children, she is noticeably rather frustrated when there is nothing else to "stretch" her. During the last two or three years she has benefited from the great amount of voluntary social work she has done.' Many men happily acknowledged their wives' mental abilities – as another man put it: 'She is an energetic bundle – mentally and physically – for whom the maintenance of a houschold would be psychologically quite unsatisfactory!'

There was general agreement among both husbands and wives that full-time work would not be possible. There was also a feeling that a paid job might not provide the same social satisfactions and mental stimulation that was needed. Voluntary part-time work, teaching or nursing were the most frequently mentioned activities. These were the energetic laity of the welfare state's priesthood. They were the new radical middle class, anxious to serve. One husband put it like this: 'Since she had a higher education and is capable of dealing with problems far removed from domestic trivia and cosy coffee mornings it would be wasteful of her professional training not to apply it both for the good of the community and her own fulfilment.'

Most of the wives knew fairly or very well the parents of the children with whom their own children played; those whose children went to nursery school knew an even wider circle. Husbands were very much aware of their responsibilities to play and be with their children, two thirds of them spending two or more hours a day with them and a quarter spending three or more hours. They liked speaking about their children and the problems of bringing them up and it would be wrong to imagine a sharp division between 'men's talk' and 'women's talk'.

Finding baby-sitters was a problem and prevented many going out together as much as they would have liked: some were able to get teenagers to help but a more general difficulty was the expense of paying for them. They would have preferred to work on a reciprocal basis with neighbours but it always seemed that neighbours did not want to go out so frequently. Hence husband and wife were obliged to go out separately. 'Meetings' of one sort of another were very popular: discussion groups, political meetings, lectures and so on. One couple took it in turn to go to the Film Society, another couple went out separately most nights of the week but went out together rarely more than once a month. Each of them going out once or twice a week separately seemed a familiar pattern. Only one respondent mentioned that she and her husband had personal friends not so well known by the other partner, but it was clear that when husband and wife joined separate groups they moved in different social networks.

Entertaining and being entertained in each others' houses in the evenings was popular and there was much emphasis on the conversation which such occasions generated. 'As our cultural, political, etc., interests are wide, conversation is never lacking when we are with friends . . . it . . . moves rapidly and varies greatly.' The emphasis was on 'ideas' and 'stimulation'. 'As so often happens the hostess has to spend too much time in the kitchen, therefore misses interesting conversation.' Wives did in fact enjoy talking about children, but there was a great fear of missing out on general talk. There was a feeling that conversation ought to be varied; for example, 'I find our social circle rather limited. Most of our friends are in education, the majority from comparable backgrounds. I have found our efforts to meet other people rather difficult as many of the sports and social groups throughout the town have a very high proportion of teachers and teachers' wives in their membership.'

This group was not concentrated in any one street or area of New Town. It was scattered in a variety of houses rented from the Development Corporation throughout the town. Although they were mainly non-manual workers, the incomes of the group were much the same as many of the highly paid manual workers. How did individuals fit in with their neighbours and did they have many friends? Nearly a third of the wives knew at least a dozen people within easy walking distance on whom they could call for help, such as getting shopping. Such people lived in the same street or cul-de-sac and their children played together, or they met each other when collecting their children from nursery school. Many of them had moved into the housing area together and the common experience drew them together. Only four women had three or less such friends, the remainder having between four and a dozen people on whom they could call.

This socially confident group was not typical of New Town as a whole; many women were conscious of their distinctiveness and two thirds of them knew other women who were said to be lonely. Those who keep themselves to themselves were pitied. In this child-centred society working wives were unlikely to make contact with their stay-at-home neighbours: children helped to make friends. The situation of the isolated and lonely was discussed with some perception: 'Sometimes they feel torn from their roots and are always hankering to be back in London or "up North". They miss their parents or old friends so much they seem unable to accept new friends.' The secretary of one of the local nursery schools went further; she felt 'some women are rather frightened of others with conflicting views, maybe they are scared that theirs are wrong. Friends I am really myself with, are those I have met through the local CND. Women are very friendly here, one can spend a whole day bumping into them and chatting for twenty minutes at a time. Many seem very lonely . . .' This woman was in full-time education until the age of 20. She had confidence and little status-anxiety. She met like-minded middle-class radicals at CND meetings. Yet even she did not understand that loneliness was functionally related to class and mobility. 'The more articulate immigrants "join things" – there are any number of associations and clubs in the Town.' But this was not so easy for the woman who left school at 14 and whose family, school contemporaries and the friends she made at work before marriage have been left in London. It was understandable that such people should be afraid of taking a false step. Those who tried to be friendly to them complained of 'clannishness' or of aloofness: in fact it was fear and uncertainty. Women without the necessary confidence and social skill withdrew from a situation in which they might be hurt or embarrassed.

It is important to remember that I am describing a particularly sociable group, who in turn were describing those they felt must be lonely. They were also asked about the ideal qualities they looked for themselves in a neighbour: their answers gave some indication of the quality of their own pattern of social relationships.

I'm afraid I'm 'English' enough to like my neighbours to be friendly but not too friendly – I do *not* like the habit of popping in and out – and we do not have this, but we are all on very good terms and cooperate in taking children to school and help in an emergency.

(30-year-old librarian)

I had the ideal neighbour who had three children. We baby-sat for each other's children (often at a moment's notice) during the day as well, borrowed things and always returned them, cheered each other up when bored, were loyal about each other, had long discussions about many interesting things; on the other hand we did not go into the other's house without knocking and didn't see each other socially in the evenings more than once a month and our husbands had little in common.

(35-year-old ex-secretary)

Someone who makes an effort to see the other person's point of view! Plus no bickering over children.

(30-year-old ex-children's nurse)

A number of women made a particular point of mentioning a tolerant attitude towards noisy children as an essential quality of a neighbour. It was perhaps the fear of offending a neighbour on account of the children which helped to keep some women isolated.

A great need of women living isolated lives in New Towns is someone reliable with whom they can leave their young children while they shop, have their hair done, relax, take a course etc. Why not each other? There seems to be a great fear of becoming too familiar with another family. Some don't want the responsibility even though it frees them on another day. Others can't believe their children would go happily to another woman. Some children's first day at school is their first day away from Mother!

(32-year-old social worker).

For many of the women there was insufficient space on the form for them to say all they had to say and they showed readiness to be interviewed at length on a later occasion. They enjoyed thinking about themselves and their social situation. For example, one woman wrote: 'I value my independence too much to expose it to living near to my friends – am sure this tells something about me; with our friends we share interests, ideas etc. but not everyday lives.'

An interesting theme, which it was not possible to explore in detail, was the degree of overlap between wives' and husbands' friendship patterns. At one extreme was the wife of one of the few manual workers in the group who said: 'My husband and I may be unusual in that we don't seem to need outside friends when we are together. He has many workmates but only one calls here (without his wife). I have my friends here but we only meet during the day.' At the other extreme was the woman with at least twenty-four friends in the area whose husband was said to be just as friendly with them as she was. Altogether over a third of the couples claimed that all their friends were joint friends.

This account adds little to the more extended treatment of this subject by Elizabeth Bott and Josephine Klein. Newcomers in a New Town may all be in a similar situation, looked at from one point of view, but there was no doubt that some were more able to cope with the problem of creating new patterns of social relationships more easily than others. The radical middle-class islands were surrounded by a sea of others: distinctions in values and lifestyles were understood and discussed. The affluent manual worker withdrew into his own small family circle and was criti- cized for his lack of 'interests' (in a middle-class sense). 'The women go out to work for money – they always say they can't manage but they're just bad managers. Some wives go out solely to buy and upkeep the car.' Their husbands were not interested in politics because 'they don't feel it particularly involves them'. Stimulated by this lack of firm ideological commitment by those who may have much more money coming into the house, the radical middle-class minority was acutely conscious of its dis- tinctiveness, despite frequent face-to-face contacts. 'I can never get very far with them,' said one 32-year-old mother, 'they just sort of close up when you talk of politics. There's some you almost put off being friends with for fear of what you'll say next.'

Clearly one must be very wary of rash generalizations about 'New Town People'. The articulate minority I am describing was highly self-aware and had some general knowledge of social processes. Social links started with the children but very soon the ideological feelers worked out through the various clubs and associations to bring the like-minded elements together. The usual status differentials of home ownership, cars or consumer durables did not work in the New Town where the houses were for rent, and wage differentials were slight. 'Ideas' sorted out the middle from the working class: people very soon moved into a social network that linked them together. Many of those who were politically Conservative and more self-consciously middle class left the New Town as soon as they possibly could. Refugees from the New Town were scattered over the surrounding rural districts. They tried hard to become 'integrated with the village' and approved of status-assenting, deferential rustics. Since those who did not like the New Town left it, those who remained were to some extent self-selected. Only the social and political activists who did not mind living next door to the working class appeared to enjoy living in the town. There was a fellowship in the mental activity; they saw the same familiar faces at lectures, political meetings and discussion groups. They enjoyed 'the Welfare State' and what it stood for, but while complaining of the political apathy of those around them, they were angry when I discussed problems of social stratification. 'Class does not exist in New Town' they assured me, yet everything they told me confirmed that the barriers were there.

NEWCOMERS IN A VILLAGE

During the 1950s this south Cambridgeshire village had been losing population. Men were not needed on the land and there were good employment opportunities in north Hertfordshire, particularly in Letchworth. Indeed between 10,000 and 12,000 workers – nearly half as many as the Garden City's total population – came into Letchworth from the surrounding towns and villages each day. Manual workers were forced to leave the village or commute, while many managerial and professional people chose to live in a village and preferred to commute. Hence depopulation of one element may be disguised by the immigration of another. However, in this village the arrival of the newcomers could not be thus hidden: in 1959 the population of the village was 610, in 1962 660 and in 1963 it was 700.

The small cluster of new houses more or less discreetly tacked on to a village is now a familiar sight in many parts of the country. How do the people in these houses relate to the established villagers? Is it possible for there to be a feeling of common interest between the middle-class commuters, whose network of social relations extends widely throughout the country, and those more locally oriented? How do the newcomers become integrated into village clubs and organizations?

The first step was to gather data on the various voluntary organizations in the village. We wanted to get information on membership and meetings; in particular we wanted the names and occupations of all the office holders (secretary, treasurer, chairman etc. and all committee members): we also wanted some general information from the secretary on the purpose of the organization and how successful it was in achieving it. We therefore devised a simple questionnaire asking for this information and explaining that the information provided would be used in the class on 'Our Changing Rural Community'. A class member who lived in the village spent many hours distributing, collecting and editing the forms. Without a local informant the data would have been much more difficult to obtain. For example, 37 per cent of all the names on the electoral roll were divided between five families and their names appeared frequently on the lists of office holders. Without detailed knowledge of kinship links further analysis would be impossible, as there would be no way of distinguishing between those with both similar surnames and similar initials.

A somewhat unusual feature in the pattern of voluntary associations was a Welcoming Club, with a membership of about fifty, founded in 1964 'to introduce new residents to the village – its people, organizations and services'. It was initiated by the Parochial Church Council 'to integrate newcomers' and the vicar was made president with two other members of the PCC as vice-presidents. New residents were visited and given a Diary of Village Activities – a stencilled sheet with details of the Churches, headed by the Church of England, followed by the Methodist Chapel, and then other nearby denominations, sports clubs, WI, British Legion, Civil Defence etc. Information was also given about evening classes, the children's clinic and the nearest doctor. Coffee mornings were held once a month in members' houses and twenty-five to thirty wives attended. At a sherry party in the house of the vice-president fifty people came, and 140 came to a Hallowe'en Party in the village hall. Remembering that the stated purpose of the club was to introduce new residents to the village it seemed odd that only eighteen months later it was considered to have achieved its purpose, despite the fact that it was openly acknowledged that 'village people will not join' and few new-comers took an active part in any other village organization apart from the Church.

An attempt was made to analyse systematically the composition of all the committees. It was clear from a superficial inspection that there was a good deal of overlap, office holders in one organi-zation having similar positions on various other committees. After a certain amount of trial and error the following method showed interesting results. The eighteen members of the Village Hall Committee were listed in the centre of a large piece of paper and whenever one of these names appeared on the committee or as an office holder of any other organization a line was drawn from the names to the appropriate box. Cross-affiliations were such that sixteen out of the eighteen had thirty-eight other positions between them, six having three each and one man hav-ing six. Furthermore, half of the Village Hall Committee were Methodists and an analysis of all office holders in Methodist organizations showed that the cross-affiliations of Methodist committee members and Village Hall Committee members intermeshed very tightly. The summary diagram opposite shows clearly the interlocking character of village organizations as determined by their most influential members.

Further analysis of office holders by occupation failed to pro-duce such striking results. The most common occupations were farmer, smallholder and farm worker. It was clear that village organizations catered for like-minded groups and only in the football and cricket clubs, the Young Farmers and the British Legion was there much mixing between the distinct social elements of village 'gentry', the Methodists, the Church and the new commuters. Both the Conservative and Labour clubs refused to complete the form and so it is not possible to do more than note some association between the Church of England and the Con-servatives and the Methodists and the Labour Party.

This was clearly a Methodist village. Average attendance in Chapel was about fifty and in the Church twelve. The Methodists were a tightly knit group with a very large proportion sharing four or five surnames between them. Non-Methodists were needed to complete the teams in the sports clubs and were accepted on the common ground of the Young Farmers' Club. The newcomers were likely to be both Conservatives and Anglicans and it is hardly surprising that quite apart from fundamental differences in styles of life, chances of 'integration' with the village were slight. *Some* commuters' wives met *some* of the more elderly village women at the Women's Institute but because the energetic Methodist group did not join the WI the newcomers were not drawn into the more important village net.

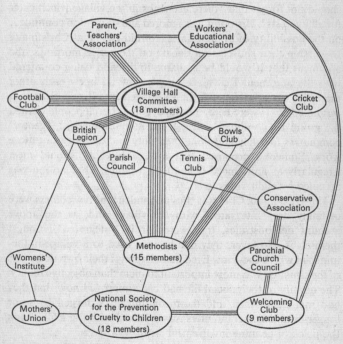

2. Web of Affiliations

Eighteen months after the foundation of the Welcoming Club an extraordinary general meeting was held in the afternoon in the Village Hall, which I was able to attend. The business was to decide the future of the club. The vicar reminded the sixteen commuters' wives present (others were absent at work) what the club had done. The committee recommended that the club should be disbanded since there could be no further building (and no more newcomers in large numbers) and 'members have all met each other now'. It was unanimously agreed that the club had achieved its purpose (presumably of integration with the village? Or of strengthening the Church of England?) Some discussion centred on alternative activities for the club: someone suggested a mime group; someone else suggested that theatre trips could be arranged. The vicar interposed a suggestion that the meeting should not forget that 'there are clubs in the village which cater for all interests'. His point was ignored and discussion continued, on the possibility of doing mimes 'for old people at Christmas'. Discussion then shifted to a debate on the coffee mornings, the argument that it would be a shame to disband being countered with the argument that since people now all knew each other there was no need for a formal arrangement. It was clear that certain conflicts were being revealed: some church people wanted the group to continue; other local, more-established, 'gentry' commuters felt they had done their duty and did not want more work. Someone proposed that a 'Coffee Club' should meet irregularly as announced in the Parish Notes. This motion was accepted by eight votes to six.

The Welcoming Club was thus disbanded; the newcomers were certainly not 'integrated' with the village and, as the above account demonstrates, they were hardly 'integrated' amongst themselves. However, they had become used to a village-in-the-mind, in which they now lived quite happily: their own definition of the situation was more important to them than objective reality. The quality of their social life had been improved now that they had met each other, and the mediating links, forged by some longer-established commuters' wives linked with the PCC, took the place of genuine involvement with the village.

NEST-CENTRED NEWCOMERS: THE MIDDLE-CLASS
SUBURB

In March 1966 a *Review of the South-East Study* was published
by the Standing Conference on London Regional Planning. The
original South-East Study had suggested that of the 3½ million
people to be accommodated in the area by 1981 some 1·3 million
would go to 'planned' expansion – that is, new towns or officially
sponsored 'expanded' towns. However, in the *Review*, with a
total population to be housed only slightly less than the original
estimate, the proportion to be housed in planned expansion had
markedly declined. This left 2,480,000 people to be housed under
what was known as 'normal' allocations of land in the development plans of the local authorities. This meant that a population
equal to that contained in twenty-five towns of the current size of
Cambridge would have to be added on to the existing settlements
of the South East within the fifteen-year period.

Thus it was that the medium-sized privately built estate
became an even more characteristic feature of the South-East. In
an attempt to find out something of the style of life characteristics
of one of these estates, some time was spent during the summer of
1964 with a group of young wives in a Hertfordshire market-
town devising a questionnaire and interviewing a quarter of the
housewives in the new estate of some 200 houses, just over a
mile from the centre of the town.

The estate overlooked a local authority one on the west side of
the valley. The estate gave the impression of a fortress straddling
the hill, with the lower rows of terrace houses being, as it were,
ramparts to the castle. Once one had climbed up into the main
road of the estate one got a different impression. Here there was a
feeling of spaciousness: the front gardens were unfenced and there
were wide views out into the country or back over the council
estate. However, there was also a feeling of loneliness: everything
seemed still and quiet and almost all the houses looked as if they
were deserted. The net curtains and venetian blinds held back
neighbourliness. On a glorious sunny afternoon only a few
houses had upstairs windows open and only a very few had a

front downstairs window open; the few women who were out walking or visiting all wore gloves.

Everyone was a newcomer: of the 46 women interviewed in the autumn of 1964, 39 had arrived since the beginning of 1962. Most people had moved out from north London suburbs, 25 in all; of the remainder, 12 came from other places in east Hertfordshire and 5 from elsewhere, the furthest being from south Oxfordshire. Few husbands worked in the town: both Harlow and Welwyn Garden City/Hatfield attracted their share of commuters and the remainder went either to the north London employment centres such as Southgate or Enfield, or right into the City. A few were representatives who had no fixed place of work. The longest journey to work was probably made by the manager of a supermarket in Watford. Most of the husbands could be classified as junior or middle managerial or professional people. In all, 11 were described as an engineer of some sort; this might be prefaced by, for example, aircraft, electronics, civil or development. There were 11 professional people, such as mathematician, physicist, accountant or solicitor, and there were 3 draughtsmen and 4 company representatives. A further 5 were employed at various levels in commerce, insurance and banking, and the remainder included such occupations as a self-employed builder, a supermarket manager, the head of a test room, the owner of a draper's shop and a toolmaker.

The fathers of these men were generally in occupational categories of slightly lower status – junior non-manual or skilled manual workers – but 10 of the fathers were in firmly established middle-class occupations. Of their wives, as many as 28 were engaged in secretarial or clerical work before marriage, a further 5 were in nursing or physiotherapy, and of the remaining 10, 3 were engaged in professional occupations, and 7 were junior non-manual workers, such as shop assistant, or manual workers, such as a comptometer operator. The fathers of these women were of very similar socio-economic status to the fathers of their husbands. Inspection of the fathers' occupations of all the couples showed that in only two or three cases were sons of solidly middle-class fathers married to daughters from a lower social status background. Thus we are considering here the lower middle and 'new middle class' (created by the expansion of job opportunities in the new growth industries), which together had common problems in status placement and the learning of new normative and relational behaviour. Any tension was thus common to the group which made up most of the estate and was not simply related to individual differences and difficulties. In any comparison with the New Town group it is of course crucial to note that the market-town wives were much less well educated: 64 per cent left school at 16 or younger and a further 25 per cent at the age of 17. The level of education of the wife appeared to be of greater importance than the occupation of the husband when considering local interaction or assimilation.

The wives who were interviewed were generally mothers of small children since those out at work could not be contacted. Only 7 households comprised husband and wife alone; 33 had at least one child under 5 (11 had two children under 5) and 12 households had at least one child over 5.

Social life

Questions were asked about friends on the estate, how they were met, how many were entertained in the home, how many were 'real friends', and so on. In addition, respondents were asked for their general comments on friendliness on the estate.

It was clear that there was a wide range between those who led a very sociable life and those who were isolated and sometimes extremely lonely. There were sixteen people who were classified as being 'very friendly'. They had all moved in together, and during the first hard winter, when water supplies were limited, there had been a fair amount of visiting each other's houses. Children also provided a means of effecting introductions. All in this category entertained frequently and there was little discrepancy between those entertained and 'real friends'. It is perhaps significant that *without exception* those classified as 'very friendly' (by the number of friends they had and the remarks and comments they made) were from the highest status level on the estate, the husbands being in established professional or managerial occupations. Of the fathers of the 'very friendly' wives, only three or four were manual workers and where this was the case the husband and husband's father were in established middle-class occupations. Strikingly, the 'very friendly' also had more relatives close enough to visit or be visited, variously described as 'many', 'hordes', 'lots', 'countless', 'hundreds' and so on.

Most of the sample – 25 people – were classified as of 'average friendliness' (and of these only three had no children). None of these 25 respondents was without help if it was needed, and none relied on relatives for this help. Like the 'very friendly', they were seemingly able to accept and integrate a *variety* of friends incorporating different aspects of their lives. Among the 'averagely friendly' group, too, by far the largest category of 'real' friends had been carried through from their previous address. The 25 households in the average friendly group had between them a total of 297 people whom at one time or another they had entertained. Of these, 170 were considered 'real friends' and of these 170, 35 were carried through from the previous address, 26 were wife's friends before marriage, another 26 were wife's local friends and 23 were wife's old school or college friends. Husbands supplied fewer real friends – 23 were colleagues from work, 17 were old school/college friends and only 6 were friends the husband had met locally.

The young women with young children, who arrived with the rest during the early days of the estate, generally felt the estate to be a friendly place – especially those with relatives nearby to give confidence and to supply a stable background of friendliness on which to draw. However, the old or those out at work during the day might find it difficult to break into the friendly net. For example, when one man's wife was dying no one offered to help, and when she was brought to lie by the window, neighbours complained that she was prying, since she could see into their back gardens. The world of the wives appeared strikingly insular, with an outward friendliness, but little interest in people and activities outside their narrow world. For those without relatives nearby it might be difficult to escape from the local mould: 'be one of us or be lonely'.

There was no baby-sitter's club or crèche on the estate at the time of the survey, and it seemed as if mothers did not want to engage in any different sort of social activity. Many wives did not like to leave children with baby-sitters at all, and some would not go out without taking the baby: it was clear that the majority preferred to spend the evening watching TV. Money was not mentioned as a factor influencing out-of-home activities and though it may have been important, only eleven couples went out together for pleasure more than once a month.

This was a child- and home-centred society. Respondents were asked how much they looked forward to various alternatives when their children were grown up. The following table summarizes their answers.

Wife	Per cent positive	Per cent negative	
Being a grandmother	60	40	
Freedom to travel	77	23	
Doing a full-time job	20	80	'Don't mind'
Going out more with husband	85	15	classified as
More local activities	37	63	negative
More relaxation at home	58	42	
More attention to husband	55	45	

If the above table is compared with the following, which shows the extent to which respondents wanted their husbands, when aged 50, to have various characteristics, some interesting conclusions emerge.

Husband	Per cent positive	Per cent negative
Wealthy and successful	60	40
Contented family man	100	—
Respected member of local community	60	40
With power and influence but no great wealth	10	90
Pleasant companion to do things with	100	—

Interviewers had the impression that wives gave little thought to what a man of 50 might really want. They assumed that being a contented family man, doing pleasant things with his wife and family would be enough for him, and indeed this may well be true. There was, however, something slightly sinister about the fear of husbands having power and influence (without great wealth). One imagines many men would be disappointed if in their various careers they were not able to have some power and influence at the age of 50. Clearly the wives did not want their husbands to move away from the nest on account of their interest in their jobs: maybe they also feared that the job might stretch them beyond their capabilities.

In an attempt to understand the wife's conception of her role in the home, a question was asked about the wife's ideas of what importance, in her opinion, a number of choices would have for her daughter. This question elicited a most interesting series of responses and the results are tabulated in full.

	Essential	Very important	Important	Don't mind	Not important
Healthy, happy children	17	14	9	1	—
Specialist training for a career	4	6	17	13	—
Wealth	1	1	4	17	17
An exciting and adventurous time	—	3	10	12	12
Someone like a doctor or MP for husband	—	—	8	16	15
A nice house with a kind husband and steady income	10	10	10	5	1
Freedom to be herself	21	8	10	1	—

When these results were described to the New Town group of mothers they were very surprised: many imagined that although children would certainly be important for their and other people's daughters' happiness, they would not be as important as the

replies suggested. Similarly, the more radically minded middle-
class mothers expected a greater emphasis on specialist training
and were surprised at the relatively high proportion which did not
appear to mind about this. The aversion to wealth may also be
unexpected. Since this question was answered very seriously,
with a deliberate weighing up of alternatives it is perhaps reasonable to assume that mothers were imposing their own values and
attitudes on to their daughters. One might have expected some
sort of fantasy, relating 'freedom to be herself' to career or
adventure. Instead the 'freedom' leads to *kinder, kuche* and the
nest. Respondents do not have very high-status husbands, their
own careers have been brief and they have found themselves with
children early in life; they seem to want their daughters to be the
same. Is this because they dare not face the alternative for themselves?

An attempt was made to make respondents face various
changes in their lives such as a sudden increase in their husband's
income or a possible change in his job. It was hoped that by
asking respondents to put themselves imaginatively into new
situations they would reveal more of their own image of themselves and their aspirations and ideas of 'the good life'. In a
question which postulated a sudden doubling of the husband's
income, respondents were asked to choose from a list of fifteen
ways of spending the extra money, but were warned that they
clearly could not have everything and that some restriction on
spending would still remain. Far and away the most important
item was felt to be a bigger house; 60 per cent would consider
this seriously and a further 21 per cent would certainly not disregard such a move, this despite the fact that respondents were
new arrivals in new houses. Second in importance was spending
money on children's education, which would be considered
seriously by half the respondents.

Turning to the wife's attitude to her husband moving his job
under various conditions, the strongest feelings were expressed
against any form of shift work, despite the increased income this
might involve, and the strongest encouragement was expressed
for the job which was better for the husband but involved more
help and understanding from the wife. This is an interesting

indication of a latent demand for a more companionate style of marriage: as these women get older their resentment against their husbands' 'careers' may increase. In general most wives were against their husbands moving. Most strikingly this was shown in the response to the situation where the 'new job would stretch him to the limit of his capacity'. Only 17 per cent would encourage this, and 69 per cent would discourage it. The other situation which most wives felt they would discourage would be if the new job, although better paid, involved a longer time away from home. Opinions were fairly evenly divided on the situation where the new job was less well paid but the work was more interesting and satisfying. The fact that there was not unanimous approval for such a move may imply that, in this, respondents were being realistic financially, or that they were relatively unconcerned about the work satisfaction of their husbands. When wives were asked what they thought the main purpose of their husband's job was, 32 mentioned that it gave him satisfaction, 18 mentioned the provision of income, and a further 11 mentioned support for the family, supporting the home, and so on. Only two respondents thought that the job should satisfy their husband's ambition. Rather they felt that the satisfaction he should get should perhaps inhibit ambition. As one said: 'If he's satisfied at work he's more contented and satisfied at home with his family', or again: 'He should leave a happy balance for the family', 'He should be satisfied with his job but it should leave a happy balance for the family', 'He should be satisfied with his job but it should not be a be all and end all'.

No one seemed to think that her husband was dissatisfied with his job. They all, apparently, enjoyed their work, found it interesting and were by no means concerned about more money or status. Wives had to think this, presumably, to give force to their concern that their husbands should not be stretched further. There is clearly some tension here. Many would *like* a bigger house, second car, and so on, but seemed reluctant that their husbands should work harder to get more money. Similarly they did not appear keen to go out to work themselves. I got a very strong impression that an ordinary, comfortable existance was the highest goal. These wives seemed afraid of too successful husbands. Many had vaguely idealistic ideas about their husband's work serving the community and so on, but it must be other people's husbands who rise to the top to take the major decisions and responsibility in society. No one felt that her husband was being held back, no one felt he lacked scope. If the export drive meant that some of these husbands would be obliged to work in the evenings their wives, I suspect, would be against it. The woman who said, 'I don't mind what he does as long as he gets a reasonable [*sic*] salary and he's happy' summed up the opinions of many. A fear of 'nervous strain' or otherwise endangering health was widespread – maybe this is due to the sort of studies in women's magazines or on TV – the ideal is 'a good happy medium position'.

Another woman felt 'any great success or interest in his work would inevitably bring sacrifice of family life'. Quite exceptional was the comment: 'Ambition is a good thing in a man.' It was understandable that wives should wish to discourage their husbands from staying away overnight, from excessive travel and from dirty or monotonous work, which was, of course, the view of the majority. Perhaps more significant was the statement: 'I'd be against anything which disrupted home life and I'd discourage anything too new and experimental.' In the light of these comments the aspirations expressed on behalf of their daughters are much less surprising.

When respondents were asked generally: 'In what do you find your chief sense of security', 33 mentioned their husbands, 16 of these mentioning children; 2 others also mentioned children, making 18 in all. Twelve respondents mentioned their 'home' as providing a sense of security, but all these combined it with other things such as husband or religion; 3 other respondents mentioned the material security of their own home as their chief source of confidence. Parents as a source of security were mentioned by 4 women, and 3 others mentioned their own happy childhood or upbringing. Only 2 women mentioned 'other people' and 'friends' and only 2 mentioned education and training; a further woman claimed 'growing experience' provided her chief sense of security.

NEWCOMERS AND SOCIAL CHANGE

In this final section I want to draw on my more extended research on three Hertfordshire villages. Without providing a summary of all my work (which I list at the end of this essay), I would like to make explicit a line of argument which may put the more limited studies described above in their context.

I do not want to refer to the villages by name since what I am doing now is to create 'ideal types' which I can fit into a model or continuum of change. In the first village almost everyone is engaged in or retired from agriculture. Apart from the church, the school and one or two other houses the squire owns the complete parish and the estate is run with an efficient and enlightened paternalism. Newcomers may be a shepherd from Yorkshire or a gamekeeper from Norfolk and everyone soon gets to know them. Since, in one way or another, most people see each other when they are about their day-to-day business, there seems little point in meeting together in the evenings. The women are more isolated – as the gamekeeper's wife said, 'It would seem funny to have a neighbour' – and so the Women's Institute meetings are welcomed for the opportunity to get out of the home. Thus there are two groups: the squire who owns the village and the villagers who are economically dependent on the squire and interdependent on each other. The squire refuses to sell land to potential newcomers.

The second village is in a different category. The squire still owns most of the parish but he does not exert the same sort of influence. Tenant farmers are responsible for the management of most of the land and the squire is more concerned with his strong financial interests in London. The local RDC has chosen the village as a centre for local authority housing and an estate caters for a number of surrounding parishes, in addition to local needs. In keeping with the squire's stronger financial interests, land has been sold to private developers who have built suburban-style houses for junior white-collar workers who commute. Nevertheless the squire still owns most of the village and exerts influence as chairman of the RDC's housing committee: he controls most people's housing whether as council tenants or private tenants.

However, the squire does not control the jobs of the majority, who commute out to local factories or work for builders, transport contractors and so on: their houses are in the village because they were born there, but their main economic life is elsewhere. People such as the Rector or the area youth officer believe there ought to be more local activity – dances, clubs and so on – they do not understand that the community is in transition and sees no purpose in itself for itself. Those white-collar newcomers who work for a large factory in a near-by town can get all the social facilities they need in the firm's 'country club' for employees, which is just down the road. Their children may go to the local school but, for them, the village is simply a bus-stop in the country. They have a cheaper house and a larger garden than they could find elsewhere.

It was difficult to know where 'the village' was. The old-age pensioners in condemned houses in the village street? The people in council houses who have moved in from a neighbouring parish and who work in a neighbouring town? The agricultural workers in their tied cottages out near the farms or in tiny hamlets? The newly arrived 'privates' who commute from their smart suburban houses? Only the squire 'is' the village, and he is only interested in it from a financial point of view.

In the case of the third village the squire sold much of the land after the First World War and only the ex-governesses or butlers, who still live in the village, remember the old order. One manor house is a school, another is divided into flats, and a third is smaller and is still used as a private residence (open to the public on Sundays). This village is much further along the continuum of change. During the 1930s the near-by Garden City drew out men to work in factories and they could easily commute by bicycle. An area of woodland, just over a mile from the village, began to be developed by professional and managerial immigrants. Individuals bought two or three plots of land so that substantial houses could be built and remain hidden in the trees. This set a precedent which was continued after the Second World War.

Since the junior white-collar workers were in a very small minority the 'village' was divided between the manual workers at one end in council houses and the managers in privately owned houses at the other. The two broad groups had quite distinctive styles of life and lived in distinct social worlds (see Chapter 1, above). The differences between manual and non-manual workers in terms of educational opportunity, conditions of employment (holidays, hours of work, pension rights) and so on have been well-documented by sociologists and are summarized by Klein. The village provided an arena in which the two value-systems and ways of life could confront each other. In order to understand each system the sociologist is forced away from the local milieu to the wider industrial situation. Employment and level of wages or salaries depend less on local and more on national or international decisions. For example, the reassessment of an international defence commitment may lead the government to cut back on an armament contract which may lead to the redundancy of a worker from the council estate as much as a manager in the wood. The manager may be obliged to move house on taking up his next job, possibly some distance away.

In the same way that the villages round the towns expand as immigrants move in, so also do the towns round London expand as people move out of the conurbation in search of a cheaper house, from which the men commute back. New Towns, to provide jobs and better houses for Londoners, are just part of a broader process of peripheral expansion. The centrifugal move-ment out of the cities and out of the smaller towns hits the villages which are themselves in a process of change, as I have just described. New industries create new jobs which mean new occupational categories (or status groups) with distinctive value systems. 'Traditional' jobs and values come up against 'non-traditional' jobs and values, as Margaret Stacey shows so clearly in her study of Banbury. The son of a coal-miner who is now a tutor-librarian in a college of Further Education does not see himself living next door to the tea-importer in his wooded retreat, even if he could afford it. Similarly the daughter of a bus-conductor who was a typist for a few years after she left school, before marrying a salesman in the firm, would find the radical, graduate wife too frightening and confusing. Both are doing what is expected of them: the nest-centred wives of the small town estate reflect values which are still typically found in women's magazines of the traditional sort, whereas the radical wives are more self-conscious and read *New Society* and the *Guardian*.

Sociologists are much concerned both with the way existing communities work and also with broader changes in the national class structure. Studies by Goldthorpe and Lockwood and, more recently, by Runciman, stress the importance of values, self-rated class and style of life in an understanding of our changing social structure. Some of these broader changes can be fully understood only by detailed analysis at the local level. Occupational groups are becoming more sharply segregated, not only by residential area, but also socially and culturally. The cultivation of a particular style of life may be linked not only to present occupation and life-chances but also to social origins. That is to say, in any one occupation not only is present salary important but so also is access to capital, however limited. For those without any capital, apart from what they can save, the housing market forces them into a particular sort of house at any given stage in their life-cycle. For those with capital, however, their choice is considerably extended and their style of life may be significantly different. Again social networks may depend very considerably on the level of education of the wife. Even when the middle-class husband does not commute long distances to work he is still very dependent on his wife for maintaining social contacts.

Given these changes, which Klein and others have commented on in a general way, there is a need for many more careful studies at a local level, describing distinctive, normative patterns of behaviour (or styles of life) and the relations between these increasingly segregated worlds. In the New Town study I probed the values of one atypical minority and at the time there was no way of finding more of their pattern of social relationships. In the commuter village the introduction of the religious element added a further complication to the local configuration. In other parts of the South-East where the local status hierarchy is more complex – in an area of smallholdings for example – the response to newcomers will again be different. In some places those who have established themselves in the recent past may act as mediators or gatekeepers linking newcomers to the local situation. It would be interesting to know more of such people and how easily they can move between social worlds. Is their position in the local social structure ambiguous because of their occupation or because of their length of residence or something else? If some groups expect more from a local place, in the way of active voluntary associations and so on, than others, is it possible to define these more precisely, possibly relating them to occupation or house type (in effect income)?

Adult classes in sociology or local studies could perhaps discover the basic structure of their established community and relate it to their own continuum of change or to the morphological continuum suggested by Frankenberg. They might characterize the newcomers in terms of distinctive styles of life and relate these to the local configuration. Local situations of conflict – over schools, local planning decisions and the provision of other services – or the action of resident's associations or local councils provide opportunities for mapping out lines of tension between social worlds. The distribution of power – whether economic, political or social should be an important part of the analysis, and studies such as those by Vidich and Bensman or Lowry provide readable introductions and give valuable hints, even if they are not close parallels to the British situation. Making conscious the processes of which we form a part is a challenging and yet necessary task if we are to remain self-aware people and not puppets.

REFERENCES AND FURTHER READING

Bott, E., *Family and Social Network*, Tavistock Publications, 1957.
Durant, R., *Watling: A Survey of Social Life on a New Housing Estate*, P. S. King & Son Ltd, 1939.
Frankenberg, R., *Communities in Britain; Social Life in Town and Country*, Penguin Books, Harmondsworth, 1966.
Goldthorpe, J. H., and Lockwood, D., 'Affluence and the British class structure', *Sociological Review*, N.S. 11(2), 1963, 133–63.
Jefferies, M., 'Londoners in Hertfordshire', *London, Aspects of Change*, edited by Centre for Urban Studies, MacGibbon & Kee, 1964.

Klein, J., *Samples from English Cultures*, Vol. 1, Routledge & Kegan Paul, 1965.

Lowry, J., *Who's Running This Town?*, Harper & Row, 1965.

Morris, R. N., and Mogey, J., *The Sociology of Housing: Studies at Berinsfield*, Routledge & Kegan Paul, 1965.

Pahl, R. E., 'Education and social class in commuter villages', *Sociological Review*, N.S. 11(2), 1963, 241–6.

—, 'The old and the new: a case study', *New Society* 29 October 1964.

—, 'Class and community in English commuter villages', *Sociologia Ruralis* 5(1), 1965, 5–23. Reprinted here as Chapter 1.

—, *Urbs in Rure: The Metropolitan Fringe in Hertfordshire*, London School of Economics, Geographical Papers No. 2, 1965.

—, 'Commuting and social change in rural areas', *Official Architecture and Planning*, July 1966.

—, 'The social objectives of village planning', *Official Architecture and Planning*, August 1966. Reprinted here as Chapter 2.

—, 'The rural-urban continuum', *Sociologia Ruralis*, 6(3–4), 1966. Reprinted in *Readings in Urban Sociology*, Pahl, R. E., (ed.), Pergamon Press, 1968.

Runciman, W. G., *Relative Deprivation and Social Justice*, Routledge & Kegan Paul, 1966.

Stacey, M., *Tradition and Change: A Study of Banbury*, Oxford University Press, 1960.

Vidich, A. J., and Bensman, J., *Small Town in Mass Society: Class, Power and Religion in a Rural Community*, Doubleday Anchor Books, 1960.

Chapter 4 Social differences between urban and rural societies

Both village and town retain many characteristics of the family; the village retains more, the town less. Only when the town develops into the city are these characteristics almost entirely lost. Individuals or families are separate identities, and their common locale is only an accidental or deliberately chosen place in which to live. But as the town lives on within the city, elements of life in the Gemeinschaft, as the only real form of life, persist within the Gesellschaft, although lingering and decaying. On the other hand, the more general the condition of Gesellschaft becomes in the nation or a group of nations, the more this entire 'country' or the entire 'world' begins to resemble one large city. However, in the city and therefore where general conditions character-istic of the Gesellschaft prevail, only the upper strata, the rich and the cultured, are really active and alive. They set up the standards to which the lower strata have to conform.

FERDINAND TÖNNIES, 1887[1]

It is important to remember that Tönnies was concerned in his work to explore not only the situations in which *gemeinschaftlich* relationships continued within the *Gesellschaft* but also to relate his dichotomy of social relationships to the social structure. He expected *gemeinschaftlich* relationships to continue amongst, say, women, artists and the poor whereas the merchants, the rich and those in authority would be typically *gesellschaftlich*. The *Gemeinschaft* of place was but one type: there was also the *Gemeinschaft* of kin and friendship.

Today I think we would all be extremely cautious in attributing a particular style or pattern of social relationships to particular categories of people or places. Perhaps I should emphasize that in this chapter I am drawing primarily on the situation in Britain where the majority of the population is *culturally* if not physically urbanized. Hence the *size* of settlement may not be a significant variable when people listen to the same radio and television programmes, read the same newspapers and consume the same goods, no matter where they live. Tönnies was concerned with the qualitative effects of quantitative changes. The important question still remains: what *are* the significant variables which affect the style and pattern of social relationships?

Few would argue that there are sex-linked characteristics, so that in all societies, no matter what the pattern of socialization, women, say, are more or less calculative in their social relationships than are men. Similarly it would be hard to contend that 'peasants' – however we may define that term – are more or less shrewd, calculative and rationalistic than, say, industrial managers. Indeed the recent work of Homans and Blau[2] suggests that much of social behaviour is of necessity calculative, based on the norm of reciprocity and the principles of social exchange: even in the case of love – the polar case of intrinsic attraction – 'each individual furnishes rewards to the other, not to receive proportionate extrinsic benefits in return but to express and confirm his own commitment and to promote the other's growing commitment to the association'.[3]

Modern sociological analysis has also cast considerable doubt on the thesis that industrialization, urbanization and bureaucratization necessarily and inevitably lead to atomization and the break-up or disappearance of primary groups. There is an enormous literature on the importance and persistence of small face-to-face groups in factories and offices; links with extra-familial kin have been studied in a variety of contexts and, although the nature of the links may be changing, there is no evidence of any collapse of such ties. This point is elaborated on by Litwak and Szelényi in their paper on primary group structures.[4] Despite the unanimity of sociological research on this point a popular view of the destructive effects of the sheer size of urban agglomerations on the pattern of social relationships still prevails. It is important to recognize this as a product of an anti-urban ideology which is unfounded on empirical fact.

The important point is that the immediate locality does not *necessarily* generate a pattern of social relationships for an *in-*

creasing proportion of the population in *advanced* industrial societies. Modern methods of transport and communication have enabled men to leave the primary group of the work situation, which is often physically some distance from home, in order to retire to the privacy and autonomy of their domestic situation. However, for the poor and those in certain distinctive occupations the immediate locality imposes itself upon them. The poor may lack the resources to escape from immediate social relationships. These local social relationships act as an important basis for social control which may be seen either as a necessary support or as an objectionable tyranny. Those encapsulated from the rest of society in this way may be in 'urban villages' or 'rural villages': in either case they simply lack the resources or perhaps the motivation to escape to another social world. The constraining influence of these social worlds depends on the housing and employment situation elsewhere. The most highly skilled or highly qualified can get employment, and probably housing, almost anywhere. This gives them power, so that the highly qualified professional and managerial strata may be the most reluctant to live in places which they define as less suitable for their style of life. The poor have less choice but also fewer demands: the less-well-educated do not miss concerts, bookshops and intellectual companionship. Perhaps the most isolated and constrained in this way are the old who lack money and have few, if any, living relatives.[5] Physically and economically such people are trapped. This, of course, creates a vicious circle: the more that specific milieux acquire concentrations of the deprived the less attractive such places then appear to those with more power (that is more choice) and the more likely that those trapped there will be more deprived.

Certain occupational categories may also find themselves socially, and even physically, cut off from the rest of society. Clark Kerr and others have noted that occupational groups such as miners, dock-workers, deep-sea fishermen and the like, in a number of societies, are more strike-prone than other groups, such as shopkeepers or agricultural workers. They argue that where all the employees do much the same work and have much the same experiences, and the industrial situation is such that large numbers need to be brought together – in the mining town or waterfront district – then localities will develop their own 'codes, myths, heroes and social standards'.[6] This combination of industrial and physical isolation enables such workers to develop a relative immunity from the normative pressures of the wider society. The skills of such men are not transferable and it is thus hard for them to move either up or out. 'Protest is less likely to take the form of moving to another industry and more the character of a mass walkout.'[7] Workers encapsulated in these community and industrial sub-cultures may be in physically urban or rural situations: indeed lumbermen and certain types of miners may be more isolated from cities and urban life than many agricultural workers, whereas, of course, dockers are often in the heart of industrial cities. Social isolation does not necessarily involve physical isolation, particularly in societies where distinctive class cultures have emerged.

Similarly physical isolation does not necessarily involve social isolation: the large capitalist farmer or landowner in Britain or America may spend most of his life living in comparative isolation on his land. However, his network of social relationships and his reference group are ever-present, however much these significant others are physically scattered. Proprietors of agri-businesses have the means and the motivation to overcome any potential spatial restraints and to live instead in their class culture. I believe there is an increasing tendency to live in occupational if not class cultures: the community of the profession is replacing the community of the locality. But my membership of the occupational community of professional sociologists depends on *communication*. Unless I can write to, say, colleagues in Czechoslovakia, exchange books, papers and information and also exchange visits and attend conferences from time to time, then we cannot keep in the same occupational community. The same applies within a nation: if occupational and other categories of people are not able to keep in touch with each other through the free use of the media of communication then proximity is essential. If, say, intellectuals feel obliged to move together to the same place then this is more likely to be a reflection of the difficulty of other means of communication rather than something inherent in the place. For example, those people who write to the London *Times*, which is generally held to be the paper for the nation's élite, do not all live in London. Indeed, they are more likely to live in villages or isolated houses throughout the country: Bertrand Russell lived in an isolated part of Wales and many more such examples could be cited.

My argument is, therefore, that in advanced industrial societies 'Any attempt to tie particular patterns of social relationships to specific geographical milieux is a singularly fruitless exercise.'[8] Some people are of the city but not in it, whereas others are in the city but not of it: the *Gemeinschaft* exists within the *Gesellschaft* and the *Gesellschaft* within the *Gemeinschaft*. Now this is a strong point which is unlikely to hold true in Eastern Europe where those that are not in the city suffer in certain respects. If that is the case it still has to be demonstrated that this is due to the *size* of the settlement: when the urban dweller moves to his weekend or summer cottage is he any less 'urban'? The fundamental variables in determining styles of life will still be class and life-cycle stage, even though size of settlement may be an ancillary variable. Furthermore, even if it can be demonstrated that, within a given society, and controlling for age/sex structure, religious belief and socio-economic status, small settlements have a higher or lower rate of fertility, suicide, deaths due to cardio-vascular diseases or whatever, the *sociological* significance of such variation in rates has to be demonstrated. For example, the higher rate of deaths due to cancer of the stomach in parts of rural Wales *may* be due to the value attached to fried food and the frequent use of old fat when frying, or it *may* be due to physical properties in the local water supply or indeed some other cause altogether. Similarly *if* it is shown that there is a lower rate of social mobility in small settlements than in larger ones, it still has to be demonstrated that this is directly related to the size of the settlement rather than, say, the occupational composition of the population. There may be populations encapsulated *within* cities numerically as large as other complete settlements and with as low or lower rates of inter-generational social mobility. Larger settlements are more likely to have employment in the tertiary or quaternary sectors of the economy which are growing most rapidly. However, new research-based industries or academic power houses are often sited in new or expanded centres outside cities. Where new sources of employment need a large amount of land, whether for playing fields or laboratories, they are obliged to move away from urban centres. Furthermore, this change in the occupational structure may give the illusion that there is more opportunity for upward mobility in the cities than there actually is. However, with the decline in urban unskilled and semi-skilled employment it may be more difficult for the migrant from rural areas to be socially mobile. This blockage in mobility potential is seen in its extreme form in the plight of the American Negro who has been lured by false hopes to the northern cities of the United States.

Finally it would be wrong to see the large settlement as the inevitable destroyer of the small settlement. The linkages between economic growth and change and the hierarchy of settlement structure are still only imperfectly understood. It seems clear that different relationships are appropriate at different times and it is extremely dangerous to make generalizations between different historical and socio-cultural contexts. It now seems clear that the period of urban concentration is typical only of the *early* stages of industrialization and has given way in many advanced industrial societies to a more diffuse and dispersed form of urbanism.[9] The same settlement structure may be evaluated quite differently at different historical periods with different levels of technological development. Thus at one period, for example, the intellectual may flee the small town for the big city in order to get more stimulation, whereas at another period the intellectual may withdraw from the noisy and traffic-congested city to the peace and more leisurely pace of the small town. The latter situation can only arise when accessibility between the different-sized centres is quick, cheap and efficient. Thus one gets the links between economic growth, technology and the spatial pattern of social relationships.

In the past some sections of the population achieved social mobility by physical mobility to the towns. Certainly the élite in pre-industrial cities recruited its religious acolytes and apprentices from a wide area. In a recent paper[10] Wrigley has made some very interesting calculations to account for the addition of

275,000 people to the population of London between 1650 and 1750 when an average of 8,000 immigrants a year would have been needed throughout the period to cover the shortfall of births over deaths. During this period London grew to be the largest city in Europe reaching some 575,000 by the end of the century and continuing to 900,000 in 1800. Assuming it to be the young and unmarried who are most likely to migrate, and since this category would represent a birth population half as large again and since, finally, the average surplus of births over deaths in provincial England at that time was 5 per 1,000 per annum, then London's growth was absorbing the natural increase of a population of some $2\frac{1}{2}$ million! This is even more remarkable when one remembers that the population of England, excluding London, was only about 5 million at this time, and that in many areas of the West and North there was little natural increase, or indeed there was a decrease in these areas.

I have stressed this example because in many ways the demographic situation of London between 1650 and 1750 is very similar to that of Prague or Budapest today. The interesting problem to debate is why this 'pre-industrial' pattern should be paralleled in Eastern Europe when the pattern now is a movement to the periphery of cities and city regions in many industrial societies. Central parts of cities are losing population as the outer suburbs and fringe areas expand. The reasons for this dispersal are complex. Partly this is a product of the way the housing market operates,[11] partly it may be seen as a way of acquiring prestige or enhancing status,[12] partly it may reflect the demand to escape the noise and congestion of the centre for the relative quiet and better facilities (particularly for education and socialization of the young) in the periphery, or it may simply be the result of industrial relocation.[13] Perhaps new technological aids such as the computer and video telephone may help to stop the recent trend of the concentration of office employment in urban areas. What has been called 'the routine processing of paper' may take place not at the centre but at the periphery of urban concentrations within the very near future. Communication provides the key to what is both possible and desirable.

Having said all this I now want to pose some issues which do seem to me to be related to differences between rural and urban societies, as these terms are commonly understood.

1. The low density of population in rural areas must mean that the *availability of facilities* is in certain ways restricted. Holding class and life-cycle characteristics constant, the spatial constraint will always operate inequitably. Of course facilities are not equally easily available for those living in urban centres, but given a public transport system and so on, the poor in urban areas may be less deprived in this respect than the poor in rural areas.

2. The *density of role relationships* declines from the rural to the urban. Where relationships are single-stranded, social control and social pressures are less intense and the more highly educated may value this 'freedom' in urban areas. Those of higher social status in rural areas are less able to withdraw from interaction with those of lower social status than may be the case in urban areas, where there is greater opportunity for social segregation. This is a particularly important issue when considering the education and socialization of children.

3. Almost by definition the range of *occupational choice* in rural areas is small. Where agriculture and related occupations are dominant young people may be inadequately socialized to adopt new work cultures or occupational styles. This same point may, of course, also apply to other isolated occupational communities discussed above. However, whilst sharing some characteristics with solidaristic, collectivist occupational groups such as miners and dock-workers, the agricultural worker also shares much of the occupational ethos of those at the other extreme, such as lorry drivers and small shopkeepers who stress individual autonomy. It is this combination of isolation and independence, as Marx described in the Eighteenth Brumaire, which characterizes the peasant or agricultural worker in industrial societies.

4. The new *adventitious or commuting rural population* which has been moving into rural areas over the past twenty years in many industrial societies is creating a whole series of new situations and new problems, which have not been adequately portrayed and discussed in the traditional and well-known sociological studies and texts.

5. Attitudes to rural and urban societies are rarely free from *strong ideological bias*. These may be based on antagonisms related to a previous situation with regard to the landlords or the ruling class. In societies where the landowners typically lived in the cities and exploited the rural peasantry, rural–urban ideologies are likely to be very different from those societies where the landed élite lived out on the country estates in their manors or castles. But whatever the basis of the antagonism, links between urban and rural sub-systems of the parent society are unlikely to be free from tension, based on the unequal economic and political power relations between them. For example, many socialist societies appear to be strongly pro-urban and cut back on investment in the rural sector. On the other hand many ex-imperialist capitalist nations – and indeed the specialist branches of the United Nations – have adopted a strong anti-urban bias, concentrating investment in the rural sector in Third World nations. It is interesting that one recent American commentator on the issue was apparently personally disturbed to discover that the socialist ideological bias produced the quickest results.[14]

1. *The spatial constraint and lack of facilities in areas of low population density and dispersed settlement*

The lack of facilities in rural areas implies both that the rural poor are particularly disadvantaged and, secondly, that social welfare policies are likely to demand that there should be as few poor in rural areas as possible. Of course, even if agricultural workers are paid more than some industrial workers they may nevertheless remain relatively poor. Since it is the rich who are more likely to be the first to acquire private transport, there is likely to develop, in an advanced industrial society, a situation where only those who have the means to overcome the spatial constraint will want to live in a dispersed settlement pattern. The poor and the old will prefer to be closer to facilities in larger concentrations. No society can completely disregard the cost of communication and the provision of services. The result may well be that rural areas will be polarized between the poor whose work keeps them there and the rich who have chosen to be there (perhaps only at week-ends and holidays).

This problem may be illustrated by a case study of the English county of Norfolk.[15] There are some 500 villages in the county and nearly four fifths of these are in areas of population decline. A prosperous agriculture has led to a marked and continuing decline in the demand for full-time workers. Furthermore the market towns are replacing the villages as the main service centres for the surrounding countryside. Over 75 per cent of the parishes in Norfolk have a population of less than 500 and in only 10 per cent is the population over 1,000. The problem is how many of these 500 villages could (economically) or should (socially) survive. It has been calculated that agriculture alone would be able to support about fifty villages of 1,000 population each. At the moment there seems to be an acute shortage of alternative employment opportunities. None of the school leavers from grammar schools can find a job in their home village. The provision of facilities is poor – 77 per cent of the population live in parishes without a doctor's surgery and 75 per cent live more than fifteen miles from hospital facilities. For 27 per cent of the population there is no daily bus service. Despite these trends parts of the area are attracting a new commuting population and in other parts of the county 80 per cent of the houses for sale are bought by retired people. In some areas the depopulation of one element of the population is masked by the arrival of newcomers. The local planners have calculated that a support population of not less than 5,000 is needed for everyday facilities. On this basis and with the present pattern of population, a decision has to be made whether to allow most villages to sink into rural micro-ghettos of the poor, the old and the deprived, or whether ruthlessly to destroy the majority of the county's villages. The social costing of such an exercise is not easy.

2. *Social segregation in areas of dispersed settlement*

There seems to be a general demand in most advanced industrial societies for those in privileged positions in the occupational hierarchy to hand on something of this privilege to their children. Perhaps the most important means of doing this is to ensure that the socialization of young children is reinforced by a peer group of the same social status so that, for example, children of managerial and professional workers become accustomed to practise role distance, functional autonomy and more complex and logical patterns of speech.[16] In non-socialist societies the privileged rich who live in rural areas are able to send their children to fee-paying private schools in order that they may not be socialized by their social inferiors. In socialist societies or in countries such as Britain, moving towards a system of comprehensive state education, we may expect a trend towards greater social segregation in both rural and urban areas, assuming that rents and house prices are governed by the market to some degree. Hence some areas will become predominantly for the managerial or professional categories, others for the junior white-collar workers and so on. Alternatively the dispersed settlement pattern may deter the more affluent from moving to rural areas until their children have been through the educational system. These are the sort of issues which need to be explored in the appropriate national and social situation. It is extremely difficult to arrange the same educational provision for those differentially located – whether socially or spatially.

3. *Occupational choice in areas of dispersed settlement*

In their attempt to define a theory of occupational choice Ford and Box state the following proposition: 'In choosing between alternative occupations a person will rank the occupations in terms of the relation between his values and the perceived characteristics of the occupation: the higher the coincidence between the characteristics and his values the higher the rank.'[17]

This may not be an entirely appropriate proposition in an area of declining population, promoted by the mechanization of agriculture where the alternatives are to be unemployed or to migrate. Perhaps the young person has to make the choice after migration to an urban area. Much will depend on the distance from the urban area, the amount of information which has come back from previous migrants to the city, the formal organizations and informal networks which help to ease the migrant into the urban system and so on. Work by Mayer, Epstein and Touraine[18] helps to classify and clarify the processes in modernizing societies, but of course the situation may be broadly similar in more advanced industrial societies.

The important point is that occupational choice takes place in a different milieu for the rural–urban migrant. Of course the break for an agricultural worker going to a factory-based job may be no greater cultural change than would be the case for a miner or a lorry driver. It is often assumed that the move out of agriculture is more distinctive and exceptional than would be the move from any other declining industry. It is difficult to see why this should be so, particularly when the increasing mechanization of agriculture is making it less of a craft industry and more closely akin to production line methods – certainly this seems to be the case for advanced dairy farming and types of meat and egg production. Hence whilst migrants from certain types of farming try to maintain out-of-doors work with more autonomy and may prefer to move into, say, the building and construction industry, others may find no difficulty in adopting the rhythms and work norms of more advanced production technology.

4. *The new adventitious or commuting population*

First of all, those rich enough to buy or rent a cottage or house in the country may simply go there for holidays in the summer or their wives and children may go there at intervals. Later, with the increasing use and ownership of private cars these second homes may be used every weekend. Finally, possibly, people will prefer to live in their country homes and either commute in by car every day (thus making the city congested) or keep a small flat in the city in which the chief earner lives for four nights a week. Different societies have different traditions of urbanism and one must be cautious in projecting the same trend for all societies. However, it is clear that given such a situation of a new urban-employed population living in rural areas a number of problems will arise. New facilities will be demanded by populations below the appropriate economic thresholds. Conflicts and tensions arising out of the use of land for farming or recreation, or relating to the speed and nature of local development, will emerge. The local power situation will be disrupted and those who would otherwise hold office in voluntary associations will be resentful at being displaced. Since girls are more likely to be socially mobile than boys, it is likely that more local girls will marry offspring of the newcomers, obliging the local boys to look for spouses elsewhere. This will produce more tension and conflict. It is possible that local communities will be polarized between the 'established' and the 'newcomer' element.[19]

5. *Urban and rural ideologies*

Once one has reached a certain level of technology, population concentration or dispersal becomes largely an ideological issue. In more technologically primitive times settlements developed in central places, for defence, as trading centres, communication centres and so on. Once established such centres continued, partly through inertia and partly because of the market value of centrality. The place where most people passed had the highest potential to attract customers and so the rents for stalls (or later shops or other uses) were highest. However, with advancing technology the advantages of centrality were subject to the law of diminishing returns. Electric power, the motor-car, the telephone and so on enabled the various functions to be decentralized without being any less profitable, although farther away from each other in time and so forth. Indeed, the same market forces, which under one set of technological conditions led to concentration, at another period led to dispersal (e.g. out of town shopping centres) under different technological conditions.

Parallel with the technological and market forces were ideological forces; for example, conservatives in capitalist societies feared the concentration of workers and argued for decentralization. A fear of concentration may also exist in socialist societies, since social control of non-party members is easier in small settlements. At a later period, but at different levels of economic development, in capitalist societies progressives argue for decentralization in terms of regional balance and diseconomies of scale, whereas in socialist societies progressives are arguing the reverse, claiming economies of scale and greater choice in large concentrations.

Some awareness of the degree of choice between concentration and dispersal, which is now possible, has led planners to seek some super logic, some absolutes, by which they can decide where to put homes, employment centres and facilities. This forces planners to make judgements about the good life, or rather the distinctive 'good lives' based on differing goals and values in society. But planners, like everyone else, are not free from values and ideologies. Some planners will operate with a consensual model of society and others with a conflict model. Some planners will aim to devise *the* plan and expect to find an answer to the question of the optimum size of a city; other planners will envisage a *number* of plans and will understand that the 'optimal size' is an unresolvable issue.

In modern society, with a division of labour based on highly differentiated skills, a minority, who accumulate intellectual resources through the educational system, gain considerable power in society. Inevitably power is concentrated and planners generally plan for those with most power. Those with most power generally wish to maintain that power, which means that they will try to ensure that plans do nothing to diminish their power. Thus in a conflict situation, where power, wealth and prestige are unequally distributed, any plan or any system produces its set of constraints and disadvantages for some section of the population (those with least power). Different sections of the population will have different goals and values and different amounts of power. Conflicts between bureaucrats and workers, provincials and metropolitans, highly educated and less-well educated, working women and non-working women, party members and non-party members, agricultural workers and factory workers, large families and small families, the young and the old are all inherent in society to a greater or lesser degree. Indeed these conflicts are essential to society. It is only within the context of these conflicts that the ideologies of rural/urban balance can be seen and assessed.

REFERENCES

1 Tönnies, F., *Community and Society*, Harper Torchbook Edition, 1963, translated and edited by Loomis, C. P. (first published in German in 1887), p. 227.

2 Homans, G. C., *Social Behaviour: Its Elementary Forms*, Routledge & Kegan Paul, 1961; and Blau, P. M., *Exchange and Power in Social Life*, John Wiley & Sons Inc., 1964.

3 Blau, op. cit., 76.

4 Litwak, E. and Szelényi, I., 'Primary group structures and their functions: Kin, neighbours and friends', *American Sociological Review*, 34(4), August 1969, 456–81.

5 Townsend, P., *The Family Life of Old People*, Routledge & Kegan Paul, 1957.

6 Kerr, C., and Siegel, A., 'The interindustry propensity to strike – An international comparison', in Kornhauser, A., *et al.*, *Industrial Conflict*, McGraw-Hill, 1954. Reprinted in Kerr, C., *Labor and Management in Industrial Society*, Doubleday Anchor Books, 1964, 109. See also the argument of Parkin, F., 'Working-class conservatives', *British Journal of Sociology*, Vol. 18, 1967, 278–90.

7 Kerr, C., op. cit., 110–11.

8 Pahl, R. E., 'The rural-urban continuum', *Sociologia Ruralis*, Vol. 6, 1966, 299–329. Reprinted in *Readings in Urban Sociology*, Pahl, R. E. (ed), Pergamon Press, 1968.

9 Schnore, L. F., *The Urban Scene*, Free Press, Glencoe.
Dobriner, W. M., *Class in Suburbia*, Prentice-Hall, Englewood Cliffs, N.J., 1963.
Pahl, R. E., *Urbs in Rure: The Metropolitan Fringe in Hertfordshire*, London Scool of Economics, Geographical Papers No. 2, 1965.

10 Wrigley, E. A., 'A simple model of London's importance in changing English society and economy 1650–1750', *Past and Present*, No. 37, 1967, 44–70.

11 Clark, S. D., *The Suburban Society*, University of Toronto Press, 1966.

12 See Pahl, 'The rural–urban continuum', 303–10, and Dobriner, op. cit., 1963.

13 Berger, B. M., *Working Class Suburb*, University of California Press, 1960.

14 Sjoberg, G., 'Rural–urban balance and models of economic development', in Smelser, N. J., and Lipset, S. M. (eds.), *Social Structure and Mobility in Economic Development*, Routledge & Kegan Paul, 1966.

15 Green, R. J., and Ayton, J. B., 'Changes in the pattern of Rural settlement'. Paper read to the Town Planning Institute Conference on *Planning for the Changing Countryside*, October 1967.

16 Ford, J., *et al.*, 'Functional autonomy, role distance and social class', *British Journal of Sociology*, 18, 1967, 370–81.

17 Ford, J., and Box, S., 'Sociological theory and occupational choice', *Sociological Review*, 15, 1967, 287–99.

18 Epstein, A. L., 'Urbanization and social change in Africa', *Current Anthropology*, 8(4), 1967, 275–95.
   Mayer, P., 'Migrancy and the study of Africans in towns', *American Anthropologist*, 1962, 576–92.
   Touraine, A., 'Industrialisation et conscience ouvrière à São Paulo', *Sociologie du Travail*, 1961, 77–95.

19 Pahl, R. E., 'Class and community in English commuter villages', *Sociologia Ruralis*, Vol. 5, No. 1, 1965, 5–23. Reprinted here as Chapter 1.

Part 2 Spatial patterns and social processes

Introduction

The four chapters in this part are all concerned with the relationships between the spatial and the social and were written more for planners and geographers than for sociologists. The concerns of Chapters 5 and 6 have been extended by Peter Hall and others in *The Containment of Urban England* (two volumes, Allen & Unwin, 1973). However, it still appears to be the case that Edward Craven's analysis of planning applications and of a sample of companies concerned with private residential development is one of the very few empirical studies based on such detailed evidence and is still extremely relevant. To quote from Chapter 7: 'The built environment is the result of conflicts in the past and present, between those with different degrees of power in society – landowners, planners, developers, estate agents, local authorities, pressure groups of all kinds, insurance companies and so on. As the balance of power changes and ideologies rise and fall, so the built environment is affected' (p. 151). Chapter 7 further raises the point that planning plays an important role in a mixed economy in redistributing spatial resources and hence real incomes. This point was more original in 1968 when it was first written but it provides the starting-point for Chapter 8 which attempts to explore in some detail how planning policies in London may serve to penalize the poor still further, particularly if the policies with regard to recruitment to the New Towns are considered. Again this latter point has been elaborated in the Hall volumes mentioned above. Planners have come to be increasingly aware of the social consequences of spatial policies. However, that is no reason why researchers should not continue to document as precisely as possible who does gain and who does lose as a result of their decisions.

Chapter 5   Residential expansion: the role of the private developer in the South-East*

(with Edward Craven)

It is truly remarkable that we know next to nothing about the basic processes that determine the nature and distribution of the most important consumer of urban land – residential development. Despite all the research funds and effort that have been put into this problem, particularly in the United States, the results are ambiguous and inconclusive. Brian Berry, in a survey of recent studies, concludes that 'we should not be sanguine about our knowledge of the residential pattern of cities . . .', and calls for new and more comprehensive studies.[1]

This chapter attempts a preliminary exploration of an approach which might be fruitful in providing planners with significant insight into the residential development of the London Metropolitan Region. Before proceeding it may be useful to examine the relationship between planning and research, since our project was designed partly with the needs of planners in mind.

PLANNING AND RESEARCH

Planning is essentially the making of decisions and choices in accordance with a set of values. These values must spring, not from 'the simple aggregation of individual values' or from the values of sectional interests within the community, but from the planner's conception of his role and the approach to his task.[2] No

*This is a slightly revised and amended version of the published article.

longer does the planner see himself as simply the regulator of physical form but as a major creative participant in channelling change within the complexity of the physical environment. This role involves the definition of specific goals and the development of successful means of attaining them.

In this means-end process, there is the assumption that planners must be the interpreters of community needs, as far as the physical environment is concerned. Successive planning Acts since 1947 have recognized this assumption and have given planners the legal powers to execute their proposals. One of the claims to be such interpreters must surely rest upon a greater knowledge of the workings of society than any individual or organization within it can hope to have. This knowledge of what *is* becomes naturally a sound basis for saying what *ought to be*. The intelligent design and use of research should enable planners to enlarge their understanding of society and how it works. Whether such increased understanding makes planning action and politics easier or more difficult, is another matter.

The need for rigorous investigation and new concepts by planners is made all the more urgent by the fact that they are dealing with a society that is growing daily more complex. This might seem an unwarranted emphasis, but the mechanics of advanced industrial society are so little known, even to the social scientist, that planning for it in some cases must appear presumptuous and decisions are taken which, inevitably, have little theoretical and empirical support. Some planning departments collect 'facts' and describe patterns, even though they, as yet, have little knowledge of the processes behind them; indeed, with the acute shortage of planners, it is less likely that research without immediate pay-off can be attempted.

However, this is not meant to devalue some most useful research studies undertaken by some local authorities in the South-East. Such studies tend to be limited to descriptions of static patterns: snapshots in time are useful in themselves but have greater relevance if seen as first stepping-stones to an understanding of the *processes* of change. This is, perhaps, where research can make its best contribution. If planners define their task as attempting to control the physical expression of a changing society, then rigorous and imaginative research into the processes which help to create that physical expression must be necessary.

THE SETTING

The background to change and expansion in the South-East since the war is familiar. Both the Barlow Report of 1940 and the South-East Study in 1964 emphasized the 'excessive' growth in employment and population in the London Region in comparison with other parts of Britain. This expansion, and the principles and means adopted to cope with it, have been a prime concern for local, regional and national planners since 1945. In the main, the dominant element in the resultant physical growth, either in New Towns or in the fringe expansion of old settlements, was houses and the services they required. Ever since World War II, with growing preferences for large family houses in the suburbs with gardens and garages and pleasing environmental facilities (all of which involve more and more space), the residential sectors of settlements have been expanding disproportionately.

Not only has there been a 'natural' pressure for housing land in the South-East, which could have constituted a problem in itself, but the immigration of young families in search of better employment opportunities (both in quantity and quality) has augmented this demand. However, this migration involves not only the young but also an added influx of elderly people wanting to retire in the coastal resorts south of London, especially in Kent and Sussex. Growing affluence has placed an ever-increasing proportion of the population in a position to realize their needs for higher housing standards.

This pressure for land for housing has become all the more serious as it is by no means uniform, but has become concentrated in certain areas. The inner and outer country rings of the Metropolitan Region are experiencing more than natural demand. First, slum clearance and redevelopment in London has resulted in an intra-regional movement out from the metropolis:

many London families have been obliged to make their homes twenty to forty miles from the centre. Secondly, the rigid maintenance of the Green Belt (as far as was possible) resulted 'foreseeably' in greater pressure for land immediately beyond it. This is clearly shown by the Kent County Council Social Survey for the Mid-Kent area, where 70·5 per cent of immigrants in a commuter centre such as Paddock Wood gave the availability of housing as the reason for moving there. However, away from the major railway lines in strong local employment centres such as Maidstone or Sittingbourne, proximity to work, as might be expected, becomes of greater importance. For many immigrant commuters, this was the most convenient area with regard to housing and travel-to-work, given the Green Belt farther west.

It is clear that the proportion of houses built by the private builder/developer since the War has also been increasing, although, compared to local authority efforts, it was fairly stagnant up to the early 1950s. This period saw the removal of building licence controls, more available supplies of building materials, together with generally higher income levels. A change of government at a national level also tended to create greater reliance on the market mechanism to meet demand.

Table I indicates that from the middle fifties in all the areas considered, the private developer has been responsible for well over half of all new houses built and the trend is upward. The local authority, after its exhaustive task of re-building and re-housing, necessary through war damage, has declined in importance. The private builder/developer is seen to be more prominent in the South-East than in England and Wales as a whole and similarly more prominent in Kent than in the rest of the South-East: over three quarters of new houses built in the period 1960–66 in Kent were privately built.

Finally, it is important to consider future prospects for expansion in the South-East. The South-East Study gave rough proportions for the division of new population up to 1981 between 'planned' expansions and 'natural' growth. The Standing Conference in March 1966 adjusted these figures in the light of population growth in the period 1961–64. A total population increase of 2,910,000 is expected, of which 22 per cent will be

TABLE I The private sector's share of total housing completions in Great Britain, the South-East and Kent, 1951–66

	Great Britain		South-East		Kent	
	Total houses completed ('000s)	Per cent built by private sector	Total houses completed ('000s)	Per cent built by private sector	Total houses completed ('000s)	Per cent built by private sector
1951–5	1,419	23	427	31	37	33
1956–60	1,450	48	477	56	39	66
1961	296	60	95	66	10	78
1962	305	57	95	61	10	74
1963	299	59	90	65	10	76
1964	374	58	111	66	14	77
1965	382	56	114	61	13	76
1966	386	53	119	56	12	68

Source: Ministry of Housing and Local Government, *Housing Statistics*, No. 5, April 1967.

accommodated by planned expansions, leaving 78 per cent to be taken up through 'normal allocations'. Strict and effective control can be exerted over the expansion of the planned settlements, but over three quarters of the population growth in this period will be catered for in the 'unplanned' expansion of older settlements, in which the private developer, as we have seen, is likely to play a vital part. Therefore the pressure for residential land comes now largely from the private developer who has met, and will continue to meet, the growing demand for homes.

THE PRIVATE DEVELOPER: THE SKELETON IN
THE CUPBOARD?

It can be argued that the interests of the planning authorities in the South-East, outside London, and the interests of residential land developers are often in conflict. The restriction of population growth and the preservation of the countryside are major concerns for the planning authority, while the building of houses is the *raison d'être* of the developer. Many developers tend to regard planning policy, without real understanding, as merely a barrier to be overcome in order to bring their plans to fruition. Many planners see the demands of the builder, for land especially, as a major threat to the successful application of principles they regard as vital for the sound growth of the community. Very little consultation or discussion is found between the two, at the local level in particular, and contact is often made only when disputing proposals for development. It is incongruous that on the one hand the developer constantly complains of lack of land for building, and on the other hand, authorities assert that ample provision of land has been made available for population growth for a considerable period ahead. Secondly, it is interesting to note that land that has long been released for residential development has not been taken up. Given the fact that such land is in short supply, one must presume that the land, for a variety of reasons, is not regarded as 'suitable' or 'available' by developers.

These issues suggest that it would be of value to examine the residential development process in which the developer plays a major part. Generalizations concerning growth over long periods and on a regional and city scale abound, but neither can give the planner the necessary information on residential growth, which basically involves the taking up and development of numerous individual sites in numerous individual settlements by numerous individuals and organizations. An explanation of this process by suggesting it is controlled by improved transport facilities or an increase in the headship rate or the differential growth of industry is likely to prove inadequate. It can be strongly argued that this understanding can be gained only by applying a microscope to the process of growth and by concentrating on the groups who, involved in the process of residential land development, initiate and sustain the physical development of settlements. Our problem is a basic lack of knowledge about these people and the way they interact.

THE POSITION OF THE PRIVATE DEVELOPER

The importance of the private developer/builder in terms of the sheer numbers of houses built is evident, yet this in itself does not justify our approach. The housing market in the South-East and the whole process of residential expansion, especially with regard to planning policies, add to the case.

The South-East, except in times of shortages of credit, particularly for mortgages, has seen an excess of demand for dwellings over their supply, whether provided by the local authority or the private builder. A number of explanations have been advanced for the slow growth of supply. Bowley's recent study[3] indicates clearly that the characteristics of the building industry itself, such as its conservatism in introducing new methods or the problems of communication and cooperation between the building owner, the designer and the construction contractor, are important here. The shortage of building land, partly produced, it is suggested, by planning restrictions, and the shortage of labour in times of full employment can be cited as other contributory causes. Builders, rightly or wrongly, insist that the delays encountered in the process of application for permission to develop are a further restriction. On the demand side, the desire to own one's home reflects both the expansion of white-collar occupations and growing affluence since the early fifties. Furthermore, the desire and the ability to buy a house is becoming more common among manual workers also. The South-East, with its growing share of national wealth in its new and expanding light and service industries, has felt a heavy demand for private housing, a growing proportion of which is catered for by a relatively small number of large firms building a variety of types of housing mainly in estates, in the Outer Metropolitan Region. It has been estimated that over half of all new private housing is built by the large builder/developer (with over 100 employees), whose internal organization is such that he is able, as one operation, to buy the land, prepare the site, develop its services, build the houses and act as his own marketing organization.

The South-East therefore appears to be a seller's market for housing. Hence, consumer preferences concerning location and type of housing built are substantially reduced in importance, as the house-builder, within broad limits, can be assured of selling most of the houses he builds. What then appears as more significant than *actual* household preferences may be the conception of such preferences in the builder's mind. Market conditions permit him to lead and educate rather than to follow demand. As far as we know, the builder/developer engages in little market research and attempts to gauge consumer response to his 'products' are arbitrary. Furthermore, houses are not a luxury product: they can be placed in the same category as food or clothes when considering expenditure of any household or individual. However, it can be argued that a proportion of expenditure on housing is taken up in obtaining differences in quality; demand can be seen as stratified into the need for shelter and the desire for varying qualities of housing, dependent on such factors as the stage in the life-cycle or socio-economic status of the household involved. This need for shelter is often provided for by the stock of old houses rather than the flow of new ones. Nevertheless, the possession or otherwise of a place of shelter is *not* something that is subject to the changing preferences and circumstances of a household to the same extent as are consumer durables. A dwelling can be classed as a 'basic' necessity that has a high priority in the allocation of resources. This further strengthens the producer's control over his market. In a spatial context it has been suggested in the United States that 'differential population growth is primarily determined by the distribution of differential housing opportunities and especially by the differential patterns of building activities evidenced in various sub-areas'.[4]

While we believe that the conditions creating the seller's market in the South-East make this concentration on the private developer particularly appropriate, it is obvious that the complete process of residential expansion must involve a number of groups: these are the landowners, the private developers, the building contractors, individual households and government authorities at a national and local level. Certain important decisions are likely to be taken by government authorities which Chapin sees as the starting-point of the process. Such decisions, called 'priming' decisions by Chapin,[5] usually include major transportation

improvements, important planning policies such as the maintenance of the Green Belt and general credit facilities. However, if
any one of the groups mentioned was to be chosen as being
strategic to the process, a strong case could be made for studying
the private developer.

We have shown that over two thirds of all new houses are
privately built. Furthermore, the developer tends to be the prime
mover in the process. In the case of the landowner, it could be
argued that the scarcity of land places the latter in a powerful
position *vis-à-vis* the developer. The latter may have limited
choice in the land he buys, in the same way that the consumer has
limited choice in the house he buys. On the other hand many of the
major companies would bid for suitable land even before the
owner had decided to put it on the market. The developer, realizing the profitability of meeting a particular housing demand,
would seek out suitable land: this process of search has the odd
name of 'bird-dogging' in the United States. Bird-dogging is also
a feature of the long-term planning by development companies in
order to ensure a continuing production effort and the economies
gained thereby. The relationship between the developer and the
supply of land needs particular attention.

Planners are another important group engaged in the process of
growth. Planning policies, however, such as density controls,
zoning or amenity, exist in a vacuum until the developer decides
to take positive action, at which time alone they can have an
effect on the course of events. While a knowledge of what is
acceptable to the local planning authority can deter some applications and modify others, the real effectiveness of planning
policies in the process of residential expansion lies within the
context of the applications for development submitted and the
initiative for this is with the applicant. This is, perhaps, a function
of the rather negative nature of the planning machinery. Even
given both the importance of planners in their decisions to allow
or refuse development and the need for flexible planning policies,
pressures for residential development, which in type and location
might be contrary to planning policy, can be sufficient to overcome basic planning principles.

Looking finally at the role of the developer from a planning point of view, we have seen the broad limits which can be imposed upon his activities by 'priming' decisions. We have also discussed the negative role which the planner is apt to play in the process of growth itself. It would seem that the planner often has to deal with the unforeseen or uncontrollable results of his own decisions in this respect. This springs from a lack of knowledge about what happens after the granting of permission and approval for residential development and before the new demands and pressures which result from the development make themselves felt. This might be termed the 'planning gap'; using a geometrical analogy, planners so often touch the process tangentially at these two points but not in between. The importance of this 'gap' is easily illustrated. The planner has little control over the type of people who will live in the houses built by developers on a variety of sites. Detached houses at a low density will attract different socio-economic groups, generally speaking, than maisonettes at a high density. Similarly, differences in the age characteristics of the households and their work place can have an important effect on the future demand for local services such as schools and transportation facilities. Again, a site developed with a particular physical layout by a local builder might well differ markedly in respect of subsequent householders from the same site developed in the same way by a regional builder/developer. The size of site, the size of development and the type of housing built might be important variables in the social, economic and demographic characteristics of the householders. These factors, however, at the moment, seem to be outside the interest of the planner as well as his control.

The need to fill in this gap in knowledge and control has at least been implicitly accepted by some local authorities. Kent County Council has released some land in its portion of the Metropolitan Green Belt for residential development, inspired in part by Ministry circulars urging local authorities concerned with the Green Belt to reconsider the allocation of housing land in that area in light of the high level of population increase predicted in the next twenty years. Land has been released to District Councils and to at least one housing association, so that control over the occupancy of houses built can be exercised, in which local people working locally would be favoured. This type of control over the characteristics of the occupants as well as the location of their houses has significant possibilities of extension.

THEORETICAL ORIENTATION: THE FUNCTIONALISTS

A range of disciplines has observed the land use arrangement in cities and attempted to provide an explanation of their growth and change. Such explanations rest upon the assumptions first, that objective analysis is able to discover and evaluate forces within the system; secondly, that a full knowledge of the characteristics of the units within the system is required, so as to provide an understanding of the ways in which they respond to these forces; thirdly, that these responses, *en masse*, are similar enough to allow generalizations to be made. In the context of the city, these explanations have been aimed at the distribution pattern and as a result they have a strong spatial component. So strong was this tendency that little attempt was made to examine other implied forces which were operative; nor could it be assumed that because patterns *expressed themselves* spatially they could be *explained* spatially. This criticism can perhaps be more justly applied to the first broad group of theories to be examined, 'function' theories, than to 'behaviour' theory which escapes to some extent the determinism assigned to space restraints. This division into function theory and behaviour theory is as much one of convenience as of significance, as recent work has tended to incorporate both in comprehensive studies of land use development, yet it does provide a useful framework within which analysis of contributions can be made.

The functionalists see the city as the regulated establishment of its social and economic units, be they individuals or households or firms, in accordance with components within the urban structure which allow it to function effectively. These components are made manifest through an analysis either of the land-use pattern, the intensity of development or the movement of goods or people. The functionalists tend to emphasize the parameters which set the limits of action. These parameters exist independently of the active units and spring from the urban environment as a whole. This is not the place to present a full critique but comment is appropriate on one major theme of their work.

The restraints imposed in overcoming space or distance in the urban environment are of central importance. Since the city is essentially a system which depends upon movement and interaction between its highly specialized parts, the tax of space is the effort of overcoming distance in making these movements and contacts. The input of effort varies, dependent on location, in relation to the centre where contact is most easy. Since accessibility is said to decline at a roughly constant rate from the centre, a gradient of accessibility is set up which creates some locations more favourable for development than others. The land use economists in the 1920s, leaning heavily on Ricardo's concept of economic rent, suggested that the various land uses become arranged around the city centre according to their ability to profit from, and therefore pay high rent for, accessible locations. At one end of the land use spectrum are commercial uses, at the other residential. Stone quotes average auction prices for land in Britain in 1960–62 to illustrate this inequality in competitive power between different land users: land for commercial purposes sold at £25,000 per acre on the average: land for residential purposes at £5,000 per acre.[6] The human ecologists at Chicago, also in the 1920s, saw the city as a complex of social organizations controlled in their spatial distribution by biotic 'forces' such as 'dominance', 'invasion' and 'succession', with a struggle for 'the most favourable sites' where 'the most intensive (i.e. dominant) uses of space occupy the most accessible locations'. In ecological dominance, as in economic competition, accessibility and space controls are vital.

More sophisticated functionalist approaches have concentrated on the residential sector which the classical economists and ecologists tended to neglect: the latter were in fact much more convincing in explaining the location of profit-making concerns. Residential development was seen almost as the poor relation occupying that amount of space left over after the other more competititive or dominant land uses had become located at the most favourable sites. It has been realized that this was not the way to account for what constitutes over 60 per cent of the total urban areas of most cities. Important historical perspectives have recently been added to the study of the growth of residential areas in some of Britain's industrial cities. Similarly, Rex's and Moore's analysis of housing classes in Birmingham contributes a new sociological dimension to the purely spatial approach, avoiding the conceptual simplicity of the early ecologists.[7] Other contemporary writers, however, still rely on the control of space: the effort of overcoming distance in travel to work is thought to be important in the location of households, especially as travel to work involves at least two journeys a day. Add to this the fact that land becomes cheaper away from the city centre and the choice of location depends upon balancing the cost of travel with the cost of residential land. Given these two variables, choice in location depends upon income and preferences in residential space. This approach has been well developed by Kain[8] and mathematical models have been formulated by Muth and others.[9] A genuine attempt is made to integrate a number of factors affecting location rather than suggesting a simple, sweeping statement based solely on spatial controls. The inclusion of income takes cognizance of the different locational choices of different socio-economic groups. This approach has been exposed to doubt from various quarters. Chapin and Hightower[10] have calculated, from empirical work, that households were indifferent to the time-cost-distance factor below a value of about a quarter of an hour, while Marble, working in Washington, discovered that only socio-economic variables proved significantly related to the levels of transport inputs of households: spatial variables showed little or no correlation.[11]

More general criticism of the functional approach and its emphasis on space is on three counts: first, the tax of space is usually taken with reference to one point in the city, the centre; secondly, the city is considered as a highly organized but separate entity where the forces controlling the land use pattern are generated from within the city itself and external influences are minimal; thirdly, that cost is the most important factor affecting a household's choice of location. The growth of metropolitan regions, the decay of the centre areas of the city and the growing ability to communicate speedily both within and between such regions invalidate the first two points. Man is able now to distribute himself widely in the metropolitan region and still remain part of the urban system. General increases in income have seen a partial demise of 'economic man', who was at least tacitly accepted by the classical ecologists and land use economists. Choice is no longer made solely through balancing the cost-effect of one action with that of another; new sociological and psychological insights have demonstrated the narrowness of this view. The first half of this essay has suggested that a more relevant way of considering household choice is through a consideration of the differential pattern of housing opportunities. Choice of houses is taken less between the narrow limits imposed by external parameters and more within the range of alternatives which urban society presents. The city and its inhabitants are far too complex and diverse to allow of such simple explanations as economic competition or biotic dominance, or to allow the isolation of a single component such as space restraint. This simplicity in explanation is further threatened by the increase in interference in the physical form of cities by governments whose broad concern with the needs of the 'community' often conflict with 'natural' forces. This emphasis on space results in more of an interest in static patterns rather than dynamic processes. Many of these criticisms can be related to the level and scale of investigation attempted. If knowledge of the detailed working of the residential process is required, a large-scale, deep-level investigation would seem appropriate, for which the above 'factors' or 'forces' would act as a backcloth to, not as a substitute for, understanding.

THE BEHAVIOURISTS

The functionalist approach is, therefore, useful for setting the stage upon which the actors engaged in the process of residential expansion will perform. The action of these actors must take place within the limits imposed by this scenery, although the traditional limits at least are becoming wider and their control over the course of events is weakening. No one doubts the general importance of overcoming space in making contacts in the urban environment and the effect of this on location, but this relationship is not specifically determined or universal in space and throughout the social structure. A site in a settlement on a newly electrified railway does not automatically become developed. Before and during its change in use, decisions on its suitability for development by land developers, decisions to sell by owners, decisions to allow or refuse development by planners and many more must be taken. It is these decisions which make significant or otherwise any causal link between development and the electrification of the railway. Research must now be directed away from this general and slightly superficial level and, using the functionalist's variables as the environment for change, must examine the process in detail through an investigation of the typical actors and their interaction with each other and with their environment.

W. H. Form was one of the first writers to suggest a shift from the examination of land use development at a 'sub-social impersonal' level.[12] His comments mark a movement towards an appreciation that through the social organizations most concerned with land use one can understand the dynamics of land use change. He sees this change not as competition between different land uses as such based on a maximization of investment, but as the interaction, whatever its nature, of the various *groups* in the community. Firey, in his classic study of Boston (and later Emrys Jones, in a similar study of Belfast) reacted against the impersonality and determinism of the Chicago School of ecologists.[13] He substituted the value systems within the urban population as the significant field of study. He argued that groups of individuals have values and desires and that it is their acting upon these values which locates them in space and sets up the observable land use pattern. Space is a restraint only in as much as it is given value and differentiated by man himself, who alone utilizes space and makes it significant.

This emphasis on value systems, the actors and their actions has recently been elaborated convincingly by Wilhelm's study of the land use zoning process in Austin, Texas.[14] He sees the clash of different value systems as being vital for a study of land use change, in the same way as Firey's 'rational' and 'cultural' values in Boston. He discovers two major groups of values: one economic, which involves bowing to the inevitability of 'economic' forces within the community by allowing a piece of property to be utilized to its full competitive value; the other protective, which aims at maintaining the existing pattern, especially in residential areas, against any encroachment by commercial or any other uses which would 'lower the tone' of the area or the value of the property. These two systems were examined through a study of the zoning process, and the attitudes and opinions of appellants, defendants and decision-makers in public inquiries were the source of the final conclusions. He points out that decision-makers on the Planning Committee had much the same goal in mind in deciding on applications for zoning changes: they all indicated that the land use pattern must be such as 'to benefit the public and people who live in the city' and 'to foster the health, welfare and safety of the community'. The very vagueness of this goal, however, allows a wide range of alternative choices as means of attaining it and this results in the growth of a series of competing value systems.

Much recent research has employed behavioural orientations although not to the same extent as Willhelm. Harvey and Clark, in their study of urban sprawl, suggested that the manipulation of the tax system by land owners was important.[15] An owner is taxed less, if he sells his land in small parcels over a period than if he sells in one large parcel at one particular time. This means that 'instalment contracts' are made with developers for taking up portions at suitable intervals. Other developers must therefore find land well in front of or away from existing lines of growth. This increases what appears to be random urban sprawl. Similarly in this process, the financiers of developer/builders insist on financing sites which can be completed in one to three years. This limits the size, physical characteristics and location of developable sites.

Perhaps the most exhaustive and far-reaching contribution to this field is by F. S. Chapin and his associates at the University of North Carolina. Land use development, it is suggested, can be studied at three levels: first, the physical structure and patterns of land use. These were the realm of the early functionalists. Secondly, there are the variables which control the land use pattern, making themselves felt through individual or group action: this combines the functionalist and behaviourist approaches. Thirdly, there are the values which determine the action that is to be taken through the 'choice' of variables which control it: this is the pure behaviourist approach exemplified by Willhelm. Chapin is concerned with the Piedmont Industrial Crescent in North Carolina, and he has studied particularly the residential development pattern, following closely the sequential course set out above. Much of the recent work lies at the second level, i.e. the identification of the variables affecting individuals and groups. For this purpose, the residential process has been divided into two, the producer section and the consumer section, and work is being conducted into producing two parts of an interconnected model to simulate growth patterns. Chapin's work shows the possibilities of using both approaches to develop meaningful relationships within the process of growth and also the practical application of such work to planning, as his model is designed to show different patterns of growth which might be produced by alternative planning policies (the 'priming' decisions).

In Chapin's terms, our own research project has decided to concentrate on the producer end of the process and within that on the private developer rather than the land owner.

In America, computer techniques and simulation models are particularly well-advanced. Such techniques are slowly becoming known here, although adaptation to peculiar local circumstances is necessary. The accuracy of the prediction of future trends must basically rest upon the quality of the input information and the assumptions concerning future events. This project aims at providing basic information on the process of residential growth which will give planners sound basis for prescribing future land use patterns. It will give planners some knowledge of the mechanics of growth through an investigation of the main agent of expansion, the builder/developer who, within limits imposed by planning and other government authorities, etc., controls, through his choice of sites, the pattern of residential growth.

Planners may well be familiar with the decision variables affecting local authorities in the development of residential sites. Such decisions have a strong anti-profit element and are taken within the peculiar system of legal powers available to local authorities in the acquisition of land. Familiarity with the actions of private developers working in a relatively 'free' market for land and with profit-making a high priority, is less assured. Knowledge of the variables which affect his choice cannot fail to increase the likelihood of the successful application of planning policies aimed at meeting the needs of an expanding metropolitan society. Consultant feasibility studies and policy documents of very great significance sometimes seem to be based on an almost complete lack of relevant data; an understanding of residential development seems to be a case in point.

Acknowledgement

This research was financed by the Kent County Council.

REFERENCES

1 Berry, B., 'Research frontiers in urban geography' in Hauser, P. M., and Schnore, L. F. (eds.), *The Study of Urbanization*, Wiley, 1965, 419.
2 McLoughlin, J. B., 'Notes on the nature of physical change' in *TPI Journal*, December 1965, 397. See also 'The planning profession: New directions', in *TPI Journal*, June 1965.
3 Bowley, M., *The Building Industry*, Cambridge University Press, 1966.
4 See Schnore, L. F., 'The growth of metropolitan suburbs' in *American Sociological Review*, 22 April 1957.
5 Chapin, F. S., Jr, and Weiss, S. F., *Factors Influencing Land Development*, University of North Carolina, 1962.
6 See Stone, P. A., 'Price of building sites in Britain', in Hall, P. (ed.), *Land Values*, Sweet & Maxwell, 1965. See also McAuslan, 'Residential land values, 1962–5', *The Chartered Surveyor*, May 1966.

7 See Checkland, S. G., 'The British industrial city as history: the Glasgow case', *Urban Studies*, Vol. 1, No. 1, May 1964: also Robson, B. T., 'An ecological analysis of the evolution of residential areas in Sunderland', *Urban Studies*, Vol. 3, No. 2, June 1966; and Rex, J., and Moore, R., *Race, Community and Conflict*, Oxford University Press, 1967.

8 Kain, R. S., 'The location of residential areas', *Papers and Proceedings of the Regional Science Association*, 1962.

9 Muth, R. F., 'The spatial structure of the housing market', *Papers and Proceedings of the Regional Science Association*, 1961.

10 Chapin, F. S., Jr, and Hightower, H., 'Housing activity patterns and land use', *Journal of the American Institute of Planners*, August 1965.

11 Marble, D. F., in *Studies of Highway Development and Geographic Change* by Garrison, W. L., *et al.*, University of Washington Press, 1959.

12 Form, W. H., 'Place of social structure in the determination of land use: Some implications for a theory of urban ecology', *Social Forces*, May 1954.

13 See Firey, W. F., *Land Use in Central Boston*, Harvard University Press, Cambridge, Mass., 1947: also Jones, E., *A Social Geography of Belfast*, Oxford University Press, 1960.

14 Willhelm, S. W., *Urban Zoning and Land Use Theory*, Free Press, Glencoe, 1962.

15 Harvey, R. O., and Clark, W. A. V., 'The nature and economics of urban sprawl', *Land Economics*, February 1966.

Chapter 6 Private residential expansion in Kent

Edward Craven

INTRODUCTION

Two thirds of all houses built in the South-East since 1955 have been built by the private sector. This in itself is not surprising; anyone working or travelling in the region is repeatedly confronted with new private estates springing up along major routeways and at the edge of many settlements. Our awareness is further increased by the constant cries of woe from planners, architects and sociologists about the threat to the physical and social environment which such developments present. The speculative builder is seen as a *bête noire* responsible, amongst other things, for evils such as urban sprawl, pressure on natural rural attractions, the standardized boxes of many estates and the psychological troubles of those who live in them. It is important to recognize behind these suggestions, whether they be true or false, the implication that the developer is an *independent* element in the process of urban growth. He does not, apparently, respond passively to comprehensive land use controls or to public capital investment decisions or to the requirements of his consumers. If this were so the accusations would be unjustified. Being more explicit, my argument is that the developer is a catalyst who interprets, albeit inaccurately, major forces in the urban environment; an initiator of action based on this interpretation and a challenger of public policies which obstruct such action. What is surprising, therefore, is the lack of scientific, as opposed to speculative and anecdotal, knowledge of the process of residential expansion and the role of the private developer in it.

One reason for this may be that studies of housing in Britain have often been undertaken in a 'public-social welfare' context. This has led to a concern firstly with the central city where the quality of housing is at its worst and social problems most evident, and secondly with the public authority whose policies are, or should be, aimed at improving housing conditions through the elimination and replacement of sub-standard housing. The Milner Holland Report on Greater London[1] and Rex's and Moore's study of Sparkbrook[2] are recent examples of where these two interests coincide. Attention is directed upon an underprivileged section of the community living in crowded and insanitary accommodation, often with little hope of helping themselves given their unenviable position in the housing market. A basic task is to see how effective government action has been and how it can be improved.

Such attention is necessary and has a high priority. Moreover, the importance of government at a national and local level in all forms of land use is beyond question; Professor Donnison has demonstrated this quite clearly in the case of housing.[3] Nevertheless there has been a neglect of research on other facets of housing in which the public-social welfare approach has little meaning. In the South-East a growing number of families have made their homes away from the central city in the metropolitan fringe, in new rather than old housing and in owner-occupied rather than rented property. In these extra-city areas, the public authorities have provided only a small fraction of new housing. In the period 1956–66 approximately 1 million houses were built in the South-East. Of these, only 25 per cent were in Greater London and of the 75 per cent built in the rest of the region, only one third were built by the public sector. (This includes the New Towns.[4]) These figures put housing in the central city and the role of the public authority into perspective. In the future the dominance of the private sector is likely to be maintained especially after the cutback in public spending on housing announced in January 1967. 'Natural' growth of existing settlements, to which the private developer is the main contributor, will account for about 70 per cent of total population increase up to 1981[5] and even in the new and expanded towns the government hopes that the private sector will contribute up to 50 per cent of the housing provision. It is the private developer, then, who has been and will be the most important supplier of housing and the major agent of change. Yet we know little or nothing about the way he operates.

Furthermore, residential development by the private developer in the Outer Metropolitan Region cannot be wholly explained in terms of the system of land use controls in the hands of government. Public control over land use, however advanced our planning machinery, presents a framework within which the developer must act. This framework has wide limits which allows the developer considerable scope for initiative. This is especially likely in some of the rural counties around large cities where restrictive planning policies are found. The aim of the counties on the whole is one of preservation of traditional villages, good agricultural land, statutory Green Belts, Green Belt extensions, large areas of natural landscape value and a plethora of historic buildings. In such a situation initiative for change must come from the developer, not the planner. Indeed, a recent White Paper has admitted that in the past 'the system [of land use planning] has been better as a negative control on undesirable development than as a positive stimulus to the creation of a good environment'.[6] Secondly, there is a tendency for some geographers and economists to lump together individual sites and developments when describing the residential growth of an area. The patterns produced by this aggregation are then often explained by the effects of space restraint, especially upon the housing consumer. However, more important is the view that each site and its development represents the productive output of a building/development company. The significance of these *separate* developments should be seen in the context of the operations of the development companies themselves, which alone are the vital intermediaries between the social, political, economic and physical environment and the pattern of residential expansion on the ground.

However, each development company itself operates within a housing market and among 'competitors' of various kinds. These firms together constitute a house-building industry which has a form and structure based on certain objective criteria such as size, area of operations, type of housing built etc. It can be suggested that changes in this structure might well have an effect on both the distribution and nature of residential development. While an examination of these changes might therefore be a first step in understanding private residential growth, two qualifications are necessary. Firstly, an investigation of the structure of the house-building industry might indicate a relationship with the pattern of residential growth. It is, however, no substitute for understanding the processes which create this relationship. Secondly, it can be argued that the structure of the house-building industry and changes within it merely reflect 'basic forces' in the environment such as housing demand or land availability. As has been suggested before, the significance of both these two qualifications can be gauged only through an examination of the development companies themselves, to see how they view their environment and how these perceptions are translated into action.[7]

Given this approach to residential growth, there is little or no work in this country which can give us guidance. Only in the United States has any substantial research been done. It is of course necessary to guard against the wholesale transference of findings from America to Britain. With regard to land development, differences in the systems of land use controls and in the availability of, and attitudes towards the use of, land for urban purposes have been particularly noted.[8] Nevertheless, certain key points emerge. All the studies emphasize the importance of the size of a company upon the nature of that company's residential building activities. Maisel, working in the San Francisco Bay area, showed that the site requirements, the housing markets catered for (in terms of price) and the internal organization of the company itself varied with the size of the company.[9] An increase in the number of larger companies might well result in radical changes in the type and price of house being built and the size of sites being taken up. Wolfe's study of Seattle similarly indicated the importance of size but further suggested that the size of a company greatly affected its locational activity patterns.[10] The large developer tended to locate farther from the city, partly due to high land prices close to it, and partly due to the increasing difficulty of assembling land in parcels large enough to achieve the economies of scale commensurate with their scale of operations. Kaiser, working in Greensboro, N. Carolina, discovered that the large developer tended to locate *closer* to the city than the small developer, a finding which is the reverse of Wolfe's in Seattle. However, it is clear from both studies that there is a relationship between the size of developer and his locational behaviour, although the exact nature of the relationship must be empirically established.[11] Lastly, Hertzog shows, for the Los Angeles area, the startling change which took place in the size structure of house-builders between 1950 and 1960; in that period, large-scale builders (100 dwellings per year or more) increased their percentage of houses built each year from 32 to 74.[12]

Therefore, by looking at the producers of housing for the private market, both *in toto* as a house-building industry and individually as actors in the process of residential development, significant insights into metropolitan expansion can be gained. These American studies show clearly that temporal and spatial variations in private residential development seem to be strongly associated with the changing structure of the house-building industry. Within the limits of available data, our research was concerned with finding if such a relationship existed in the London Metropolitan Region in the period 1956–64 and, if so, what sort of relationship it was.

THE SURVEY

Kent was used as the geographical context for the study. It could be argued that the county is unrepresentative of the Outer Metropolitan Region as a whole, especially as regards new industrial growth since the war. However, a similar argument could be applied to any selected area since each would be distinctive in one way or another. Given that a study of the whole region was not possible, a choice had to be made. Kent has the advantage of including within its boundaries all the significant geographical zones in the OMR – the Inner Country Ring, the Outer Country Ring, and the Outer South-East. More practically, since Kent

County Council were supporting the project, county data was easily accessible.

Collecting data from the builders themselves was rejected for a number of reasons. Small builders in particular keep inadequate written records or no records at all of their developments. This would place reliance largely on memory. Moreover, not only would we have great difficulty in defining a universe of builders who had been active in the country over the last decade, but also there would be practical difficulties in collecting data from builders located throughout Kent and the South-East. A better source was residential planning applications submitted to local authorities in Kent. Here there were distinct advantages: there was a permanent written record of each planning application; the applications were submitted on a standardized form and were ordered systematically on the shelves of the planning department by year and local authority, which made sampling easier and more accurate: lastly applications were concentrated in only three centres, Canterbury, Maidstone and Gravesend.

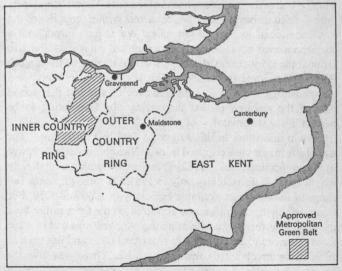

3. Kent: Regional Divisions and Green Belt.

The survey consisted of a 20 per cent sample of planning applications in each of three sample years 1956, 1959 and 1964 which correspond roughly to the beginning, middle and end of the period in which the private sector established its dominance over the public sector in Kent. It was decided to gather detailed information from residential applications for 5 dwellings or over; for applications of less than 5 dwellings, the number of dwellings involved and their locations were recorded. In all, 8,305 applications were examined; 2,035 were residential and 138 of these were for developments of over 5 dwellings. Three new variables were available from this source:

1. Size of development in dwellings;
2. Type of development; i.e. house type and number of bedrooms;
3. Developer type: (a) local developers, (b) non-local developers with headquarters in the county, (c) non-local developers with headquarters outside the county.

The first two variables are straightforward and present few problems, except for the fact that house price was not available, which is one of the main drawbacks of the data. 'Local' developers were defined as having their headquarters within ten miles of the site, 'non-local' as beyond ten miles. We assume throughout a correspondence between these geographical categories and size groups; the extra-county developers would tend to be the largest, the local developer the smallest. This is obviously in many ways unsatisfactory and crude as an indicator of size but the second part of the research project is proving our assumption to be correct in the vast majority of cases.

Certain difficulties in this source of data had to be faced. The size of site in acres was required from applicants only after a change in the application form in 1962. Therefore information on density would apply with reliability only to 1964. On some forms the full range of data was not available especially in 1956 and 1959. For example only the agent's name appeared on the form rather than the developer for whom he was acting. Applications had in some cases therefore to be recorded in truncated form and not used in tabulations involving its missing variable. There was also the danger of double counting, i.e. two applications submitted at different times for development on the same site. This was overcome in two ways; first, many local councils physically attached subsequent applications for development of a particular site to the initial application; secondly, a precise grid reference for each site was recorded so that, by constant checking, no two applications with the same grid reference would be included. Also we had the problem of the variability of the number of dwellings involved in each 'large' residential development. One application might represent 5 or 150 houses and their relative importance is obviously unequal. Therefore it would be misleading to use numbers of applications alone in tabulations and each application was 'translated' into the number of houses it represented for all tables.

Even though our source of data was planning permissions to develop issued by Kent County Council, the results will be presented in terms of developments which have taken place and are visible on the ground. It is however obvious that permission to develop does not necessarily lead to the development of the site either at once or at any time in the future. (In the absence of any checks, it could be suggested that the acute land shortage in the South-East at the time would ensure fairly speedy development.) In the case of developments of 5 dwellings or more, we tried to eliminate sites which had not been developed in three ways. First, any sites with *outline* planning permission but without *detailed* planning approval were excluded from the tabulations. In such cases, we assumed that the site had not been developed for a variety of reasons varying from difficult physical conditions for building to change of ownership. Secondly, it was often clear from the files relating to the detailed approval of estate layout, house design etc. that the physical development of the site had started. In many cases, there was a series of detailed approvals corresponding to changes in the developer's plans for the site while he was in the process of building. Thirdly, even though it might be reasonable to assume that developers submitting costly detailed plans in all probability develop the site as soon as possible, a visit to the site was undertaken if it was not clear from the files that development was under way. As far as developments of under 5 dwellings were concerned only the first two checks were employed: the large number of developments involved made visits to the site impractical. It is quite likely, therefore, that we have included a number of sites in this size category which have not been developed. This would tend to overestimate the importance of small developments in the tabulations which follow.

RESIDENTIAL DEVELOPMENT IN KENT, 1956–64

In this section the basic findings will be presented. Certain qualifications made necessary by the distinction between developments of more and less than 5 dwellings are to be found for each major sub-section.

1. Size of developments* (See Table I)

(*a*) in 1956, only 19 per cent of all houses were built in developments containing 36 or more dwellings; by 1964, the proportion had reached 57 per cent. This is a clear illustration of the remark-

TABLE I Size distribution of developments in Kent by area and year

Size of development (dwellings)		Under 5	6–15	16–35	36–75	76 and over	Total
1956	No. of houses	444	146	77	161	0	828
	Per cent of total	53·6	17·6	9·3	19·4	0	100
1959	No. of houses	562	185	239	352	266	1,604
	Per cent of total	35·0	11·5	14·9	21·9	16·6	100
1964	No. of houses	537	322	438	555	1,194	3,046
	Per cent of total	17·6	10·6	14·4	18·2	39·2	100
ICR	No. of houses	188	89	212	250	0	739
	Per cent of total	25·4	12·0	28·7	33·9	0	100
OCR	No. of houses	359	180	220	524	1,281	2,564
	Per cent of total	14·0	7·0	8·6	20·4	49·9	100
EK	No of houses	996	384	322	294	179	2,175
	Per cent of total	45·8	17·7	14·8	13·5	8·2	100

* Figures include *all* residential applications for development, regardless of size.

able increase in the size of developments. It is made all the more remarkable by the speed of the change as the average size of developments alone rose from 29 to 63 in less than ten years. While there was an absolute increase in the number of houses being built in the small development, its relative importance decreased steadily.

(*b*) It was in the Outer Country Ring of Kent that this trend was most pronounced. In this area, developments were significantly larger than in any other, with 70 per cent of all houses in the period being built in developments of over 36 dwellings. Indeed, by 1964, *70 per cent were built in developments of over 76 alone.* In East Kent, developments did tend to increase in size but not spectacularly. Even in 1964, developments of 15 dwellings and under accounted for over half of all houses built.

(*c*) The large development was much more common in urban than in rural areas of the county.* In the former, 56 per cent of houses were built in developments of over 36 dwellings, in the latter 53 per cent were built in developments of under 15 dwellings.

2. *Type of Housing*†

(*a*) There has been a marked change in the type of house being built in Kent. Three-bedroomed semi-detached and terrace houses accounted for 35 per cent of all houses built in 1956; by 1964, the figure had almost doubled to 60 per cent. The striking dominance of these 'middle-density' house types seems to have occurred at the expense of the semi-detached bungalow. Even though the semi-detached house was by far the most important single house type being built, it was the terrace house which most rapidly increased its absolute and relative share of the total.

(*b*) It was in the Outer Country Ring and, to a lesser extent, the Inner Country Ring, that the semi-detached and terrace house were most prevalent. In East Kent, due to its attraction as a retirement area, bungalows were much more important although

*'Urban' refers to Urban Districts and Municipal Boroughs, 'rural' to Rural Districts.

†Figures refer only to developments of 5 or more dwellings.

the trend towards the middle-density house types was appearing strongly in 1964. In the Inner Country Ring, detached houses were significantly more important than elsewhere, probably due to the high price of land.

(c) On the whole, urban areas in Kent saw a much higher proportion of the middle-density dwellings than rural areas. This applied more to East Kent than West Kent. In the latter, rural urban differences in house types being built were much less significant.

(d) There is a strong correlation (see Table 11) between the size of development and the type of housing being built. The large development tends to consist of semi-detached and terrace houses (or semi-detached bungalows); the small development of detached dwellings or high-density flats and maisonettes. This is especially true of semi-detached houses; 76 per cent of those appearing in the sample were found in developments of over 36 dwellings. Detached dwellings, which were built in large developments, tended quite often to form a minor part of an estate dominated by semi-detached or terrace houses. This sprinkling of detached houses is included presumably to increase sales through raising the potential social status of the estate.

TABLE II   Size of development by type of development in Kent, 1956–64

Size of development	5–15	16–35	36–75	Over 76	Total
Detached house	129	125	171	60	485
	26·6	25·8	35·3	12·4	100
Semi-detached house	100	208	550	435	1,293
	7·7	16·1	42·5	33·6	100
Detached bungalow	149	120	128	61	458
	32·5	26·2	27·9	13·3	100
Semi-detached bungalow	94	120	155	186	555
	16·9	21·6	27·9	33·5	100
Terrace house	59	103	26	207	395
	14·9	26·1	6·6	52·4	100
High density (flats and maisonettes)	122	54	38	22	236
	51·7	22·9	16·1	9·3	100

3. Developer type*

(*a*) Over the decade, there has been a striking growth in the percentage of housing in any area built by developers from outside it (see Table III). By 1964, the non-local developer accounted for 60 per cent of all houses built, compared with 48 per cent in 1959 and only 10 per cent in 1956. A good deal depends upon the definition of 'local' and 'non-local'. Our definition of a 'local' developer was rather arbitrary. However, the position of the non-local developer can also be judged without facing the difficulties of the arbitrary definition, through examining the importance of developers whose headquarters are outside the county altogether, in the metropolis itself. In 1956 these London-based developers accounted for 7 per cent of houses built, for 26 per cent in 1959 and for 42 per cent in 1964. The importance of the non-local developer is one of the strongest trends of the survey.

TABLE III Developer type by area and year in Kent, 1956–64

		Non-local	Local (over 5)	Local (under 5)	Total local	Total
Total houses		2,623	1,244	1,543	2,787	5,410
Per cent of total		48·5	22·9	28·6	51·5	100
1956	No. of houses	80	304	444	748	828
	Per cent of total	9·6	36·8	53·6	90·4	100
1959	No. of houses	787	292	558	850	1,637
	Per cent of total	47·9	17·8	34·1	51·9	100
1964	No. of houses	1,756	648	541	1,189	2,945
	Per cent of total	59·6	22·0	18·4	40·4	100
ICR	No. of houses	307	244	188	432	739
	Per cent of total	41·5	33·0	25·5	58·5	100
OCR	No. of houses	1,634	571	359	930	2,564
	Per cent of total	63·7	22·2	14·1	36·3	100
EK	No. of houses	682	429	996	1,425	2,107
	Per cent of total	32·4	20·4	47·3	67·7	100

*Figures are calculated on the assumption that *all* developments of less than 5 dwellings were built by the local developer. This assumption would tend to *underestimate* the importance of the non-local developer.

(*b*) The dominance of the non-local developer was least marked in East Kent and in rural areas in general. The non-local builder had least influence in rural areas in East Kent where he built only 40 per cent of all houses. However, even in East Kent, he had become much more important by the end of the period. The local builder in the Outer Metropolitan Region and in urban areas generally was totally overshadowed by the non-local builder. For instance, in the towns of the Outer Country Ring in Kent, over 80 per cent of all houses were built by the non-local developer.

(*c*) Seventy-five per cent of all houses built by the non-local developer were in large developments of over 36 dwellings: only 42 per cent of the local developer's houses were in this size group (see Table IV). There was a strong relationship between type of developer and size of development. On the whole, the non-local developer built in relatively large developments and the local developer in small developments. So strong is the correlation that this pattern is observable using numbers of applications alone.

TABLE IV   Size of developments by developer type in Kent, 1956–64

Size of development (in dwellings)	5–15	16–35	36–75	76+	Total
NON-LOCAL					
No. of houses	244	420	663	1,296	2,623
Per cent of total	9·3	16·0	25·2	49·4	100
LOCAL					
No of houses	381	334	365	164	1,244
Per cent of total	30·6	26·8	29·3	13·1	100

(*d*) It is the non-local developer, therefore, who is largely responsible for the majority of the middle-density semi-detached houses: almost half of all houses he built during the period were of this type. The local developer does not tend to specialize in any one particular house type in the same way as the non-local developer, although he tends to build proportionately more detached houses and bungalows.

(*e*) However, when the non-local developer does build in small developments, there is concentration upon detached houses, detached bungalows and high density development, i.e. a pattern more similar to that of the local builder (see Table v). This reinforces the view that small sites and small developments have distinctive house patterns associated with them.

TABLE V   Non-local developer: house type by size of development, 1956–64*

No. of houses in developments of 16 and over dwellings	182	968	193	317	134	72	1,886
Per cent of total	9·8	51·9	10·3	17·0	7·2	3·9	100
No. of houses in developments of 15 and under dwellings	70	38	44	32	11	49	244
Per cent of total	28·7	15·6	18·0	13·1	4·5	20·1	100

IMPLICATIONS FOR PLANNERS

Before discussing the more general conclusions of the survey, the results seem to have fairly direct implications for land use planners. The rapid growth of residential areas is closely associated with the development of a few large sites by a few large developers and not with more piecemeal growth through a multitude of small developments. Demand for large sites or for sites which can easily be assembled is becoming more and more pressing. Land which is released either in small parcels or in a multiple-ownership pattern is less likely to be taken up as speedily as larger parcels of land, especially with only a few owners. Moreover, the social and physical character of many settlements can be altered now by one single large development in a way in which they could not by a number of small ones. It requires only *one* permission for *one* large development to

*Three developments comprising 513 dwellings are not included here as reliable information on house types was not available.

necessitate major adjustments in a settlement and its services. The impact on the services, especially schools and shopping facilities, is likely to be particularly severe. The decision-making process in planning has to be geared more and more to coping with a few applications for residential development, each with far-reaching consequences, rather than many applications with only limited implications as in the past.

Land which is released in large parcels or land which is easily assembled is likely to see a distinctive *form* of development taking place upon it. 'Middle-density' semi-detached or terrace houses tend to be built on large sites and, conversely, smaller sites tend to contain detached or high-density dwellings. Furthermore, since the type of house is strongly associated with the final selling price, selection of households with similar financial status and their concentration into certain estates is likely to occur. For instance, the large estate of semi-detached and terrace houses will offer the cheapest new houses on the market and thus attract those households which are able to meet the *minimum* financial requirements involved in buying a house through a mortgage. This will include particularly young households in the early stages of the family cycle, manual, semi-skilled and white-collar workers, immigrants from the metropolis and those moving from a lower-priced housing market in other parts of the country. The smaller developments of detached dwellings will tend to be more expensive and be more suitable for households in the latter stages of the family cycle and in the higher socio-economic groups. Therefore, the social composition as well as the physical expansion of settlements is closely associated with the selection exercised by house type and price, and size of development.

Lastly, planning policy in a particular area greatly affects the availability of land for residential developers. However, it is clear that policies affect developers differentially. Land released in large sites is more suitable and, from the financial point of view, more easily obtainable by the large, non-local developer. Conversely, land released in small parcels gives the smaller, local builder a much greater chance to obtain adequate supplies. While it is highly debatable whether the planning authority has any responsibility for ensuring a steady flow of building sites in such a way as to provide equitably for the land requirements of a *variety* of developers, the tendency of their land policies to discriminate against certain types of developer must be recognized.

CONCLUSIONS

The key to the trends in private house-building over the last decade in Kent seems to be the growing importance of the non-local developer, especially those based in London. These developers favoured the OCR and, within that area, large sites for semi-detached or terrace houses. Certain factors seem important in explaining this 'preference'. First is the availability of land, not only in terms of quantity but also in the size of sites available. As the ICR encloses the Metropolitan Green Belt in Kent, restrictive planning policies considerably limited the amount of land available in that area. Moreover, much of the land that was released tended to be infill land and, as such, to be found in small parcels. It is not surprising, therefore, that Tables I and III show small local developers and small developments more prevalent in the ICR than in the OCR farther east. Developers in search of large sites therefore tended to hop over the Green Belt into the area immediately beyond. Another land factor at work was the gradient of land prices which falls steeply away from the centre of London. Stone indicates that in the period 1960–64 residential building land per acre cost £32,000 within a ten-mile radius of the centre, £17,000 between 10 and 20 miles, £8,500 between 20 and 30 miles, dropping steeply to about £3,000 in East Kent.[13] Not only were financial problems for the developer significantly eased by paying relatively low prices for land in the OCR, but it also enabled him to build much cheaper houses and thus increase the size of his potential market.

Secondly, the large non-local developer was faced with an employment pattern and transportation system which was centred on London. A significant portion of the demand for their dwellings came from individuals who worked in London and used the transportation network to get there.[14] This again predisposes developers to build in the OMR as close as possible to the metropolis, given the Green Belt farther west. Moreover, the importance of London as a work centre has meant that only lately has the large non-local developer been attracted by the availability of suitable sites at relatively low prices in East Kent. Therefore, the local builder could dominate the market in East Kent with only occasional incursions by the non-local developer.

We have suggested thus far that certain developers have been 'forced out' into the OCR although not into East Kent. However, it can be argued that consumers are also 'forced out' to find houses at a price which they can afford, i.e. cheap enough for them to meet the building societies' requirements concerning deposit, income/house price ratio and repayments. Which is the chicken and which the egg in this situation is difficult to judge. However, the average consumer at the wide base of the home-owning pyramid can afford only the cheapest house available, which even then involves severe financial and other strains. In many cases, the house must have easy access to London for work. These cheap houses are built by large non-local developers on large sites bought at relatively low prices in the OCR: the size of the development itself and the high degree of standardization of product allows considerable economies of scale. These standardized products are the semi-detached or terrace house built at densities of 8–12 to the acre.

One response of the developer, therefore, to the constraints imposed by planning policies, land availability, the gradient of land prices, housing demand and the employment/transportation system was to build cheap semis or terrace houses in large estates on the edge of the Green Belt. A second response, and one implicit in this discussion so far, has been mobility. Over the decade, many companies have moved out from local areas in which they formerly operated and are increasingly liable to build on a county, regional and, in some cases, national scale. One reason for this has been mentioned already. Acute land shortages exist for all developers and for large developers in particular. In order to find suitable sites they must cast their net wider and wider, away from the local area which they know. This mobility can be accomplished within the existing framework of the company, or by creating regional subsidiary companies or by taking over small local firms in order to utilize their land banks. A typical advertisement in *The Estate Gazette* reads:

Wanted: Building land or builders with land.
Builders who have land and are interested in the possibility of a takeover are invited to contact us for a confidential discussion.

However, this response is by no means automatic or determined and here it is necessary to revert to the point made previously about developments being seen in the context of the activities of individual development companies. Mobility in production is just as much a response to the *internal* circumstances of the company as to the external environment. In fact, the external environment and the constraints it poses become most relevant only when the company wishes to expand its house-building activities. The predisposition to growth from *within* the company is of vital importance.[15] Mobility in production is one way of expanding turnover and increasing profits. Developers who do expand are motivated by a set of economic values to which they give high priority. They see success both for themselves and their company in terms of growth. Given this commitment to expansion, they then have to decide what form growth should take. In the case of many developers, as we have seen, this involves widening the geographical basis of their housing demand by moving away from local areas. Mobility in production therefore can be seen as response to economic motivations aimed at achieving greater turnover and profit.*

By no means all development companies respond to land shortages and a desire for growth by the dispersal of house-building activities. Many increase their potential market by expanding their price and house type range, which to some extent precludes the need for greater geographical mobility. Some achieve growth through diversifying away from house-building altogether, into local government contract work, civil engineering etc. Some companies make no response at all, even though they

---

*For the purpose of this paper, the economic aspect of growth has been simplified considerably. The situation is of course complicated by the effect of tax laws, both on the individual entrepreneur and upon the company as a whole. Tax considerations can greatly affect the decision to expand.

perceive their productive opportunities and how to grasp them. This variation in response is largely due to the ramifications other than purely turnover/profit ones involved in growth.

First, the internal manpower and capital resources of the company at a particular point in time have a great effect on the direction of growth. Developers will tend to see opportunities for growth in terms of utilizing their existing resources to the full. For example, a developer in East Kent employed a manager with civil engineering experience to act as supervisor of house-building on the site. The developer was committed to growth and suggested that he would use the experience of this manager by taking on local government civil engineering contracts in the future.

Second, there is the problem of risk. Once a developer moves out of a fairly circumscribed local area of which he has great knowledge, based on many years' experience, of local land markets, consumer demand, planning policies and officials etc., risk and uncertainty must increase. He is moving into areas of which he does not have the same degree of knowledge. Knowledge can of course be acquired but not, in the first instance, through experience. Either the developer must continue to rely on intuitive experience-based methods of site assessment, which in new areas may be irrelevant or completely misleading, or introduce more systematic research techniques which he probably has never used before. The increasing risk and uncertainty and/or the means of reducing it might well act as a deterrent to growth. Thirdly, and related to the latter, growth through mobility in production might well require basic changes in the organization of the company and in the division of responsibility. This particularly applies to the fairly small private company owned and controlled by an individual entrepreneur who was its founder. In the past, he had probably been able to supervise personally even the most detailed actions of his employees with the bare minimum of administrative personnel and his decision was required before almost anything could be done in the office or on the site. In many cases, expansion through geographical dispersal (as well as the other means mentioned) requires an increase in management/administrative staff both in the office and on the site, and at least some measure of devolution of responsibility to the area manager, site supervisor etc. This must mean a significant change in the personal position of the entrepreneur and it is possible to suggest that the nil response indicates resistance to such changes by the entrepreneur himself. In this instance, therefore, it is not economic man who is dominant by seeking out and grasping his opportunities but socio-psychological man concerned with his own personal status within the organization.*

It seems, therefore, that 'attitudes to growth' is a much better indicator of the behaviour of developers than 'size', which was prominent in the American studies. The latter is a rather static concept which does not emphasize change and which does not allow for the dynamics behind the variations in behaviour already mentioned. Change in size by a development company involves the interaction of a number of factors, some of which have been briefly explored. Four elements seem particularly important. First, there are environmental forces which, on the one hand, act as constraints upon the actions of the developer and on the other provide opportunities for increasing production and profits. Secondly, the internal resources of the company can influence the way that growth is achieved. Thirdly, the existence or otherwise of economic values within the company which result in a desire for greater profits through expansion, often, in our case, involving geographical dispersal of house-building activities. Lastly, the socio-psychological values of the entrepreneur in deciding about his own personal position within the company after it has undergone the change associated with growth. These two value sets can often be in conflict within the entrepreneur and within the company. By looking at the relationship between these groups of factors, we can start to understand the variations in behaviour and the physical pattern of residential development that results.

Acknowledgement

This research was financed by the Kent County Council to whom the writer wishes to express his thanks.

* This kind of factor is again important in deciding about the desirability of the private company becoming public.

REFERENCES

1 'Report of the Committee on Housing in Greater London', Cmd. 2605, HMSO, March 1965.

2 Rex, J., and Moore, R., *Race, Community and Conflict*, Oxford University Press, 1967.

3 Donnison, D. V., *The Government of Housing*, Penguin Books, Harmondsworth, 1967.

4 Ministry of Housing and Local Government, *Housing Statistics*, No. 5, April 1967, HMSO.

5 South-East Economic Planning Council, *A Strategy for the South-East*, HMSO, 1967, Annex C, Tables 4 and 11.

6 White Paper, *Town and Country Planning*, Cmd. 3333, HMSO, June 1967.

7 For a full discussion see Craven, E. A., and Pahl, R. E., 'Residential expansion: a preliminary assessment of the role of the private developer in the South-East', *Journal of the Town Planning Institute*, Vol. 53, No. 4, April 1967. Reprinted here as Chapter 5.

8 Delafons, J., 'Land use controls in the United States', Report to the Joint Center for Urban Studies, Massachusetts Institute of Technology, 1962; and Cowan, P., 'Developing patterns of urbanisation', Paper to the SSRC/CES Joint Weekend Conference, July 1968.

9 Maisel, S. J., *Housebuilding in Transition: Based on Studies in the San Francisco Bay Area*, University of California Press, 1953.

10 Wolfe, M. R., 'Locational factors involved in suburban land development', unpublished Report to the Weyerhauser Company from the College of Architecture and Urban Planning, University of Washington, 1961.

11 Kaiser, E. J., *Toward a Model of Residential Developer Locational Behavior*, Center for Urban and Regional Studies, University of North Carolina, Chapel Hill, 1966.

12 Hertzog, J. P., 'The dynamics of large-scale housebulding', Research Report 22, Real Estate Research Program, Institute of Business and Economic Research, University of California, Berkeley, 1963.

13 Stone, P. A., 'The prices of building sites in Britain' in Hall, P. (ed.), *Land Values*, Sweet & Maxwell, 1965.

14 For detailed statistical information see 'Report on the Survey and Analysis; Part 4, Vols. 1–4', Kent Development Plan Quinquennial Review, 1963.

15 For a full discussion see Penrose, E. T., *The Theory of the Growth of the Firm*, Basil Blackwell, Oxford, 1966.

Chapter 7   Spatial structure and social structure

Most sociologists, whether keen Marxists or not, would argue that the work situation is a fundamental determining variable: families take their position in the social structure by the amount of reward – of power, wealth and prestige – which the economic system allocates to the chief earner. Thus, Marxists would argue, there is not a random association between variables but rather a prime, fundamental link between the economic substructure and the social and political superstructure. And one does not necessarily have to be a Marxist to accept this link. Those, such as Clark Kerr and his colleagues, who describe a logic of industrialism based on common techniques and technology, also seem to argue for a kind of historical materialism or determinism creating *Industrialism and Industrial Man.*[1]

Certainly there are superficial resemblances between industrial societies, suggesting a certain convergence. For example, airports all have similar problems to solve and may use a similar logic to overcome them. The same may be true for international hotels or plants for the assembly of motor vehicles. However, there would be a world of difference in the social situation within hypothetical subsidiaries to assemble Fiat cars in Spain, Poland and Sweden. Different national policies and traditions with regard to industrial relations, power of the trade unions, role of the management and so on, create significant differences in life-chances for the individual and of the social situation as a whole.

Hence, if we restrict our discussion to Europe, and hold techniques and technology constant, we shall nevertheless have distinctive social structures dependent upon historical experience and the existing distribution of political power. Factories, hotels and airports may everywhere look the same superficially, but it would surely be naïve to imagine that such similarities indicate similarities of social structure. Techniques and technology mould a national social structure but conversely a given social structure uses its knowledge in a particular way.

This debate about the so-called convergence of industrial societies is now part of elementary courses for sociology students in British universities. Good students discuss international studies of the prestige of occupations and certain inevitable similarities in occupational structure but conclude that the unequal distribution of power and privilege within and between societies is likely to produce an industrial pluralism with only partial or temporary convergence in certain limited areas. However, it seems that urban sociologists have been much slower in responding to the lead provided by industrial sociologists. Even distinguished sociologists tend to make indiscriminate references to the American situation with strong implications that there is an international urban sociology which describes a *common-industrial urbanism*, with no admission of the possibility that cultural, historical or political differences might produce distinctive social structures having distinctive responses to the urban system or the spatial structure.[2]

The sheer volume of American research means that most of us spend a great deal of our time and effort rediscovering that there are important differences between our societies. For example, in my study of the careers of British middle managers I am attempting to establish the connections between a man's wife, family and community commitments and his career and how each affects the other.[3] I have found myself forced back time and again to the inescapable conclusion that the reason why my work does not fit in with previous (American) work is that, for example, British wives have different attitudes to their husbands or their local communities. These cultural differences are hard to define but crucial to an understanding of the situation. Hence I do not think that those sociologists, such as Herbert Gans, who do so much to popularize American sub-cultural styles among the sociologically unsophisticated, necessarily provide guidance to urban ways of life in Britain.[4] However, Professor Wilensky's work on the principal determinants of styles of life does seem to me to have more cross-cultural significance and I return to his work below.[5]

The spatial structure partly reflects and partly determines the social structure. The sheer permanence of the built environment means that the distribution of economic rewards which creates a social structure at one period of time becomes fossilized in, say, the housing situation, at a later period of time when the values and structure of distribution of economic rewards in the society have changed. Thus socialist Czechoslovakia inherited the large-roomed houses of the old middle class, creating inequality of living space in the new political order. Those living in the flats of those previously in a privileged position themselves gain privilege in the new situation. The problem is, given a specific historical, cultural and political situation, how does the product of a given division of labour adjust and adapt itself in space, given also a certain level of technology? Sociologists are now in debate amongst themselves about degree of choice and degrees of constraint. The urban system dominates some and is manipulated by others. This is a crucial point on which I must enlarge.

There will always be scarce and desirable resources in any society. At present these resources are mainly power, wealth and prestige, since with these other resources can be obtained. The job-market is one of the chief means of allocating these scarce resources: men who are highly paid gain security and power. Their position in the economic system determines their ability to benefit within the urban system. For example, those with sufficient wealth may have complete private mobility so that they can reach whichever facilities they define as desirable. Those with power might be expected to distribute facilities to their own advantage: spatial structure would then reflect the distribution of power in society. However, all societies intervene to redress the unequal distribution of power. The nature and type of intervention will vary according to the specific ideologies and historical experience of the society concerned and there is a wide variety of types of intervention in different European countries. Cynics might argue that, in the case of Britain, the various housing acts were simply a defence by the rich against the disease and possibly violence of the poor. Certainly for nearly a century the reforming zeal of the middle class created housing standards which forced rents to be higher than the poor could afford so that collective responsibility to subsidize them was necessary. Similarly the reforming zeal of a more recent generation for Green Belts has forced a tax on those obliged to cross them between home and work.

Briefly, then, the rewards from the occupational structure are not enough to avoid absolute or relative deprivation, in terms of desirable resources such as houses or access to facilities, such as shops or clinics, for certain sections of the population. Town planning, *together with other instruments of social policy*, plays a crucial role in a mixed economy in redistributing spatial resources. In some cases the power position of a minority may be reinforced by planning decisions – as for example when local trade and business interests concentrate resources in city centres, raising land values and banishing the poor to the periphery. The effect of this is doubly to penalize the poor: they get fewer rewards from the economic system anyway; now, in addition, they are further from urban facilities and so may have to pay more to get the same services as the rich. Local authority tenants may be further penalized since the national subsidy in the form of a reduction in income tax to those repaying mortgages is, I think, still greater than the subsidy for local authority housing.

However, in other cases, planning decisions and social and political policy may redress the balance to the disadvantage of the more privileged minority. Musil's study of the development of Prague's ecological structure illustrates this very well.[6] In the 1930s the spatially most isolated or segregated group of the population were the manual workers, whereas after the war white-collar workers became the most isolated group and manual workers were more uniformly distributed throughout Prague. Until the new Rent Act 1965, rents formed a comparatively small item in the family budget – i.e. only about 5 per cent – and so for most people rent did not determine the choice of housing: there is no close correlation between size of income and quality of housing. Hence there is no massive concentration of population groups, with those with lower incomes in dwellings of poor quality. If, for example, old people do live in such dwellings, this is not exclusively the result of their economic conditions.

Since rents are also not differentiated according to the location of the houses within the city (so that a dwelling of the same quality and equipment is rented for the same price in the suburb as in the city centre), another economic factor determining spatial distribution of population, according to the classical ecology theory, is excluded.

The influence of economic factors was replaced – especially at a time when most dwellings were built by the state and almost all dwellings of the existing housing stock were under the direct control of local authorities – by a housing policy which allocates new dwellings by preference to young families with children, to employees of 'key economic branches' and to families living in very bad and unhealthy dwellings. The first two categories contained almost exclusively families with small children. Middle-aged and old people remained therefore in the old housing stock. For this reason there is in Czechoslovakia a strong correlation between the age of houses and the age of their inhabitants, i.e. also between the age of dwellings and the average size of households. The older the houses, the smaller and older the households who live in them.

The result of this housing policy is socially mixed neighbourhoods or districts, and an almost complete disappearance of the social status of some areas of the cities, as an ecological factor. The population, according to housing surveys, does, of course, prefer some parts of a city more than others, but these preferences are determined more by physical and geographical conditions than by social forces.

During the last few years (i.e. after 1960), with the rapidly growing proportion of new houses built in Prague by cooperatives, and with the government's tendency to decrease the housing subsidies, and thus with the increasing importance of market elements in housing, a new combination of forces has started to mould the ecological pattern of Prague. These economic factors, which lost their decisive influence on ecological processes in the postwar period and were replaced by social considerations – as expressed in the housing policy – are gaining more and more in importance at present. This is, however, too short a period to ascertain the effect of these changes in the ecological structure of Prague: nevertheless there is no doubt that they will result in a new social differentiation of the districts of Prague.[7]

I have enlarged on the example of Prague because I think it is crucial that we correct the Chicago-dominated thinking from which urban sociology has suffered for so long. Certainly detailed analysis of census material reveals a pattern (one would hardly expect it otherwise). Each census produces its crop of statistical stories by the demographic enthusiasts of Chicago and Wisconsin. The research tools get more sophisticated and the data is hammered and chipped into more unusual shapes and subtle indices. Cities in other parts of the world may deviate from the structure of Middle West cities to a greater or lesser degree but this, it is tacitly argued, is due simply to different values not easily susceptible to hard empirical analysis.

Very recently there are signs that the ecologists are realizing their own limitations. Leo Schnore, for example, in his essay on *The Spatial Structure of Cities in the Two Americas* has been forced through his survey of Latin American cities' spatial structure to doubt the value of his own work – 'students of urbanization in the United States may not be justified in ignoring cultural differences even when they are studying only their own cities'.[8] Later he owns up to

a decidedly 'materialistic' emphasis or bias . . . the fact that residential location is motivated or animated by ends or goals of a wide variety is given no consideration. Finally, the fact that there are numerous institutional arrangements with respect to the use of land and the transmission of property, introduces a variability that is not considered in ecological analysis. In some respects, all these factors are treated – if only implicitly – as 'constants', or as exhibiting perfect co-variation with the variables explicitly subjected to analysis . . . It must be frankly admitted that these controversial issues remain largely unresolved after two decades of debate. These omissions – regarded as sins by some writers – have been defended as virtues by others, if only on the basis of a kind of effort at theoretical parsimony. Moreover, the debate is likely to continue, for the issues are not the kind that can be readily resolved by means of empirical research, whether grand or modest in design.[9]

I do not accept Schnore's pessimistic conclusion, which I interpret as special pleading, but at least he has caught sight of the problem after his time in the arid wilderness of the ecological fallacy. Unfortunately geographers have discovered some new tools which they hope will make their descriptions more respectable. I am all for telling familiar stories in a new language as long as we remember the limitations of the plot. The statistical or visual story-tellers take most of what I consider to be the interesting variables as constants. Given a uniform plain, perfect competition, complete knowledge of the market by all concerned, no conflict or competing ideologies, no other sources of power than can be obtained from the economic system through the division of labour, the ability of the poorest to obtain shelter through gradually increasing prosperity and a number of other factors as well, *then* it might be possible to develop ecological models of an urban spatial system. However, sadly for the ecologists and geographers, the real world is not like that: the built environment is the result of conflicts, in the past and present, between those with different degrees of power in society – landowners, planners, developers, estate agents, local authorities, pressure groups of all kinds, insurance companies, and so on. As the balance of power changes and ideologies rise and fall so the built environment is affected. It is a continuing situation, with the past constraining the present and together binding and limiting the future. The spatial structure may be more appropriately understood with game theory and conflict simulation except that we do not know how to weigh the power elements in the game and nor do we know who all the players or actors are.

The social structure is the key to the spatial structure and until we understand how a given socio-economic system places people with regard to fundamental scarce resources, such as housing, we are unable to make predictions about future spatial structures in a given society. Although it might be quite possible to view a city region in terms of an ecology of games, things are not quite as random as that. The occupational structure is still overwhelmingly important as a determinant of life-chances. However, some claim that the scientific and technological revolution will produce a situation where differences in pay, security, fringe benefits, working conditions, degree of responsibility and amount of job satisfaction will become minimized. I do not share the optimism of the futurologists: I do not see the connection between the exponential increase of scientific innovation and the more widespread distribution of power. And where power is concentrated so also will be access to scarce resources.

Professor Rex has discussed the concept of housing classes in his study of Sparkbrook:

In the class-struggle over housing, qualification either for a mortgage or a council tenancy are crucial. They are, of course, awarded on the basis of different criteria. In the first case size and security of income are vital. In the second 'housing need', length of residence and degree of affiliation to politically powerful groups are the council criteria. But neither mortgages nor council tenancies are available to all so that either position is a privileged one as compared with that of the disqualified ... considerable variations in this pattern of housing-class conflict would follow from differences in the economic, political and cultural situation in different industrial countries. The model we have posited assumes the existence of a socialist movement in relation to housing amongst the native working classes, an inability to exercise political power on their own behalf by disadvantaged groups and an aspiration to relatively detached family life in suburban conditions amongst all groups. Where these assumptions do not hold, other conflict and status patterns may emerge. Thus, in the American situation, 'Council housing' does not appear to be an important factor, and low-cost public housing is likely to be thought of as part of the destiny of the underprivileged. On the other hand, militancy among the disadvantaged in the absence of privileged working-class political power may upset the prevailing pattern. And in many countries the suburban trend may not have the same cultural importance which it has in England so that both middle-class and working-class citizens may prefer flatted accommodation near the city centre.

Such differences as these, however, call for the modification of the basic model which we have elaborated, not for its rejection. What is common to all urban situations is that housing and especially certain kinds of desirable housing is a scarce resource and that different groups are differentially placed with regard to access to the available housing stock.[10]

This article by Professor Rex seems to me to be one of the very few serious contributions to urban sociology that we have had in recent years. However, I think it is clear that it is limited in its applicability as it stands. It is questionable whether it is appropriate to use the word 'class' in this context. Perhaps 'quasi-group' in Professor Dahrendorf's usage would be a better term. Clearly men may be paid the same wage for doing the same work in different parts of the country but their life-chances will vary according to the proportion of their income they have to spend on housing, journey to work, journeys to facilities and so on. Clearly there will always be inequalities of access to facilities but the unequal distribution of public and private investment between different parts of the country produces fundamental differences in life-chances within the same occupational category. Sociology has suffered from an obsession with crude categories such as 'working' or 'middle' class. Only recently has attention been directed to the geographical or spatial dimensions of inequality – the current debate for positive discrimination in primary education being one such example.

Certainly one of the advantages of the emphasis on *constraints* rather than choice is that it is possible to get objective indices of the constraints and measure the effect on activity or consumption patterns and styles of life. Chombart de Lauwe's work on time budgets shows clearly the effect of differential journeys to work among manual workers of the same socio-economic status on their family relationships.[11] Those with longer times away from home were more tired, helped their wives less and played with the children less. It is important not only to hold occupation constant but also to construct activity patterns for all members of the family at different positions in the socio-ecological system. Hence we need to compare different ethnic or religious categories *within* the same occupational category and in different physical situations. The constraint hierarchy operates vertically and horizontally.

Professor Wilensky analysed those men who work more than fifty-five hours per week.[12] He reports that the differences *between* strata (e.g. 13 per cent between *all* the professions and low manual workers of comparable age) are not nearly as large as the differences *within* strata (e.g. 28 per cent between solo lawyers and engineers in a particular company). As he remarks 'this again emphasizes that often what looks like "class" phenomena may be rooted in more specific work milieux, career patterns and organizational contexts as well as ethnic and religious sub-cultures'.

Some possible lines of research

The problem is to relate the *occupational* structure to the socio-ecological system. If, within a specific occupational category, there are fundamental changes and differences in conditions and type of work, security, and career prospects, then I would expect this to be reflected in other behavioural patterns. It is necessary to relate work and non-work constraints together to provide an appropriate model relating such variables to style of life. This approach may appear to minimize 'choice', the subjectivity of the actor, or similar Hegelian notions. I am simply concerned to relate economic change and public and private investment to how people buy, move and use facilities. I turn now to the empirical studies which I think are necessary to relate social structure to spatial structure through the socio-ecological system.

It might be possible to operationalize the concept of what Professor Rex calls housing 'classes' by combining capital resources, mortgage repayments, journey to work costs and so on, relating income to expenditure to provide an economic index which should serve to categorize the classes. Journey to work costs would have to be taken into account since obviously the cost of a house is related to where it is. It is not easy to devise an index which takes into account access to other facilities. Housing classes may be age-specific and it is important to relate income and access to work and facilities with stage in the family cycle. Other variables such as skin colour or marital status will create important status groups within housing classes.

Housing classes will be directly related to the housing market which is, of course, geographically limited, generally by the employment structure: empty houses in Northumberland do not relate directly to London's housing problem.

I see technological innovation as the main determinant of social change within a given context. If automation helps to make certain categories of white-collar workers less valuable, their bargaining power for greater rewards declines. As a result wages and salaries of such groups do not grow as rapidly as other more 'needed' categories and this affects their life-chances for housing mortgages, ability to run one or two cars and so on. Since, following Wilensky, we see a direct relationship between occupation, intra-generational mobility or 'career' and life-style, then the occupational history of typical actors should be a critical focus of interest.

We need to know where declining industries and occupations export their manpower and from whence the growing industries and occupations recruit their new entrants. In the South-East, for example, is there a mobility blockage for certain categories – e.g. the miners of East Kent or the coloured transport workers? Social mobility is perhaps the main symptom of social change but this must be seen in the context of changing industrial, employment and occupational structures. Ideally we need studies of specific growth industries (education, information processing, electronics) and specific declining industries (coal mining, railways, textiles) comparing the constraints, the activity patterns and consumption styles of appropriate samples. Wilensky[13] has demonstrated the importance of the orderliness of career as a determinant of life-style and it would be valuable to compare careers of those in different sectors of the economy. This analysis needs to be done on a geographical basis as well, to assess the constraints of the socio-ecological system. Given a variation in educational provision, employment opportunities, flexibility of the housing market and so on, an index of mobility potential will vary considerably between and within regions. Given the inevitable inequalities and discrepancies within the socio-ecological system and the uneven pattern of technological innovation within the occupational and industrial structure, then a high degree of diversity is inevitable. What is difficult to understand is the patterns behind the diversity. A first step might be to have some kind of monitoring device which would document job and house careers of a representative sample of the workforce at regular intervals – say every five years. On the basis of this kind of data we would then be in a much better position to predict future relationships between spatial structure and social structure.

Many countries have massive market-research-type surveys which document what proportion of the professional/managerial class use swimming pools or go camping and how rapidly other categories are 'demanding' swimming pools and so on. A major

French study[14] runs to a dozen or so volumes. All these studies show a diversity of patterns and increasing demands. At the moment there is a mounting volume of such studies in Britain. We learn how many people go to Windsor Great Park on a Sunday afternoon and where they come from, or where people in places X, Y and Z shop. Enthusiastic planning officers may sponsor origin and destination studies or film traffic jams from a helicopter, all in the hope that they will find the key to what 'people' will do next. The possible spectre of 'more leisure time' haunts everyone.

This emphasis on random choice to the neglect of the fundamental constraints of age, sex, occupation and housing class is driving sociology into market research. I think we should concern ourselves with understanding the *constraints* and let the choices look after themselves. Surely the whole point about a mixed economy is that it is only partly planned. If some entrepreneur is not successful in establishing a Hippie camp at Cheltenham Spa or Worthing then this need not concern us very much. However, if as unintended consequences of public policy we get concentrations of poor people in the centre of cities or by the coast (with, in the South-East, a new middle-class poor squeezed in between in the Outer Metropolitan Area) then I think it is important that research should be focused so that decision-makers are aware of what they are doing and what alternatives are open to them.

This leads me to the issue of pure and applied research and the question of priorities. Should we direct our energies to pressing problems in metropolitan areas or should we aim at theory or model building? It seems important to try to spell out the implications of the socio-ecological system within a particular part of a particular society. Changes in the occupational structure should be related to a changing pattern of housing classes by providing firm empirical referents for each. I see consumption and activity styles as consequences rather than causes. The problem is where to start. If commuters from Herne Bay are part of London's occupational structure and are constrained by a housing market operating over much of the South-East, then their particular situation cannot be understood without detailed understanding of the overall framework. We seem to have lost sight of these overall, dominating constraints in our concern to illuminate microscopic processes. It does not really matter at which point we tap the socio-ecological system – any appropriate problem that can be conveniently investigated will do – the important thing is that we attempt to interrelate a problem-centred approach with the theoretical framework. Up to now no attempt has been made to relate the changing pattern of incomes and age structure to the cost and distribution of available housing.

The distinctiveness of our own socio-ecological system depends on the distribution of power in our society and the relative growth and decline of different occupations. It is essential that we gather the experience of other mixed economies in Europe in order to probe the subtle interrelationships between physical, economic and social planning and the operation of the market. This of course involves the interest and cooperation of other social scientists apart from sociologists.

REFERENCES

1 Kerr, C., *et al.*, *Industrialism and Industrial Man*, Heinemann, 1960.
2 Willmott, P., 'The social framework' and Burns, T., 'Urban life styles', papers read to the SSRC/CES Joint Weekend Conference at Glasgow, 5–7 July 1968.
3 Pahl, J. M., and R. E., *Managers and Their Wives: A Study of Career and Family Relationships in the Middle Class*, Allen Lane The Penguin Press, 1970.
4 Gans, H. J., *The Urban Villagers*, Free Press, Glencoe, 1962, and *The Levittowners*, Allen Lane The Penguin Press, 1967.
5 The following articles by Professor H. L. Wilensky are the most useful:
    (a) 'Work, careers and social integration', *International Social Science Journal*, 12, 1960, 543–60.
    (b) 'The uneven distribution of leisure: The impact of economic growth on "free time"', *Social Problems*, 9, 1961.
    (c) 'Orderly careers and social participation', *American Sociological Review*, 1961, 521–39.

   (*d*) 'Life cycle, work situation and participation in formal associations', in *Aging and Leisure*, Kleemeier, R. W. (ed.), Oxford University Press, 1961.

6 Musil, J., 'The development of Prague's ecological structure', in *Readings in Urban Sociology*, Pahl, R. E. (ed.), Pergamon press, 1968.

7 ibid., 258–9.

8 Hauser, P. M., and Schnore, L. F., *The Study of Urbanization*, John Wiley, 1965, 378.

9 ibid., 386–7.

10 Rex, J. A., 'The sociology of a zone of transition', in *Readings in Urban Sociology*, 215–16.

11 *Famille et Habitation*, Vol. II; 'Un Essai d'observation experimentale' by P.-H. Chombart de Lauwe *et al.*, Centre National de la Recherche Scientifique, Paris, 1960.

12 Wilensky, 'The Uneven Distribution of Leisure'.

13 Wilensky, 'Orderly Careers and Social Participation'.

14 Centre de Recherche et de Documentation sur la Consommation, *La fréquentation et l'utilisation des services et équipments collectifs par les ménages*, Vols. 1–8 (mimeo), Paris, 1966.

Chapter 8   Poverty and the urban system

The main purpose of this chapter is to explore one aspect of the relationships between certain long-term trends in the industrial and occupational structure of the population and the ecological structure of British cities. There are certain indications that the distinction between the skilled manual workers and the semi-skilled and unskilled manual workers is gaining a new significance in its urban spatial context. However, it is important to be clear at the outset that firm empirical evidence for the main outline of the argument is still lacking; a secondary objective of the chapter therefore is to argue for more research to be focused upon this issue.

CHANGES IN THE INDUSTRIAL AND OCCUPATIONAL STRUCTURE

It is initially worth adumbrating some of the well-established trends of changes in the country's occupational structure. Overall, it is evident that the total labour force has been growing very slowly – at about 0·3 to 0·4 per cent per annum in England and Wales from 1931 to 1961. This rate of change masks more substantial changes at different levels, with more rapid rates of decline at the bottom of the occupational hierarchy and more rapid rates of increase at the top. The population as a whole is getting more skilled and the number of male semi-skilled and unskilled workers has declined absolutely in recent years.[1] This decline in the proportion and number of less-skilled workers is not taking place at the same pace between industries and occupa-

160 *Spatial patterns and social processes*

tional categories. Certain industries are showing a very rapid
decline in the number of semi-skilled and unskilled male workers
they employ. Thus, taking the railways as an example, from 1961
to 1966 the number of porters, ticket-collectors and lengthmen in
Great Britain declined by a third and the proportion of railway
guards by just over a fifth. These losses were offset during the same
period by increases in other sectors; e.g. office- and window-
cleaners of 19 per cent, caretakers and office-keepers by 11 per
cent and hospital and ward orderlies by 7 per cent. In absolute
terms, the railway occupations mentioned above declined by
35,000 and this was offset, for example, by the increase in the
number of those employed as drivers of road goods vehicles
alone.[2]

Such changes in the occupational structure reflect well-
established trends in industrial structure and there are indications
that the rate of change is accelerating. Thus, from 1951 to 1961
workers in the manufacturing sector in England and Wales
increased by 0·8 per cent per annum and those in the services
sector increased by 0·6 per cent per annum. However, from 1961

TABLE I England and Wales: industrial structure of employment in
1951, 1961 and 1966, and Greater London in 1966

Industry group	England and Wales			Greater London 1966
	1951	1961	1966	1966
	(percentages)			
Primary (Orders I–II)	8·6	6·4	5·2	0·2
Manufacturing (Orders III–XVI)	35·8	36·8	35·4	29·9
Construction (Order XVII)	6·3	6·8	7·7	6·9
Services (Orders XVIII–XXIV)	49·3	50·0	51·7	63·0
	100·0	100·0	100·0	100·0
Total (thousands)	19,940	20,913	22,325	4,430

Source: Greater London Council, Greater London Development Plan,
Report of Studies, County Hall, 1969, Table 3.6.

Poverty and the urban system 161

to 1966, manufacturing workers increased by only 0·6 per cent per annum while numbers in the service sector grew by as much as 2·1 per cent per annum. Table 1 shows how the industrial structure became weighted towards the service sector from 1951 to 1966 and illustrates the overwhelming importance of the service sector within the Greater London Council area.

TABLE II Great Britain: the growth of the proportion of less-skilled workers in the service sector, 1951–61 (males and females combined)

Industry	Semi-skilled manual	Labourers and unskilled
	(thousands)	
(1) xx. Distributive Trades		
1951	1,249·7	202·1
1961	1,394·7	271·1
Per cent change	11·6	34·1
(2) xxi. Insurance, banking and finance		
1951	7·7	37·7
1961	6·7	49·8
Per cent change	−13·0	32·1
(3) xxii. Professional and scientific services		
1951	124·2	219·2
1961	146·9	383·4
Per cent change	18·2	74·9
(4) xxiv. Public administration		
1951	140·6	331·0
1961	205·1	284·1
Per cent change	45·9	−14·2
(5) (1–4)		
1951	1,522·2	790·0
1961	1,753·4	988·2
Per cent change	15·2	25·1
(1–4) as per cent of total occupational category: 1961	28·1	25·8

Source: Ministry of Labour, *Occupational Changes 1951–1961*, HMSO Manpower Studies No. 6, 1967, Table 1A.

This growth in the service sector of the economy is accompanied by a dramatic increase in the number of less-skilled workers in service occupations. Table 11 shows that, for the four main service sector industrial orders in Great Britain between 1951 and

TABLE III   Great Britain: the twenty lowest-paid occupations, September 1968

	Full-time male workers earning less than £17 for a full week's work (per cent)
1 Gardener, grounds-keeper	70·3
2 Caretaker, office-keeper	66·2
3 Farm worker	61·9
4 Cleaner	54·1
5 Goods porter (not railways), materials-mover (hand)	46·9
6 Shop salesman/sales assistant	46·4
7 Coalminer (surface)	45·9
8 Clerk – routine	45·3
9 Storekeeper, storeman, warehouseman or assistant – unskilled	41·1
10 Butcher, meat-cutter	35·1
11 Guard/watchman	34·6
12 Male nurse, etc.	34·3
13 Labourer	34·0
14 Chef/cook	29·7
15 Storekeeper, storeman, warehouseman or assistant – semi-skilled	28·9
16 Packer, bottler, canner	28·4
17 Roundsman – retail sales	28·3
18 Postman, mail-sorter, messenger	25·5
19 Storekeeper, storeman, warehouseman or assistant – skilled	21·4
20 Manager – retail shop	20·5

Source: Department of Employment and Productivity, 'Results of a New Survey of Earnings', *DEP Gazette*, May 1969, Table 4.

1961, the number of men and women in semi-skilled manual occupations grew by 15 per cent whilst the unskilled increased by 25 per cent. Workers with the least skills are being increasingly concentrated in the service sector of production. This trend is shown to an even more marked degree in a large urban area such as Greater London.

THE LOW-PAID WORKERS

Turning now to consider which are the lowest-paid occupations, it is evident from Table III that the typical low-paid worker is much more likely to be working in the service sector than in manufacturing or primary industry. Of the twenty lowest-paid occupations in Great Britain, fifteen are in urban-based, service-sector jobs, probably in scattered work situations with a relatively underdeveloped trade union structure. Some indication that the lower-paid workers are not increasing their wages as rapidly as more highly paid workers has been provided in reports prepared by Incomes Data Services Ltd (IDS):

In the last five years retail prices have risen by 24·7 per cent. During this period, in 25 out of 53 Wages Councils, the lowest minimum rate of pay for men has risen less than 24·7 per cent. Since September 1968, prices have increased by 12·1 per cent. In 30 of the 53 Wages Councils pay has gone up more slowly. Not only have the lowest paid become relatively worse off. [The differentials between the minimum pay rates of the lowest grade of workers in traditionally low paid industries and the lowest grade in more highly paid industries is significantly widening – IDS *Report 97.*] In some cases, those actually on the minimum are worse off now than they were two years ago or five years ago. They have suffered an actual cut in their standard of living. Their real pay has decreased.[3]

It would be a task beyond the scope of this paper to explore in detail the social geography of the poorest-paid workers, who are gradually getting relatively poorer.[4] However, it would in general seem likely that such workers are in the declining industrial towns of the North and North-West and in the centres of the large conurbations. Certainly, it would not be a surprising conclusion to find that those with the lowest pay were living in the worst urban environments. This is most clearly confirmed in evidence provided by the London Housing Survey undertaken by the GLC in 1967.

Over three quarters (77 per cent) of households in the high stress area have a head of household in a manual occupation compared with just under one half (45 per cent) of those in the low stress areas. This is accentuated in both the 'service and semi-skilled' and 'unskilled' groups, where, although the total numbers in the groups are nearly equal for the two areas, they account for 34 per cent of total households in the areas of high stress, but only 10 per cent in the areas of low stress. With such a difference in socio-economic groupings it is hardly surprising that lower incomes prevail in the areas of high stress. One half (53 per cent) the heads of households in the low stress areas have a weekly income of £20 or more, but this applies to only 23 per cent of heads of households in the high stress areas.[5]

It must be made quite clear that direct connections between these data cannot be readily made. Thus, it is not possible to assert categorically that broad shifts in the industrial and occupational structures are leading to a growth of low-paid workers in the service sector, concentrated in city centres. There are certainly some *indications* that this is taking place and there are stronger indications that the differential between the lowest-paid manual workers and better-paid manual workers is increasing. However, it must be remembered that skilled workers in some industries earn much less than semi-skilled and unskilled workers in other industries. Also some unskilled workers in the service sector gain substantial additions to their stated income in the form of tips, though this may be offset by uncertainty and instability of employment. These issues are discussed in Marquand,[6] Sinfield and Twine[7] and Atkinson.[8]

The most up-to-date evidence on earnings is provided in the most recent DEP Study.[9] Some attempt to relate low pay to housing conditions in London was made in the supporting research for the *Strategic Plan for the South East* and the Report concluded, 'Generally housing takes a higher proportion of income in London than elsewhere in the country ... but the proportion spent by those with low incomes, who generally have the worst housing, is higher still and annually increasing'.[10]

THE EXAMPLE OF THE CITY OF LONDON

It is paradoxical that when the dominant trend in all cities in advanced industrial societies such as Australia, France, Sweden, the USA and Britain is that of dispersion and diffusion, with a general fall in population within administratively designated urban areas, the poor may be concentrating and may be becoming poorer – certainly relatively, and probably absolutely. Part of the reason for this localization is given in a recent economic analysis of the City of London, which emphasizes the professional and financial concentration without acknowledging explicitly the similar concentration of service workers.

The most noticeable feature of the City of the future will be 'specialisation within specialisation'. Not only will the type of activities carried out be almost entirely in 'rights to goods'; *within* each activity only those functions involving decision taking and close contacts with people – clients, customers or competitors – will remain . . . The interrelated network of activities will be even more closely associated with each other.[11]

This same research group did a random sample survey of firms and gathered detailed information on all the communications made by 526 respondents in senior positions. In all, these people collectively took part in over 28,000 communications in one day. Of these communications 1,482 or nearly three per head were carried by special messengers.[12] A quarter of all male postmen, mail-sorters and messengers in 1968 in Great Britain received less than £17 for a full week's work and a half received less than £20.[13] In the City of London in 1966 there were 3,610 postmen and mail-sorters and 6,440 male messengers. These 10,000 workers are clearly just as concentrated as the 11,230 professional accountants, company secretaries and registrars who also worked in the City at that time.[14] The continued development of the City as a financial centre is confidently expected[15] and if Britain enters the European Economic Community then, in *The Times*'s words (23 October 1970), 'the City of London will become the Wall Street of western Europe'. Unfortunately there appears to be no research which can give the multiplier effect of increasing financial and other activities in the City. There are 70,000 clerks and cashiers in the City but only 22,000 administrators and managers; there are over 10,000 men and women serving and working in the catering trade as waiters, counter hands, cooks and kitchen hands; there are over 10,000 men and women working as shop assistants or managers; there are over 7,000 men and women working as warehousemen, storekeepers, packers and bottlers; there are 6,000 female office-cleaners; and so on. Admittedly of these 33,000 service workers some 13,500 are married women working part-time, but even if we limit our discussion to the 19,000 full-time male workers and add the postmen and messengers, the total is considerably greater than the total of administrators and managers in the City.

Quite evidently the City of London is an extreme example to choose: its characteristics are closer to those of other world cities, such as Paris or New York, than to those of other cities in Britain. However, it does highlight the point that increasing specialization and increasing concentration of highly qualified professional and managerial workers carries with it a similar concentration of service workers, some of whom appear to be in the lowest-paid categories. The City is also exceptional in that the concentration is extreme, with some 360,000 economically active people in 1966 on a mere 274 hectares (677 acres). Clearly, other London Boroughs house all of these people except the small minority of workers who commute from outside the Greater London area or who actually live in the City. If, as appears to be the case, the routine and non-specialist office functions can be more readily decentralized to suburban situations and beyond, then evidently the changing occupational structure of the City will have important implications for housing and the provision of other urban resources and facilities. Thus it is not surprising, for example, that no messengers live in the City, but that in 1966 over 5,000 lived in the three boroughs of Islington, Hackney and Southwark, which immediately adjoin the City and include some of the very worst housing conditions in the whole of London.[16]

A cautionary note must be added here: it is not possible to show that those low-paid workers who are becoming relatively poorer are necessarily the same people who work in the City and that, in turn, these people are the same as those who live in areas where the housing conditions present a problem 'more acute and intractable than any to be found in the remainder of the country'.[17] Until further detailed research based on surveys of the incomes, occupations and workplaces of those in bad housing conditions is carried out, we are left with inferences based on fragmentary evidence.

THE REDISTRIBUTION OF REAL INCOME AND THE EQUITABLE DISTRIBUTION OF PUBLIC SERVICES AND FACILITIES

It has been stated that there may be a process of pauperization engendered by changes in the country's industrial and occupational structure. It is necessary to consider, therefore, other sources of real income apart from the labour market.

The orthodox view that life chances are directly related to income gained from the work situation alone is perhaps too limited. Thus, for example, wage differentials might have been decreasing but the poor could still be getting relatively poorer if their greater income were relatively less valuable as a means for getting scarce urban resources and facilities. Differentials in *real* income could increase, as differentials in wages decrease. Hence the operation of 'the urban system' could lead to a process of pauperization independently of the situation in the job market. In Eastern Europe, attempts to redistribute resources in favour of less-skilled workers were frustrated by the distributional effects of an urban system which appeared to be creating new or deeper patterns of inequality.[18] It is evident that even in a socialist economy the inability to understand urban distributive mechanisms can inhibit the move to greater equality, based on earned income alone. It is evident also that the availability of some of the more important urban resources and facilities is not dependent solely on the ability to pay. Those provisions which are administered by local or national government are critical determinants of life chances. Such facilities may be compulsory – such as primary or secondary education – or may be provided upon request as a right or may be granted as a privilege. One strand in the ideology of the Welfare State as a type of society was that need should be a more important criterion than wealth to determine access to facilities. If this ideology had been comprehensively pursued and supported, we might have expected a considerable redistribution of real income within and between localities. Thus, to take the example of the physical distribution of primary schools, the state attempts to provide schools in relation to the age structure of the population, the pattern of residential development and the distance a small child can be expected to walk. This contrasts with schools in the private sector which need not bear any relation to catchment areas but which rely on the wealth of their clients to transport pupils, often to inconveniently situated converted mansions.

If the provision of public services followed such a principle systematically, we would expect to find a positive correlation between the need for public services and facilities and their provision. Thus, the Welfare State and notions of citizenship would be a reality and the inequalities following from wage differentials would be compensated for, so that the poor would not be doubly penalized. However, it is a commonplace to observe that this does not happen, although detailed documentation presents many complicated methodological problems.[19] The provision of public services and facilities has its own pattern of inequalities. It can be argued that the exploration of the systematic structuring of such inequalities provides a useful focus to students of stratification working in urban areas.[20] The pattern of territorial injustice exemplified in the work of Davies for Britain can be found in every industrial society[21] and the elimination of such inequalities could well be extremely difficult, even in a post-revolutionary situation. The hidden mechanisms of redistribution operate in socialist as well as in capitalist societies: one of the tasks of a radical sociology might be to expose such mechanisms and to consider how an understanding of the urban redistributive system can be used to develop new theories of stratification in industrial society.

Regard should not simply be paid to those services which are traditionally discussed by students of social administration and social policy – what might be called the Seebohm services.[22] It is also important to consider all other aspects of public policy which have a redistributive effect. The siting of power stations, hospitals or motorways all help to redistribute real income. Externality effects, as economists call them, are an important element in the system. And the central problem is to understand how policies and programmes designed to reduce inequalities may actually increase them. It is a matter of exploring the distribution of 'fringe benefits generated by changes in the urban system', to take Harvey's phrase.[23]

The public provision of health and welfare services, roads, public transport, fire and police protection, libraries, schools, swimming pools, parks and so on, is financed out of public rates and taxes 'for the community at large'. No one openly denies that the poorest man has as much right to walk in the park, use the public library, call out a fire engine or have domestic help under certain circumstances as the richest man. If this does not happen we must ask whether the public sector generates its own system of inequality, or whether it simply reflects the economic system within which it is encapsulated.

Unfortunately, a systematic sociology of public provision has hardly started, despite the contention of one urban economist that 'local public services bid fair to become the chief means of income *re*distribution in our economy' (present author's emphasis).[24] Only educational provision has been systematically studied, although something of a start in the sociology of the Health Service and the physical planning process has been made. If we compare the amount of effort and energy that has been devoted to the sociology of industry (mainly private) with that devoted to the sociology of public services, the contrast is striking. Certainly something is known of *The Faith of the Counsellors*,[25] the ideologies of teachers, planners and social workers; but it is not very helpful to talk of 'bourgeois' values in these professions if very similar values are found in socialistic societies. Thus, for example, planners in both socialist and capitalist societies may share similar goals and values, even if the means at their disposal are different. The same applies to many other caretaking professions and to the managers of the public sector. To some extent, their power and ideology derive from the political party or council that employs them. However, it would surely be naïve to assume that managers of the urban system are merely tools of their political masters, ready to shift policies and programmes according to political fashion. Clearly, there is a considerable tension between administrator, professional and politician which the Fulton[26] and Maud[27] reports document for national and local government respectively. Such managerial tensions are likely to produce different patterns of resource allocation in different localities as the distribution of power shifts between the three contending groups. This point is made by Davies:

The power of a Committee over the Council may be the result of many factors. The authority may always have prided itself on the performance of one service – perhaps having been a pioneer in this field – and be generous in its allocation of funds to it. A chief officer may have built up a distinguished team and have a distinguished successor who may ensure the continuation of the department's status in the authority ... Members may be particularly sensitive to the needs of some services because of local pressure groups' activity, because of the political ideology of dominating members or because the needs of the area, as perceived by almost anyone, suggest that an above-average development of the service in question is appropriate. Such factors may vary greatly in strength between authorities, but there can be no doubt that they have a major effect on the extent and manner of provision of services.[28]

There appears to be no systematic relationship between the level of provision of public resources and facilities and the political party in power. Old people, for example, do not necessarily receive better care under a Labour than under a Conservative local authority. There exists a need for a typology of allocative structures based upon a number of dimensions. At present it is known that territorial inequality is substantial and that men with the same occupation, income and family characteristics have substantially different life chances in different localities. The systematic portrayal of such inequalities remains to be undertaken. The range of territorial inequality is probably greater in many instances than the range of inequality between certain positions in the occupational structure; moreover, the former inequalities are widening more rapidly than the latter. Authorities differ in the rules they adopt for the allocation of public services and facilities; they differ in wealth; they differ in the number and the degree of skills of the professional gatekeepers they employ; they differ in the system of administration and organization which they adopt and the degree of cooperation and coordination which may exist between 'chief officers' and the rest of their managerial staff. Max Weber was surely wrong when he described the end of the political autonomy of the medieval city as the end of a distinctive urban sociology.[29] There is still a considerable concentration of power over the allocation of scarce resources in localities. Although there may be, as it were, conflicts between the line and staff managers and the shareholders (i.e. the Council), there is a united and common ideology of the need to control, plan and provide for the lower participants or clients in the urban system. There is a vested interest in maintaining the local authority (a title with significant Dahrendorfian implications)[30] which pays the managers good salaries and provides the context for the expansion of various professions. To some extent, each professional group in an authority's management structure is an interest group, which gains power by increasing the number of its own clients or lower participants. Since few authorities have an overall programme or policy, such as may occur at the national level, the cumulative effect of *ad hoc* policies, reflecting a fluctuating power situation, may provide greater 'diswelfare' and increasing inequality for the majority of an authority's lower participants.

MANAGERS AND PROFESSIONALS IN THE URBAN DISTRIBUTIVE SYSTEM

Harvey suggests that 'it is tempting to hypothesize that any activity that generates strong external costs will be under-controlled or under-compensated-for' and that small but well-mobilized pressure groups will be able to influence disproportionately allocational and locational decisions.[31] As an example he cites 'Central Business District Imperialism' in which the well-organized business interests of the central city (with their small-group oligopolistic structure) effectively dominate the looser and weaker coalitions found in the rest of the city. This view of the city is very clearly exemplified by the nature and style of objections to the Greater London Development Plan, which formed the basis of an Inquiry which began in 1970. Individual London Boroughs engaged counsel to argue for more resources (floor-space allocations or population totals) and one of the longest and most elaborate cases for more resources was made by the institution which already had most – the City. Whatever the particular merits of the cases put forward, it is evident that the poorer areas and populations have fewer resources to compete for more resources. They are dependent on the advocacy of others.

Conflict, then, is a necessary condition of urban life:

> In the most general terms, therefore, the city is composed of group-ings of residents, clearly identified within a spatial location, who are competing for the resources that the city offers. Whether organised or not, they are competing for good jobs, good houses, good education, and all the other 'goodies' available in the urban milieu.[32]

The same authors go on to argue that slums exist and are main-tained because the people living there have insufficient influence or control over the allocation of resources.

The argument so far is that scarce urban resources and facilities are distributed by the managers of the urban system,[33] and that those professionals who, directly or indirectly, manage these resources are concerned individually to advance as professionals and collectively to maintain the boundaries between themselves and other professional interest groups. The important question which now emerges is the degree of independent and autonomous control which can be exercised by the urban managers as distinct from industrial managers or national and local politicians. How far, in terms of the main theme of this chapter, can urban managers work within the existing economic and political system to make their limited urban system operate more equitably? Furthermore, what indicators would be appropriate to measure the effects of the redistribution of real income within urban systems?

This is a difficult issue and all that one can say with certainty is that it is easier to find examples where the differentials between the poorest and the richest social groups have increased, rather than the reverse. Some interesting material is presented in *The Property Boom* by Oliver Marriott, who was financial editor of *The Times* from 1945 to 1965. Discussing the development of provincial town centres between 1948 and 1955 Marriot notes:

Building licences were only granted for replacing bombed shops or for shops on new housing estates. Each local authority was given permission by the Ministry of Housing for a certain amount to be spent in its area, and if the allocation was not taken up by the year end, it lapsed. This spurred the local authorities to busy on with redevelopment and quickened the flow of work into Ravenseft's eager hands between 1950 and 1955. In these crucial years Freedman and Maynard had virtually no opposition. One reason was that they were opening up a type of redevelopment which had previously been unknown. This was large-scale cooperation between municipal authorities and private enterprise . . .

The grapevine of local officials also helped Freedman and Maynard; at their annual conferences the town clerks or the surveyors or the borough architects would discuss the developer, which for a few years meant a word of mouth advertisement for Ravenseft . . .

Towards the end of 1953 Freedman and Maynard saw that before long they would be running out of blitzed cities. They began to look at the New Towns . . . the multiple shops flocked in to the New Towns' centres – and so did the New Townspeople . . .

In 1953 Harold Samuel's land securities bought out Freedman and Maynard and friends and took its holding in Ravenseft from 50 per cent to 100 per cent. This deal valued Ravenseft at £2,100,000 . . .

. . . By the summer of 1967, after the property share boom had cooled, Harold Samuel's holding in land securities was worth £12,400,000, Louis Freedman's £1,850,000 and Fred Maynard's £845,000. The entire company, including the much bigger stake of the public and the insurance companies, was valued by the stock market at £62,000,000.[34]

And that is how we got our nice new shops and Louis Freedman made a personal fortune of nearly £2 million. Certainly it was government policy to redevelop town centres with the profit and benefit of private developers in mind and local authorities could do little else than pass the best central sites to commercial organizations. Sites for public services and facilities had to be found away from the most accessible locations. There was little scope for policies for a more equitable distribution of real income.

The current interest in cost–benefit analysis as a managerial tool in urban resource allocation may also lead to a widening of real income differentials, since it has an inevitable bias towards the value of property and capital. In the Roskill Commission's study of amenity costs at a new international airport, it was found that the depreciation of property values near Heathrow and Gatwick was highly sensitive to the class of property. On average, for all noise levels, the percentage depreciation of high-class property was four times the depreciation of low-class property. Simply because their property values were so little affected, the poor were assumed to be little bothered by noise, and small or nil values were attached to their loss of amenity for the purposes of the cost–benefit quantification.[35] Again, although there are techniques for determining the cost of, say, an urban motorway to the owners of property in its path, other costs, less easily quantified, are not taken into account. In a working-class area of rented housing, kin links and supporting patterns of social relationships may have created a form of social capital which, on one system of accounting, is more valuable to those who have it than the gardens of the middle class. The problem is how to quantify such a value. Since the middle class are more likely to be compensated and may also suffer less from forced mobility – they normally have the means to overcome physical distance and to maintain close social distance where this has been established – they are much less likely to lose from changes in the physical structure of cities. And not only would they suffer less if they were to be disturbed (because of capital compensation and so forth), but they are less likely to be disturbed, simply because their costs are more easily quantified and because they are more articulate and knowledgeable about proposals that may affect them. Sections of the working class are much more likely to be at risk, partly because of their lack of property and partly because of their ecological position in the city. The relationship between ecology and equality is relatively unexplored.

An interesting study by Ornati, *The Transportation Needs of the Poor*,[36] demonstrates that the developing ecological structure of a city – in this case New York – has built into it certain constraints which lead to an increasing disjunction between poor peoples' homes and their workplaces. Public transport routes, originally developed to link middle-class residences to middle-class workplaces, greatly inconvenience the poor who move into old middle-class areas and have different transport needs. A consumer-oriented society is more concerned with transporting the poor to spend their money in central shopping centres, Ornati implies, than to opening up a wider range of employment opportunities. Even the cost of getting to shops may be considerable, and is well illustrated in this country by the case of Glasgow, where new flats on the urban periphery have few local shops and the people not only have to pay higher rents but are obliged to travel back to the area where they used to live, now redeveloped as a shopping centre. Such examples illustrate how differentials in real income may increase as a result, in this case, of the increased cost of physical access to urban resources such as employment or shops.

SPATIAL POLICY AND SOCIAL POLICY

A further theme which has been a focus of controversy in relation to Birmingham, Glasgow, London and many other cities concerns the decentralization of manufacturing industry. The suburbanization of manufacturing industry is a well-established trend in the United States: in Britain the development of New Towns, specifically planned to ease the pressures on the main conurbations, has accentuated the trend. Those growth industries which are expanding the most rapidly tend to be those which have a high demand for skills, a high ratio of managers to managed and a favourable ratio of floor-space to worker. Space and skilled workers are the crucial locational factors and the peripheries of city regions appear to be ideal sites. Thus, in the case of the London region, the most rapidly expanding area economically is in the Outer Metropolitan Region, immediately beyond the Green Belt.[37] The effect of this peripheral expansion may be to limit the opportunities for social mobility by those in the central cities, hemmed in by middle-class suburbs and offered employment either in old-established, and possibly declining, manufacturing industries, where the wages are often low (e.g. the textile industry), or the service sector, where opportunities for training and advancement may be less good. This point links back to the occupational structure of the expanding functions of the City of London. In the past large cities were more likely to have higher rates of social mobility.[38] Such a conclusion must now be severely questioned as urban diffusion 'decentralizes opportunity'.

This possibility that cities, which are continuing to concentrate a particular type of activity at the centre, may cause blockages in social mobility for the offspring of sections of the population now working in the service industries is a very serious issue. It is the main theme of 'Social Structure and Social Change', a chapter in *Studies Volume 2* of the South East Joint Planning Team's Report (1971*a*). Certain of the points touched on in this chapter are also discussed in that chapter. Of particular interest are the positive policy proposals for a Sector City which are elaborated at length in Chapter 6 of *Studies Volume 4*.[39] Here some attempt is being made to understand the social and economic forces at work in the urban system and to manage and organize the system so that resources may be reallocated to those at present most deprived and also to create the conditions under which rates of social mobility may increase. The interplay between social, physical (land use) and economic planning is innovatory and much more detailed research and experience are needed. It seems clear, however, that management of housing and employment needs to be phased together and that arranging the amount of coordination required seems beyond the scope of the market. If it is hard to imagine the activities of a New Town Development Corporation being undertaken by private agencies, it is even harder to imagine the coordination of urban redevelopment, renewal and industrial re-location within a city being done for private profit alone.

In a society where so much of the urban fabric was created over a century ago, during a period of rapid industrial and urban growth, it is inevitable that some people will be living in conditions defined by the rest of society as intolerable. What does not have to be inevitable is that such populations also have limited access to job opportunities, schools, health services and other facilities, which are differentially distributed within the city. If those with low wages have to bear a disproportionate amount of the costs of noise, pollution and renewal of the urban fabric then they will be doubly penalized. As Harvey aptly notes, 'almost all of this extensive literature has focused on the allocation problems posed by externalities and very little attention has been paid to the distributional effects'.[40] He goes on to remark that the 'best' distribution of incomes involves problems of equity not easy to resolve and hence frequently avoided. That there is frequently 'a quite substantial regressive redistribution of income in a rapidly changing urban system'[41] should be a matter for serious concern and one would expect this to be reflected in the political arena.

SPATIAL INEQUALITY AND POLITICAL CONSCIOUSNESS

Until now lower participants in the urban system have not developed much consciousness of their common deprivations. There are, however, some signs of change:

> For generations, the arena of action was more narrowly the workplace, the setting of production. Recently in the United States, low income persons have been organising to affect their rights to welfare and other forms of government services rather than to affect the economic market.[42]

Political consciousness may be slow to develop in the urban system because the mechanisms of redistribution are hidden. However, it may be that well-organized squatting and sporadic demonstrations against high rents, or intolerable noise from motorways, are the forerunners of more-organized locality-based associations concerned with the basic issues of urban equity. Attempts to assess the relative costs and benefits of various locational decisions have had the unintended consequence of making explicit the fact that some people benefit and some lose. When it is manifest that the *same* category tends to benefit in a variety of circumstances and situations, a more conscious pressure for an equitable distribution of urban resources and facilities may emerge.

Urban analysis may help us to reformulate our notions of the nature of our distributive system and to redefine lines of conflict based on constraints and limitations of life chances, which restrict the *use* of income and the access to rights and benefits rather than access to income alone in the labour market. It is possible that, in terms of access to urban facilities, the division between the skilled manual workers and the less-skilled manual workers may be becoming more significant than the division between the skilled manual workers and the routine non-manual workers. This might lead us to revise our notions of the conventional cutting-points in the class structure.

The inequities and possible pauperization generated by the operation of the urban system are extremely hard to document precisely. Although Harvey may well be right that the hidden mechanisms governing the redistribution of income 'seem to be moving us towards a state of greater inequality and greater injustice', such an assertion is extremely hard to substantiate. And even if the assertion were to be accepted it would be extraordinarily difficult to incorporate into a political programme policies that would ensure greater equity. It is hard to envisage a society which would accept such clear goals of equity and few would consider it legitimate to coerce, even without the use of armed force, to achieve a given pattern of distribution. We are left with arguments based on a sense of justice which assume that multiple deprivation is not part of a good society. The same people should not be at the bottom of all the hierarchies and receive the worst of all the public services and private markets. Yet even given a willingness to achieve such a measure of social justice, the means to that end are not easy to determine. Questions

of costs and benefits involve value judgements as well as calculations, and conflicts, even between those who agree on the ends,
are likely to increase.

FROM ASSERTIONS THROUGH RESEARCH TO POLICIES

It is evident that these matters are too important to leave to the
assertions and hunches of academics, journalists and politicians.
There are very important research problems with direct policy
implications which urgently deserve attention. Perhaps mentioning some of these would strike an appropriately cautious note on
which to conclude this chapter.

Firmer evidence is required on the relationship between the
employment shift to the service sector in the economy as a whole
and the relative growth of low-paid occupations. More knowledge is required concerning the spatial distribution of low-paid
occupations in all sectors of the economy. This chapter has concentrated on the inner city and emphasized the need for more
information on the multiplier effect of senior professional and
managerial jobs, which are located in the city centre, on the
growth in the number of the low-paid. Further, we simply do not
have adequate information to enable us to say with certainty
whether those in certain low-paid occupations are the same
people who live in the worst housing and receive the least of
urban resources and facilities. As an example, clear empirical
evidence is not available on the nature and degree of the limitations on social mobility amongst less-privileged populations in
the inner city. It is not known, in any precise way, how far the
activities of a professional group associated with the management
of the urban system – town planners – have, in fact, helped to
produce greater equity in the last twenty years. The example of
the redevelopment of provincial shopping centres was chosen to
indicate that differentials probably increased as a result of such
activity. No doubt contrary examples could be found: but what
would be the final balance? It is somewhat alarming that we do
not know. Quite clearly, there is a spatial dimension to the
problem of poverty which poses some of the toughest problems

of social policy. It is probably impossible ever to achieve a truly equitable distribution of resources and facilities. However, it is important to distinguish between those problems that are associated with long-term trends in the economic and spatial structure of our society – such as the decline in agricultural labour or the financial concentration in city centres – and those that are due simply to the way resources are allocated in specific localities.

Perhaps the most hopeful development in recent years has been the move to a more rational system of local authority financial budgeting. This has forced some managers of the urban system to make explicit who is to benefit from the allocation of scarce resources and when. As the distributional mechanisms become more clearly understood, the possibility of having a more equitable distribution of urban resources becomes greater. This is partly because more information can be fed into the political process and partly because it is much more difficult to perpetrate inequalities if this activity is clearly apparent to everyone. This belief that more information makes for greater equity puts a heavy responsibility on research workers. Whose problems do we tackle first?

REFERENCES

1 Knight, R., 'Changes in the occupational structure of the working population', *Journal of the Royal Statistical Society*, CXXX, 3, 1967, 408–22.
2 Department of Employment and Productivity, 'Employment changes in certain less-skilled occupations: 1961–1966', *Employment and Productivity Gazette*, 1969, 308–11.
3 Income Data Services Ltd, *Incomes Data Report 98*, September 1970, 25.
4 Sinfield, A., and Twine, F., 'The Working Poor', *Poverty*, Journal of the Child Poverty Action Group, 12/13, 1969, 4–7.
5 Greater London Council, *The Characteristics of London's Households*, County Hall, 1970, 52.
6 Marquand, J., 'Which are the lower-paid workers?', *British Journal of Industrial Relations*, 1967, 359–74.

7 Sinfield, A., and Twine, F., *The Low-Paid: The Employment Market and Social Policy*, unpublished MS, University of Essex, 1968.

8 Atkinson, A. B., *Poverty in Britain and the Reform of Social Security*, Cambridge University Press, Department of Applied Economics, Occasional Papers No. 18, 1969.

9 Department of Employment and Productivity, *New Earnings Survey 1968*, HMSO, 1970.

10 South East Joint Planning Team, *Strategic Plan for the South East*, HMSO for Ministry of Housing and Local Government, 1970, 25.

11 Economists Advisory Group, *An Economic Study of the City of London: A Summary*, Corporation of London, 1968, 28.

12 Dunning, J. H., and Morgan, E. V., Proof of Evidence to the Greater London Development Plan Inquiry on behalf of the Corporation of the City of London. Unpublished, 1970.

13 Department of Employment and Productivity, *New Earnings Survey 1968*, Table 4.

14 General Register Office, *Sample Census 1966: Economic Activity Tables for Greater London*, HMSO, 1968, 51–2.

15 Economists Advisory Group, *The Role of International Companies*, Committee of Invisible Exports, 1969.

16 Standing Working Party on London, *London's Housing Needs up to 1974*, HMSO for Ministry of Housing and Local Government, Housing Report No. 3, 1970, Table 2.

17 Central Housing Advisory Committee, *Council Housing: Purposes, Procedures and Priorities*, HMSO, Ninth Report of the Housing Management Sub-Committee, 1969, 141.

18 Konrád, G., and Szelényi, I., 'Sociological aspects of the allocation of housing: Experiences from a Socialist non-market economy', Institute of Sociology, Hungarian Academy of Sciences, Sociological Research Group, Budapest, 1969.

19 Davies, B., *Social Needs and Resources in Local Services*, Michael Joseph, 1968.

20 Pahl, R. E., 'Urban and social theory and research', *Environment and Planning*, 1, 1969, 143–53. Reprinted here as Chapter 7.

21 Scardigli, V., 'La fréquentation des équipments collectifs', *Consommation*, Annales du CREDOC, 1, 1970, 1–27.

22 Seebohm Committee, *Report on Local Authority and Allied Personal Services* (Cmnd. 3703), HMSO, 1968.

23 Harvey, D., 'Social processes, spatial form and the redistribution of real income in an urban system' in Chisholm, M., Frey, A. E., and Haggett, P. (eds.), *Regional Forecasting*, Butterworth, 1971.

182   *Spatial patterns and social processes*

24 Thompson, W., *A Preface to Urban Economics*, Johns Hopkins Press, 1965, 118.
25 Halmos, P., *The Faith of the Counsellors*, Constable, 1965.
26 Fulton Committee, *Report on the Civil Service* (Cmnd. 3638), HMSO, 1968.
27 Maud Committee, *Report and Papers on the Management of Local Government*, HMSO, 1967.
28 Davies, op. cit., pp. 114–15.
29 Weber, M., *The City*, Martindale, D., and Neuwirth, G. (trans.), Heinemann, 1960.
30 Dahrendorf, R., *Class and Class Conflicts in Industrial Society*, Routledge, 1959.
31 Harvey, op. cit.
32 Meltzer, J., and Whitley, J., 'Planning for the urban slum', in Sharrard, T. D. (ed.), *Social Welfare and Urban Problems*, Columbia University Press, New York, 1968, 173–4.
33 Pahl, op. cit.
34 Marriott, O., *The Property Boom*, Hamish Hamilton, 1967, 61–5.
35 Adams, J., 'Westminster: the fourth London airport?', *Area*, 2, 1970, 1–9.
36 Ornati, Oscar, *The Transportation Needs of the Poor*, Praeger, New York, 1969.
37 Pahl, R. E., *Urbs in Rure: The Metropolitan Fringe in Hertfordshire*, London School of Economics, Geographical Paper No. 2, Weidenfeld & Nicolson, 1965; South East Joint Planning Team, op. cit.
38 Lipset, S. M., and Bendix, R., *Social Mobility in Industrial Society*, University of California Press, 1959.
39 South East Joint Planning Team, 'The social, employment and housing problems of London', in *Studies Volume 4*, HMSO for Department of the Environment, 1971.
40 Harvey, op. cit., 273.
41 ibid., 277.
42 Miller, S. M., and Roby, P., *The Future of Inequality*, Basic Books, New York, 1970, 143.

Part 3 Urban processes and social structure

Introduction

The six chapters in this section were written between 1969 and 1974. They are all concerned with the same set of problems and my various attempts to grapple with them. Fundamentally they are concerned with these questions: Who gets the scarce resources and facilities? Who decides how to distribute or allocate these resources? Who decides who decides? Not only is there a focus on the sociology of urban distributive systems, the gatekeepers and their rules, but there is also an attempt to bring the spatial component into the analysis in a systematic way. The key words are 'access' and 'allocation'. Accessibility can be improved by physical mobility or by political activity, or both. How far the allocation of resources is determined by local 'managers of the urban system' and how far the state and private financial interests provide the overall constraints is debatable. Without doubt there is an ambiguity and an ambivalence in the last three chapters but hopefully that reflects the reality of different levels of analysis in a mixed economy. Answering the question 'Whose City?' does not necessarily determine what is to be done next.

A further theme underlying these chapters is the degree to which cities are simply arenas in which conflicts generated in the wide social structure are played out or whether new forms of conflict, related to the nature of the city *per se*, are generated independently of the encapsulating power structure. How far can one learn about the nature of contemporary capitalism by studying British cities, and how far can the study of finance capitalism help in the understanding of British cities?

Chapter 9   Whose city?

What is to become of the city? Intellectuals scorn the neatness and order of skilled-manual-worker or lower-middle-class housing in new towns or spec-built estates, and deplore huge, 'inhuman' blocks of flats. But at the same time they feel angry or guilty about overcrowding and poverty in Notting Hill or Sparkbrook. They are not sure whether the car must adapt to the city or the city to the car. Their attitude to the London motorway box seems to depend more on whether it affects their local area or on whether they have recently been ensnarled in crawling traffic for hours, rather than on any clear vision of what the city might or should be.

The attitudes of middle-class radicals to many other urban problems are highly ambivalent. Commuting, urban renewal, the location of the third London airport, urban poverty, mobility and congestion are all irritatingly confused issues on which the progressive line is not at all clear. Attempts to stay in London, by making such areas as Islington fashionable, are a potential source of guilt ('taking away houses from those in greater need'). The only comfort is that those who have done up cottages in the country are probably suffering from a similar sort of guilt.

There has been a recent spate of television programmes and articles by various pundits giving 'personal views' about the dreary creations of the planners and architects, particularly when seen in contrast to the lively, human squalor of the streets of Soho and Chelsea or the excitement of the great mobile life of California. There is a pathetic demand for a visionary, who can explain in one Sunday supplement how we should all live; and yet at the same time there is a sort of underlying resentment that the richness, diversity, variety, etc., of 'real human life' should be squashed into the moulds devised by planners who, by implication, are all unimaginative technocrats. Planners are expected to make our life 'better', but if they succeed they may be resented – because people are thereby being deprived of the freedom to plan their lives for themselves.

It seems that we are as uncertain of the problems as we are of the solutions. We know that there are slums; we know that the population is increasing; we know that the basic physical infrastructure is ageing and will have to be renewed; we know that our urban roads are congested; and yet we do not know which aspect of these various issues is 'the real problem'. New towns and new cities can help siphon off young, skilled, energetic people from existing cities. But they are far from complete solutions, since it is those most in need of help who are left behind. When the transportation technocrat is not sure what to feed into his computer, and the playwrights' and novelists' visions don't go much farther than a few bustling streets in certain parts of London, maybe the third culture, sociology, will provide the answers?

Surely the sociologist can tell us what people will want – not only now, but in 1984, the year 2000, or whatever year it is to which we have to fix the long-term financial budgeting? But the sociologist wriggles. He argues that it is for him to analyse the implicit goals of different groups in society – how they conflict and what the unintended consequences of planning decisions might be – but not for him alone to prescribe these goals. He is a member of society as much as anyone else.

However, if pressed, the sociologist will say that physical arrangements have very little effect on social arrangements. Renewing the physical environment of the urban poor does not eliminate the causes of their poverty. The poverty is largely the result of the distribution of power in society and this distribution is preserved by powerful interest groups and finds expression in spatial and physical terms in the city. The elimination of poverty necessitates a voluntary abdication of some power by the affluent majority in favour of the poor minority.

Even though buildings and land use have very little effect on people's behaviour, this is not to say that the actual house that people live in is not very important. It is hardly an agent of social change, but it is still a much more important environment than the locality. People's *social world* is best conceived of as a social network of linkages, which is not necessarily based on locality.

However, physical planners have enough of the conventional wisdom to know that ultimately they must be concerned with social welfare in the broadest sense. Certainly, some might argue that planning is simply an end in itself rather than a means to an end. Neatness, tidiness, orderliness and planning in general may be defined as good, in some abstract sense, no matter what the people being planned may think. But the current vogue is 'participation': the Skeffington committee's report on public participation in planning has had wide publicity, and so even the most enthusiastic 'drains man' or rule-book backwoodsman is probably prepared to make some small gesture towards public participation.

I have been stimulated to consider these issues by reading *People and Plans*, a collection of essays on urban problems and solutions, by Herbert J. Gans. It seems to me that, particularly for us in Britain, Professor Gans's essays could not have been published at a more opportune time. As both a sociologist and a qualified planner Professor Gans has had a long and distinguished record of research, and his books on *The Urban Villagers* and *The Levittowners* were valuable contributions to the ethnography of contemporary America. More recently he has been actively engaged in advising government committees on the nation's so-called 'urban' crisis. Few people are as well qualified, either here or in America, to discuss the relationship between people and plans.

Furthermore, Gans is prepared to forsake academic detachment and make clear suggestions on policy. He argues consistently that planning must be *user*-oriented – it is for people, not for planners; it ought to be *compensatory*, so that those who get the fewest rewards from the private sector ought to get most from the public sector; finally, it ought to be more concerned with the established needs of *today* rather than with the hypothetical needs of the future. The problems of urban slums are greater than the problems of the aesthetics of urban sprawl. He is more concerned with the *processes* than with the symptoms they create, and traces back the causes of urban poverty to the social, economic and political structure of the society.

There are some thirty or so essays collected in this book, ranging from satirical or polemical pieces aimed at a popular audience, to summaries of the sociological literature on a topic prepared for planners or social workers, and to scholarly papers, such as his critique of 'Urbanism and suburbanism as ways of life'. It is hard to think of a better book to recommend to all the planners and architects who are increasingly wanting to know what the contribution of the sociologist to their field is or could be. There is much that is wise; it is cogently expressed and it provides a fine contribution to the sociology of planning in its widest sense. Nevertheless, the book ends on a deeply pessimistic note, as Gans doubts whether the war on poverty and segregation can be won and raises the question whether the new, affluent suburbia has been achieved at the cost of withholding opportunities from the poor and non-white.

One fears that some British planners may be acting out a script which was written in the United States in the nineteen-fifties and is now increasingly outdated. The fashion in America was then to concentrate on transportation facilities, and teams of transportation experts, with economists and operation researchers, programmed their computers with alternative simulation models: thus, given the simplifying constraints of the exercise, they were able to formulate a number of alternative schemes. It would be sad if a decade later some British planners are still expecting too much from this new technical expertise, while a large part of the American planning profession has moved on to a greater concern with *social* objectives and the most rational and effective way of achieving them.

Professor Gans describes these changes in his essays on the 'Sociology of city planning' and on the 'Goal-oriented approach to planning'. In an essay on 'Culture and class in the study of poverty', Gans attacks the notion that the poor are condemned to remain so, trapped in a culture of poverty.

If the culture of poverty is defined as those cultural patterns which keep people poor, it would be necessary to include in the term also the persisting cultural patterns among the affluent which, deliberately or not, keep their fellow citizens poor. When the concept of a culture of poverty is applied only to the poor, the onus for change falls too much on them, when, in reality, the prime obstacles to the elimination of poverty lie in the economic, political and social structure that operates to increase the wealth of the already affluent.

It is at this point that the British planner may begin to assume that the discussion is no longer relevant to him.

This is the tragedy of the British situation: it is tragic for the people that the planner sees his job in such a limited way; and it is tragic, too, for the planner that his best efforts are frustrated by forces which he defines as being outside his dominion. Thus he may build houses, only to find that those for whom they were built cannot afford to live in them because wages locally are low (Manchester Corporation reported early in 1969 that this is the situation in its newest estate at Whitefield); or he may help to create jobs, only to find that he has condemned those who fill them to overcrowded housing because local land values are so high that housing is scarce.

However, we in Britain are fortunate in that we have the example of America to learn from. There, too ready an acceptance both of the most easily applicable techniques and of the values of the most powerful groups has led to the situation in which they have, for example, splendid freeways, which simply enable the middle class to ride past the poor more rapidly. Making physical changes without parallel changes in the social structure may serve to add to the problem by drawing sections of the population farther apart. Clearly no one wants British cities to be centres of poverty and racial intolerance. However, there may be some danger that if British planners feel that their main task is to concentrate on the future and to spend their time worrying about the provision of motorways and yachting marinas in 1991, they may take attention away from present problems and so, indirectly, help to make them worse.

Similarly, if they concern themselves with large areas, which have no elected representatives – such as regions – they can avoid facing local problems by claiming that they are not relevant at the larger level. Thus planning as an activity can continue indefinitely, without having to face the conflicting goals of the present at the scale on which people live. Method-oriented planners can easily lose sight of the goals, and the question which Gans poses in the American situation is equally relevant here. 'Who plans, with what ends and means, for what interest group?'

Yet Gans is one sociologist who cannot be criticized for being negative and for providing no positive suggestions. If only for his chapter on 'Planning for everyday life and problems of suburban and new town residents', any New Town social relations officer should have the book on his desk. It should be standard reading for all community activists from Glenrothes to Solent City.

The British situation is very different from that in America, but is nevertheless disturbing. Not only are planners coming increasingly under attack through the mass media at the national level but also they may feel threatened and insecure at the local level as their professional isolation is invaded by public participation. There may thus be a retreat to defending bureaucratic procedures at the very time that a more outward-looking concern with social processes and social problems is needed.

The planners are being urged to devise means to achieve social goals, but neither they nor the sociologists can determine a community's goals. These goals may be explicit – an economic growth rate of 4 per cent, a modern nation-wide transport network, a minimum standard of living which is above the poverty line; or they may be implicit – more choice for the affluent sections of society, fewer constraints placed on the poorer sections and so on.

The will of the community is mediated through the political process, so that those with the most power set the goals, which makes the planner simply the tool of the élite. This is why, in America, the profession is becoming politicized. The progressives want social planning to reduce economic and racial inequality, the conservatives want to defend traditional physical planning and the legitimacy of middle-class values. A third group wants to plan for all interest groups, but is split over whether to work for or against the establishment.

All planning is social planning, and while geographers and transportation experts have an important role in the planning process they should not be the tail that wags the dog. In America, as Gans says, 'the city planner is no longer a non-political formulator of long range ideals, but is becoming an adviser to elected and appointed officials, providing them with recommendations and technical information on current decisions'. Urban renewal should be seen as a way of dealing with the processes which force people into slums: land use studies are becoming less relevant as planners concern themselves with the provision and use of social services and the economic and political consequences of the policies they recommend.

The crucial lesson for British planners is to learn their limitations, and to make these limitations more widely known. The public, seeing, for example, the physical environment in decay, mistakenly assumes that the solution lies in physical renewal alone. However, the planner finds that the amelioration of one problem brings about a deterioration in another sphere, for he is dealing all the time with symptoms not causes.

If the planner analyses the social and economic origins of the problem, he might wish to suggest quite other solutions, even if it were outside his scope to implement these solutions. The danger is that his regard for his professional position will make him disregard the most relevant policies in favour of policies within his field of competence. The planner cannot be the *deus ex machina* of the urban condition. The trouble is that neither the planners nor the people are facing up to the fact that our power to alter the physical environment is greater than we can cope with. Participation implies that people should not only take part in making decisions about the physical environment, but should also take responsibility for the values implicit in planning decisions.

In this sort of situation it is simpler to do what can be done most easily, even if it is expensive. Enormous sums of money are being spent by planners on traffic surveys and transportation studies, but as we concentrate on physical mobility we completely ignore social mobility. Hence we do not know whether our urban areas are collecting an unskilled residue with little opportunity for occupational mobility. We do not know how easily coloured immigrants are moving up the occupational hierarchy. Published plans make pious statements about social goals and social objectives but no long-term social research, such as a continuing monitoring programme on social mobility, is being planned. There are, however, signs that the Central Statistical Office will initiate work on social indicators and this would be a welcome and much needed task.

Professor Gans's book has prompted these thoughts because I feel that in Britain, too, the physical city with its physical problems has been overstressed. The city is essentially a social entity – the product of a particular society at a particular time. It is partly because the Americans saw the city in terms of accessibility, and urban renewal as a way to more profitable uses, that they have got into their present confusions.

In Britain we more readily accept positive discrimination – we already have the educational priority areas, the urban programme and so on. Despite this we still tend to get carried away by the discussions of the physical forms and sometimes neglect to discuss the social goals we are aiming to achieve. Professor Gans says, 'I want immediate change that improves the conditions of the deprived immediately.' Are we sure that we have our priorities right in this country? The city is what society lets it be.

Chapter 10 Urban social theory and research*

In 1958 Don Martindale remarked: 'No subtlety of perception is required to determine that the contemporary American theory of the city is in crisis.'[1] He felt that students were so bored by the textbooks that were available, that they would sooner fail their course than read them. Over the last decade teachers have wearily tramped a path through the literature, boring the student and convincing themselves that previous research is conceptually confused, outdated or trivial. In an urbanized society, 'urban' is everywhere and nowhere: the city cannot be defined and so nor can urban sociology.

It seemed that urban sociology might cease to be a special type of inquiry: Manheim noted that urban society was rapidly becoming American society;[2] Ruth Glass felt that in a highly urbanized country like Great Britain the label 'urban' could be applied to any branch of current sociological study and so it seemed pointless to apply it at all.[3] As sociologists a decade ago dismissed the city as a distinctive focus of interest, courses for undergraduates became either unpopular, non-existent or soft options, based on the kaleidoscope-of-life aspect of community studies. Some sociologists in the American Mid-West continued to use the most recent census volumes to provide commentaries and tabulations of the available statistical information on areas administratively designated as urban, but there urban sociology ended.

Looking back one can have sympathy with Martindale who, writing from his heart, asked: 'Surely in this valley of dry bones

* Paul Stirling, David Morgan and Roy Haddon gave valuable critical comments on an earlier draft of this paper. Of course, I am responsible for its present form.

one may ask with Ezekiel, "Can these bones live?"[3] Faced with the possible elimination of their subject other urban sociologists remembered that in the nineteen-twenties, when there 'really was' an urban sociology, and Park and his colleagues concentrated on the zone of transition in Chicago, it was the integration of a 'rural' population to 'the city' that provided the central focus.[4] If urban sociology did not exist, urbanization in the Third World certainly did – that is, urbanization as acculturation. And so, one after the other, urban sociologists cheered each other on to India, Africa or Latin America in the hope of what Manheim called 'theoretical yield'. Sjoberg urged that urban sociologists should amass data on *the* preindustrial city and on comparative urban studies. In his contribution to *Sociology Today* he particularly deplored the lack of knowledge about cities in Japan and Eastern Europe which resulted from language difficulties: knowledge about American cities was taken for granted.[5] Ruth Glass certainly had no false complacency but nevertheless urged an interest in world urbanization or urban diffusion instead of the current vogue for 'sporadic, detailed evidence about personal relationships within individual small communities', which, she claimed, did little more than provide opportunity for 'vicarious neighbouring'. British urban sociology, she implied, was distinctly *parochial* and British sociologists too much preoccupied with 'the bric-à-brac of our own parlours'.[6] Finally, Reissman, in his book on *The Urban Process*, provided a brilliantly destructive critique of urban social theory of the first half of the twentieth century and concluded that all previous theories of the city were oversimplified. 'The path to urban analysis must run through a broader societal analysis,' he claimed, and, following the new fashion, he brought the developing societies into his typology of urbanization. His advice on future research was to use his typology and 'describe and compare cities drawn from the range of societies at different stages in their development'.[7]

Thus it was that, leaving their own cities behind them, those who called themselves urban sociologists packed their bags for the tropics. And this was reflected in teaching. The widely used Prentice-Hall series, edited by Professor Inkeles, *The Foundations of Modern Sociology*, has no title on urban sociology, although the companion series on the *Modernization of Traditional Societies* has a title on urbanization. Similarly, the Centre for Urban Studies, University of London, has a postgraduate course in Urbanization in Developing Countries but not one on urban sociology *per se*. Undergraduates elsewhere are still being taught the sociology of integration, the ecological fallacy and a rag-bag of studies, which happen to have been done in urban areas.

It is somewhat bizarre that at the time when urban sociologists were discovering the delights of what they defined as real urban problems in Third World cities, the anthropologists, who had been working there, were returning to introduce urban anthropology to the natives of Europe and America. Centres like the Rhodes-Livingstone Institute were a product of the colonial power's enlightened self-interest. Research on 'the natives' could have all sorts of practical implications for administrators and bureaucrats. It is greatly to the credit of British social anthropologists that they never allowed themselves to become tools of their masters. Careful analysis of actual social relationships by scholars such as Epstein and Mitchell provided important insights into the mechanisms which relate the formal to the informal patterns of relationships. Work on distinct *types* of relationships, *types* of urban situations, and *types* of social networks provided a distinctive focus for the study of the African townsman.[8] One of the main problems of the urban situation was the linking of different levels: the social anthropologists provided a valuable organizing framework. However, they too became worried about what constituted 'urban': Mitchell in Central Africa,[9] Mayer in South Africa[10] and Gugler in East Africa[11] tried to operationalize 'urban', with only modest success. How 'urban' are migrants with strong rural reference groups: are the Red Xhosa, described by Mayer, more or less urban than the Mambwe described by Watson[12] and so on. Gluckman was certainly making an important point when he categorically stated 'an African townsman is a townsman',[13] but as Epstein has shown there are townsmen and townsmen.[14]

However, newly independent nations were less enthusiastic to support research on 'how the natives live' and the ex-colonial powers had other problems on their hands. The anthropologists came home and looked around in New York and Manchester: urban jungles and urban villages lay waiting to be explored. Armed with some sharp concepts for dealing with patterns of social relationships, social anthropologists wait for the dramatic events of urban life to create situations to analyse. Unfortunately they are less well-equipped to anticipate the emergence of dramatic events arising out of the structural situation.

Another strand in this sociology of urban sociology is of course the stolid British empirical tradition. Life in blocks of flats or new housing estates is described in great detail and 'urban' is taken to mean simply physically constrained *informal* social relationships. Undergraduates in a variety of institutions doing a variety of courses did essays on 'Neighbourhood and Community', 'The Ideology of the Garden City Movement' and the 'Social Composition of Voluntary Associations'. Such issues did not seem very important to some sociologists in comparison with *real* sociological issues such as *embourgeoisement* (which does not exist) or the work situation of miners (who are rapidly declining in numbers).

Thus we have a situation in Britain today where students read in the newspapers of the urban crisis, the urban programme and the need for urban research but are told in the lecture hall that urban sociology does not exist. 'Certainly there are problems of racial discrimination, poverty, bad housing and educational deprivation but these are not *urban* problems' runs a well-known argument. 'The label "urban" is simply a ploy of the élite to distract attention away from the basic inequalities of our stratification system. We "know" all about that and so there's no need for research.' Alternatively, others argue that it is simply a matter of redistribution and 'policies'. 'Policies' are left to those who study social administration to think up on an *ad hoc* basis. Social administration is often seen as a kind of poor relation for those without the strength of mind to tackle the meat of sociological 'theory'. Some who are interested in the uses of sociology may feel obliged to apologize to their colleagues who are weaving their spells of conceptual purity or advancing the frontiers of the discipline in a more professionally acceptable way.

Most of the work which has been done in the name of urban

sociology is about urbanization – that is change, disorganization and adaptation. It is as if sociologists cannot define urban without a rural contrast: when they lose the peasant they lose the city too. The response to the discovery that 'sociological urban' is everywhere is, as I have suggested, to go somewhere where still it is not everywhere, rather than to construct a truly *urban* sociology. Instead of asking the sort of questions to which urban sociology might provide an answer, urban sociologists have simply looked at what the field has produced in the past and, seeing its irrelevance, lack of cumulative development, and feeble ability to explain or predict what they have defined as 'important' problems, have discarded the field, instead of asking *new* questions. The dissatisfaction with urban sociology relates more to what has been done in its name than to its potential. Certainly a subject with no problems is not worth having. Some sociologists would say that the study of stratification, the family, political and religious institutions and so on, provides an adequate understanding of society. The fact that this all takes place in an urban context is said to add nothing more than the fact that it also takes place in a certain climatic context. They would argue that organizational analysis or the sociology of industry is more acceptable because the enterprise has a unity:

The industrial system imposes its own structure of relationships on managers and workpeople. To maintain and expand the system requires the widespread acceptance of an ordered array of values by which persons in different positions in the system set their aims in life and guide their day-to-day actions, and these values have to be inculcated by a variety of means. For industrial concerns to operate at all there has to be specified a range of roles, each with a set of constraints: there have to be also disciplinary codes or social controls in order to confine admissible conduct within these constraints. In all these senses, the industrial system marks the host society with its own special imprint.[15]

Yet even the industrial sociologists have difficulty in closing their system. The studies by Goldthorpe and his colleagues on the affluent worker minimize the importance of the primary work group, supervisory styles, or the technological constraints structuring work-roles and role relationships. Rather they emphasize the attitudes towards work which workers *bring to* their employment arising from the workers' out-plant roles and patterns of association.[16]

I have been arguing in this short ethnography of urban sociology that the field exists if only because a number of individuals style themselves urban sociologists and have a common language and culture. Much of the best work in the field has, however, been accomplished by those who simply call themselves sociologists, who have applied the concepts developed by the discipline as a whole in this particular field. No one doubts that sociologists can do useful work in problem areas which, for one reason or another, have been defined as urban. However, the flow of ideas appears to have been from sociologists working in other fields rather than from urban sociology to the discipline as a whole. Even Whyte's *Street Corner Society* is more a contribution to small group studies than any cumulative urban sociology. Of course some would argue there is no reason why this should not continue: the particular body of concepts, approaches and methodology which makes up sociology can be applied in any field.

One danger of few sociologists willingly accepting the adjective urban as part of their title would be that areas of investigation are likely to be suggested from outside rather than from within the discipline. Whilst sociologists are quick to point out that expectations of the field of urban sociology are overrated, few would deny that teams designing new cities would be better equipped by having sociologists amongst them. There are still only a few hundred sociologists in Britain and urban problems are too big to leave to traffic engineers, economists and what have you.

Thus some sociologists should be obliged to make themselves aware of urban problems – and here we move from the ethnography to the sociology of urban sociology. What are or should be the *values* of urban sociologists? What problems should they choose and which groups should they advise? Why have they chosen to specialize in the urban situation – is it that they have moved into sociology from a spatially oriented discipline and/or do they enjoy the status to be gained from the, perhaps, less-discriminating audience of planners and architects? If they are working at the periphery of the profession do we suffer from status anxiety, relative deprivation or any other symptom of stress or marginality?

THE DISTRIBUTION OF RESOURCES AND FACILITIES

It is my view that the most useful contribution of sociologists to urban problems will, in the long run, depend on their contribution to sociology. This chapter represents some preliminary thinking towards a redefinition of the field, which might provide a distinctive approach to urban problems and may have possibilities of enlarging our basic understanding of the social structure of an advanced industrial society. The main propositions in my argument may be stated as follows:

(*a*) There are fundamental *spatial* constraints on access to scarce urban resources and facilities. Such constraints are generally expressed in time/cost distance.

(*b*) There are fundamental *social* constraints on access to scarce urban facilities. These reflect the distribution of power in society and are illustrated by:

  bureaucratic rules and procedures
  social gatekeepers who help to distribute and control urban resources

(*c*) Populations in different localities differ in their access and opportunities to gain the scarce resources and facilities, holding their economic position or their position in the occupational structure constant. The situation which is structured out of (*a*) and (*b*) may be called a socio-spatial or socio-ecological system. Populations limited in this access to scarce urban resources and facilities are the *dependent* variable; those controlling access, the *managers* of the system, would be the independent variable.

(*d*) Conflict in the urban system is inevitable. The more the resource or facility is valued by the *total* population in a given locality, or the higher the value and the scarcer the supply in relation to demand, the greater the conflict.

By way of example let us consider the non-random distribution of a facility, which differs in its quality even though it is distributed to all the population within a given age range: education provision is known to vary considerably between LEAs. Variation in expenditure by LEAs can be shown by comparing annual expenditure per pupil on books and stationery: this gives some measure of the importance education holds in the overall budgetry planning. It is of course extremely difficult to get good quantitative indicators of such things as the quality of education, but size of class, turnover of teaching staff, age of building and so on might be combined to provide an index of educational quality for a given school or area. Hence, for those *at the same position in the occupational structure*, different localities will offer different degrees of educational opportunity.

The same variation of opportunity related to housing. However unreliable local authority waiting lists, or statistics relating to multi-occupation or to the numbers of families in temporary accommodation, no one would seriously dispute that Glasgow is in a worse situation than Bristol. Housing clearly operates on a local, or at the most a city-regional level, since housing is clearly related to employment market areas. Furthermore, as D. V. Donnison,[17] Elizabeth Burney[18] and others have shown, access to housing is tightly controlled in some areas by various bureaucratic rules and procedures and by gatekeepers from various public and private agencies. These opportunities of access to housing are structured: 'Among those who share the same relation to the means of production there may be considerable differences in ease of access to housing. This is part of the superstructure which manifestly takes on a life of its own. A class struggle between groups differentially placed with regard to the means of housing develops, which may *at a local level* be as acute as the class struggle in industry. Moreover, the more the independence of this process is emphasized the more home and industry become separated.'[19]

The housing market and the job market need not be congruent: there may be availability of houses but jobs may be declining locally or there may be approximate parity between the total number of jobs and dwellings but the dwellings may be too expensive in relation to local wages or may not fit the household structure of the given population. Similarly, the job market may not fit the skills and capabilities of those entering the labour market or those obliged by structural unemployment or other reasons to seek re-employment; there may, for example, be a strong demand for female workers in offices and shops, whilst opportunities for male school leavers are negligible or, again, technologically advanced industries may put their factories in areas of un- or under-employment and then may be obliged to import nearly all their skilled workers.

Undoubtedly each of these examples of educational opportunity, housing market and job market is well understood by specialists in each of these fields. However, *the implications of their interrelationships* may not be so well understood. Education, jobs and housing as scarce resources are all potential sources of conflict: access to such resources is systematically structured in a *local* context. Such contexts may be physically 'urban', 'rural', or a mixture of the two: the urban or spatial sociologist is interested in the areas in which decisions crucially affecting the life chances of those living there are made. The units for urban sociology are bureaucratically defined.

There are, of course, other facilities and resources, which are not randomly distributed, which affect the life chances of those in specific localities to a greater or lesser degree. Some people, for example, have easy access to cut-price stores; others would have to travel, at the cost of considerable time and money, to reach these facilities. The larger the concentration of population the wider the range of choice and the less the danger of monopolistic price fixing. Hence, other things being equal, and they rarely are, as I am arguing, the poor would be less disadvantaged in larger settlements than smaller ones. There is, of course, a wide range of potential local authority provision, from swimming baths to specialist social services such as clinics for physically and mentally handicapped children, and these can be systematically quantified to get compound indices of opportunity.

It is obvious that the mere summation of public expenditure in basic infrastructure and facilities in given areas will not provide any kind of guide to the overall quality of opportunity in such areas. There are basic conflicts over the most appropriate form of expenditure. Hence it is not possible to devise an immensely complicated functional model to show the 'perfect' urban system in operation, providing the maximum social benefit at least cost to everyone. This would imply a static distribution of power in some kind of political consensus – we have not reached the end of ideology yet! Nor, of course, are we in a situation of war of all against all. Conflicts are structured, both socially and spatially. Analysts of the urban system cannot do without the sociologist and political scientist, but they in turn cannot do without the geographer and economist, who help to determine the spatial distribution of economic welfare and diswelfare in urban areas.

The basic framework for urban sociology is then *the pattern of constraints which operates differentially in given localities*. Fundamental life chances are affected by the type and nature of access to facilities and resources and this situation is likely to create conflict in a variety of forms and contexts: definition of the area of the locality itself is a matter of great political importance and conflict. Commissions to determine the boundaries of Local Government units always generate conflict.

THE INTERVENTION BY THE COMMUNITY IN THE DISTRIBUTIVE PROCESSES

Intervention into the market takes place in all societies to a greater or lesser degree but the mixture of market and plan rationality in Britain is peculiarly delicate. Intervention can either underline the differential rewarding system already operating or it can moderate it. In the case of some forms of intervention it is not clear how the 'punishments' and 'rewards' are distributed. A common political debate is implicit in such intervention: that is, is it 'better' to discriminate in favour of those already advantaged so that economic efficiency may be promoted to the ultimate advantage of those presently disadvantaged, *or* is it better positively to discriminate in favour of those presently disadvantaged thus engaging total support and effort for societal goals? The type and nature of intervention into the market in a given locality will depend on a number of factors, which will include:

(a) The political history of the area;
(b) The present distribution of political, social and economic power;
(c) The values and ideologies of local technocrats;
(d) Awareness of relative deprivation in respect of other localities.

It is well known, for example, that payment of capital grants by the Department of Education and Science depends partly on the amount of pressure coming from the area making the request. Outside the Educational Priority Areas new schools will depend more on this and the above factors than on any objective analysis based on the appropriate social indicators. There are, of course, some decisions which may be taken more as a result of techno-cratic calculations than political opportunism. These are more likely to be long-term budgeting decisions, such as a motorway programme, which pre-empts funds which might otherwise have gone on short-term political fund-giving such as family allow-ances or education. However, once taken, these long-term bud-getary decisions are a very strong determining factor, stronger, I suspect, than most political groups at a lower scale appreciate. This closing of options outside the political arena may be only temporarily politically neutral: it should be part of the task of a vigorous urban sociology to explore and expose these funda-mental limiting constraints on life chances. Perhaps by making explicit the conflicts at a 'regional' level the involvement of the sociologist may help to open up a new political dimension.

Much of the argument up to now implies a somewhat static situation. What are the potentialities for *mobility* within the urban system? If position in the housing market is, in certain respects and areas, *independent* of position in the occupational structure, what are the possibilities for an individual of move-ment into a less disadvantaged situation with regard to the scarce resources and facilities I have been discussing? How much will geographical mobility of individuals and families to localities where the punitive measures and diswelfares are less, *of itself* lead to social mobility? That is, can an individual's life chances be

improved *independently of his position in the job market*? There
are certainly indications that the middle class are concerned about
the *areas* to which their careers take them, and are also concerned
about the facilities in those areas, and it is at least possible that
this concern will spread. In the same way that sociologists drew
attention to the inequalities of educational opportunity,[20] thus
making the middle class more '*Where ?*-conscious' in their choice
of school, so the work of urban sociologists is likely to make the
population more 'where-conscious' generally. Instead of 'nice'
areas being considered a luxury they may be seen as a necessity
or a right.

It is evident that I have taken as my starting point the fact that
the whole society is urban, but that, since people's life chances are
constrained to a greater or lesser degree by the non-random
distribution of resources and facilities, urban sociology is concerned with *the understanding of the causes and consequences of
such distributions for relevant populations*. The values and
ideologies of the distributing, organizing and caretaking professions, or the relations between the formal and informal patterns of social relationships, are of central importance to urban
sociology.

Strauss has recently urged[21] that we need to know more about
the social world of urban types – by these he is more likely to
mean abortionist physicians, garbage collectors or radio announ-
cers. The argument of this chapter is that the *crucial* urban types
are those who control or manipulate scarce resources and facilities
such as housing managers, estate agents, local government
officers, property developers, representatives of building societies
and insurance companies, youth employment officers, social
workers, magistrates, councillors and so on. These occupations
and professions should be studied comparatively to discover how
far their ideologies are consistent, how far they conflict with each
other and how far they help to confirm a stratification order in
urban situations. These managers of the urban system provide the
independent variables of the subject. It may be, for example, that
the farther down the social hierarchy one is, the more the lack of
resources and facilities compound together, creating an urban
underclass out of which it is extremely difficult to escape.

Some sources and measures of intervention, intended to alleviate cumulative diswelfare or punitive measures on those least able to defend themselves, may often fail to meet with success. People do not always take or get what they are entitled to: certain sections of the population – apparently for a variety of reasons – fail to enmesh with more generally held goals and values of the wider society. Under these circumstances the ego-centred approach of the social anthropologist, using social network analysis, may help to elucidate patterns of social control and help to explore the defensive mechanisms based on kin or patron-client relationships as means of coming to terms with the wider society.

Some recent studies do give indications of a renewed vigour in the subject – Foster in his study of nineteenth-century towns,[22] Rex and Moore in their study of Sparkbrook and the work on housing by Ruth Glass and her colleagues in London [23] or Norman Dennis in Sunderland.[24] Little else has been done. Research has proceeded on a very *ad hoc* basis – loneliness on new estates, images of the city, a bit of social area analysis and so on: the literature is patchy, unsystematic and certainly not cumulative. A similar conclusion was arrived at by Manuel Castells who asked 'y a-t-il une sociologie urbaine?'[25] He felt that urban sociology should concentrate on interaction between different levels – local and national, formal and informal – especially where social and physical space coincide, and, secondly should relate social processes to the ecological system. His approach was very similar to mine and it seems evident that so long as important life chances are determined locally there will be a coincidence between spatial and social structure which I have elsewhere described as a socio-ecological system.[26]

Thus there can be a sociology of the organization of urban resources and facilities: *the controllers, be they planners or social workers, architects or education officers, estate agents or property developers, representing the market or the plan, private enterprise or the state all impose their goals and values on the lower participants in the urban system.* We need to know not only the rates of access to scarce resources and facilities for given populations but also the *determinants* of the moral and political values of those who control these rates. We need to know how the basic decisions affecting life chances in urban areas are made. The application of organization theory to urban contexts might well reveal authority/compliance structures analogous to those studied in other fields. This is particularly likely to be the case where the operational fields of various bureaucratic structures overlap and the same clients suffer the same subordinate position in each structure.

There are, however, two very important differences between industrial sociology or organization theory and urban sociology. Firstly, in industrial concerns and other organizations lower participants can escape 'outside' to some degree of autonomy; secondly, such organizations have some commonly accepted goals, such as making a profit, turning out a given number of students or converting peasants to new forms of agricultural production. Of course, these goals are never clear cut and most organizations have conflict over goals.

In the case of the urban system (if there be such) it is less clear where 'outside' is: to where can the lower participant escape? Even the most intimate aspects of family life may be open to the activity of some social caretaker or other. The controllers of the urban system seem to control more completely that the controllers of the industrial system. Defensive mechanisms or informal stratagems such as Goffman describes in *Asylums* may operate for the underclass in the urban system who are in some ways trapped in a total institution. The dehumanizing effect of the urban managers on the urban poor is worth further investigation.

Similarly, we are not clear what the goals of the urban system, or rather the goals of those who manipulate it, are. We agree that certain urban resources will always be scarce and that social and spatial constraints will mutually reinforce one another whatever the distribution of power in society may be. However, given that certain managers are in a position to determine goals, what are these goals and on what values are they based? Should facilities be shared round more equally or more equitably or more efficiently? How do the managers measure the effectiveness of the goal-oriented action or policies they devise? Is positive discrimination in favour of those disadvantaged in one sphere a necessary concern of all planning or only some planning and how does this relate to other managers, whose goal is to make a profit?

In this discussion of an analogy between industrial or organizational analysis and urban sociology it is implicit that the urban system has both a spatial *and* a non-spatial character. This provides its distinctiveness. Thus, groups of the population can be both spatially and socially defined, as can the resources and facilities which are in demand. Social 'problems' may or may not have 'spatial' solutions: decisions by the manipulators of the spatial structure may have unintended consequences on the social structure and vice versa. The current fashion among physical planners for 'diversity and choice' implies an acceptance that differential access to scarce resources and facilities is an *independent* variable. The whole theme of this paper, which certainly deserves much more extended discussion, is that such patterns of access are *dependent* upon the allocation by the system managers. Lower participants can be classified both spatially and socially and suffer different degrees of constraint in different socio-spatial systems.

I see that I am open to criticism by those who would use the sociology of sociology on me. Non-sociologists are wishing an 'urban problem' on the discipline and obligingly the discipline responds with an emphasis on constraints and opportunities for the underprivileged. Surely, some may argue, this is simply academic opportunism once again, this time stealing the clothes of those studying social administration. I would like to conclude by considering such potential criticisms. Firstly, most scientific activity is social; problems may seem to arise of themselves but I think they follow from the economic and social situation of a society at a given point in time. The levelling out of our national rate of growth, the rising expectations for facilities and resources, the decline and decay of the basic physical infrastructure of our cities, built or established a century ago, the 'discovery' that work is not a central life interest for large sections of the working population and the increasing concern with consumption and style – all these and many other factors, such as expanding levels of education or the increase in ownership of private cars, is leading to a concern about the access to or quality of urban resources and facilities. No one doubts that they are urban: indeed it is this common urbanity which makes for the conflict for scarce resources.

No one disputes the multiplicity of life-styles argument: this was recently argued in a paper by Professor Burns,[27] who based his argument on the flexibility/diversity/variety/choice/styles of life theme. I would not deny that there is much in the case for viewing 'post-industrial man', responding to the whim of fashion, cavorting around in mobile homes or vertical-take-off bubble planes. There is much comfort in describing the non-community of your fellow architects and sociologists as being the style for the future. There is a sort of meritocratic ideology of social capillarity which suggests that what professionals in the South-East (or California) do today the rest of the society will do in the year 2000. I have argued elsewhere against the ideology of a mobile society and also against the idea that all urban-industrial societies are converging in certain important respects (such as the pattern of access to facilities and resources for certain sections of society).[28] The important point I want to emphasize is that urban sociology may indeed encompass different ideologies: I have crudely contrasted my 'constraint-oriented' approach with the 'choice-oriented' approach and I am fully aware of the ambiguities and dangers in making such a distinction.

Far from being opportunists I think urban sociologists must stand firm against the strong pressure by planners to turn them into futuristically oriented market research consultants, by system- and model-building colleagues, who demand sociological unreality to make their models more tidy, by those who disregard underlying social conflicts in favour of *ad hoc* amelioration and by social anthropologists, who may be more interested in the mechanisms of social interaction than the source of inequalities in the wider system. I am arguing that a truly *urban* sociology should be concerned with the social and spatial constraints on access to scarce urban resources and facilities as dependent variables and the managers or controllers of the urban system, which I take as the independent variable. Whether this provides 'theoretical yield' at a general level is not dependent on subject material but on quality of scholarship. A new approach to the subject along these lines might be cumulative, might systematically aid our understanding of a complex urban society and could have great practical value. It is time that we stopped confusing our students by explaining away the urban society in which they live. I suspect that there is extraordinarily little urban sociology taught in British institutions of higher education. This ought to be a matter to cause serious concern.

REFERENCES

1 Weber, M., *The City*, Martindale, D., and Neuwirth, G. (trans.), Heinemann, 1960, 9.
2 Manheim, E., 'Theoretical prospects of urban sociology in an urbanized society', *American Journal of Sociology*, 66(3), 1960, 226–9.
3 Glass, R., 'Urban sociology', in *Society: Problems and Methods of Study*, Welford, A. T., *et al.* (eds.), Routledge & Kegan Paul, 1962, 481–97.
4 Park, R. E., *et al.*, *The City*, Chicago University Press, 1925, reprinted 1967.
5 Sjoberg, G., 'Comparative urban sociology', in *Sociology Today*, Merton, R. K. *et al.* (eds.), 1959, 334–59.
6 Glass, R., 'Urban Sociology in Great Britain', *Current Sociology*, IV(4), 1955.
7 Reissman, L., *The Urban Process*, Free Press, Glencoe, 1964, 236.
8 Mitchell, J. C., 'Theoretical orientations in African urban studies', in *The Social Anthropology of Complex Societies*, Banton, M. (ed.), Tavistock Publications, 1966.
9 Mitchell, J. C., *The Kalela Dance*, Rhodes-Livingstone Papers No. 27, 1957.
10 Mayer, P., *Townsmen or Tribesmen*, Oxford University Press, 1961.
11 Gugler, J., 'Measuring urbanization'. Paper presented to the 6th World Congress of Sociology, Évian, 1966.
12 Watson, W., *Tribal Cohesion in a Money Economy*, Manchester University Press, 1958.
13 Gluckman, M., 'Anthropological problems arising from the

African industrial revolution', in *Social Change in Modern Africa*, Southall, A. (ed.), Oxford University Press, 1961.

14 Epstein, A. L., 'Urbanization and social change in Africa', *Current Anthropology*, 8(4), 1967, 275–95.

15 Burns, T., 'Industrial sociology', in Welford, A. T., *et al.* (eds.), op. cit., 186.

16 Goldthorpe, J. H., *et al.*, 'The affluent worker and the theories of *embourgeoisement*', *Sociology* I (1), 1967.

17 Donnison, D. V., *The Government of Housing*, Penguin Books, Harmondsworth, 1967.

18 Burney, E., *Housing on Trial*, Oxford University Press, 1967.

19 Rex, J. A., 'The sociology of a zone of transition', in *Readings in Urban Sociology*, Pahl, R. E. (ed.), Pergamon Press, 1968, 215 (my italics).

20 Douglas, J. W. B., *The Home and the School*, MacGibbon & Kee, 1964.

21 Strauss, A., in *Urban Research and Policy Planning*, Schnore, L. F., and Fagin, H. (eds.), Sage Publications, 1967.
'Rather than studying the usual occupations, or those that seem important to the city's functioning, why not study those that are little noted, even in popular magazines' (p. 92); also why not look at 'some category of economic activity or some business, which is not likely to be studied for its importance to the city' e.g. antique auctions or the sale of second-hand yachts (p. 93).

22 Foster, J., 'Nineteenth-century towns – A class dimension', in *The Study of Urban History*, Dyos, H. J. (ed.), Arnold, 1968.

23 Rex, J., and Moore, R., *Race, Community and Conflict*, Oxford University Press, 1967. Centre for Urban Studies, *London, Aspects of Change*, MacGibbon & Kee, 1964.

24 Dennis, N., *People and Planning*, Faber & Faber, 1970.

25 Castells, M., 'Y-at-il une sociologie urbaine?', *Sociologie du Travail*, 1968, 72–90.

26 Pahl, op. cit., 10–20.

27 Burns, T., 'Urban life styles', Working Paper 5, Centre for Environmental Studies, London.

28 Pahl, R. E., 'Spatial structure and social structure'. Reprinted here as Chapter 7.

Chapter 11   The sociologist's role in regional planning

Urban renewal, the physical expansion of existing cities and the creation of new ones inevitably create strains, stresses and diswelfares for certain sections of the population. Greater wealth and new ways of spending it have led to new social patterns and new demands, particularly for leisure and recreation. Sociologists have been able to collect some valuable information which has documented some of the social responses to these changes. Yet this is not enough: inevitably such studies have been snapshots of a situation at a particular period of time. Systematic studies documenting experiences over a complete lifetime are still needed.[1]

Social surveys concerned with topics of particular interest to planners are becoming increasingly common. Some county planning authorities have themselves carried out or commissioned surveys to document patterns of journeys to work and journeys to facilities, relating such data to the geographic pattern of settlements and the social and economic characteristics of the households. Other surveys have documented such things as how and where people spend their leisure time, where and for how long their children go to school, the relationship of incomes to rents, the play facilities of children living in high flats, the use of public open space, and so on. Rarely are such studies cumulative: too often *ad hoc* studies produce *ad hoc* policies. Similarly, attempts to discover the attitudes of people concerned are few or very rudimentary, so that planners and other decision-makers have to make value judgements about degrees of 'choice' or degrees of 'constraint'; some argue, for example, that 'people' 'don't mind' commuting, others argue that they do, and so on. It is evident that the same social information and attitudinal surveys even gathered for a wide geographical area may be used to document a variety of proposals, and should not be taken as the sole contribution which can be made by a sociologist.

In Britain, certainly, most studies have been limited to relatively small-scale situations. Even the largest community study relates to a small country town,[2] and attempts to synthesize what is known about 'community studies' tend to put a disproportionate amount of effort into an analysis of voluntary associational life[3] or status hierarchies[4] which relate to the multiplex ties of small-scale situations. This emphasis on the family and the immediate locality is, of course, right in that they are the focus and context of most people's social relationships and meaningful social world. A national survey, commissioned by the recent Royal Commission on Local Government in England, showed that the 'home area' for most people was extremely limited, being defined as a small group of streets in a town or, at the most, the size of a parish in rural areas. Some two thirds of this English sample had either lived in this small 'home' area all their lives or had moved to it from less than ten miles away.[5]

Thus, not only is it more practical and feasible for most sociological studies to take place in limited localities, but this corresponds to the main social world of most people. Leisure and recreational needs may draw people away from the cities at weekends and holidays, giving some impression of mobility on a regional scale, but there is no supporting evidence, even in the seemingly most mobile South-East, for any dramatic increase of other necessary journeys, such as to work.[6]

Yet, at the same time, the functional unit for which planners are obliged to concern themselves has increased in size. It is not necessary here to go into any detailed discussions about the size of the most efficient unit or how big a 'region' should be. Inevitably, there must be a degree of arbitrariness in determining the size of a unit, which is significantly smaller than the nation but significantly larger than the small, traditional, administrative units of town and country. In the case of South-East England the region extends east and south of Oxford to cover an area which includes 17 million people. This population is larger than that of many nation states, so that much of what I am discussing here under the heading of regional planning might in other contexts be considered appropriate to national planning.

Traditionally physical planners at the regional or city-regional level have been concerned with the relationship between employment and population.[7] A changing employment structure, a growing population, a demand for lower densities, and statutory limits on the expansion of existing settlements is the typical situation within which the physical planner works. Basically, his concern is with *land use*, and, in determining the future distribution of population and employment, he is much concerned with other environmental aspects, such as the quality of agricultural land, the need to preserve areas of outstanding natural beauty, the location of workable gravel deposits and the like. The economic planner, working on the spatial aspects of the economy, is concerned with the costs and benefits of concentration and dispersal, the factors affecting the location, mobility and efficiency of industry, the development of a regional input-output analysis and so on. The economic health of a region is measured by the productivity of its industrial structure, activity rates and by levels of unemployment. The costs and benefits of alternative patterns of investment in basic infrastructure in different locations are evaluated to determine the most efficient future economic pattern of the region. This crucial allocation of financial resources creates a form of budgetary determinism, which fixes the future in terms of the calculations of the present. Once the basic motorway programme, for example, is fixed, budgetary allocations must be made for the next ten or fifteen years, since an unfinished motorway is of little value. From such decisions so many other decisions, of necessity, follow. Yet those who determine the motorway programme, to continue the example, are heavily dependent on the advice of other types of planners and social scientists who must make judgements on what they see as demands, or guess as needs, of the population over future decades. Nevertheless, there is a danger that the tail may wag the dog and the pattern of roads may determine the location and nature of other investment.

It is in this context that we must consider the role of sociology. A recent discussion of the participation of social scientists in planning concluded: 'Apart from the findings of an all too small number of social surveys, sociology has as yet had little to offer to the larger issues of modern urban and regional policy.'[8] This suggests that the nature and scope of the subject has been misunderstood if it is assumed that there is necessarily some kind of sociological *information* at a regional level which, if gathered, would be the main contribution of the sociologist to the planning process. This is simply to make the sociologist's contribution to regional planning that of a market research worker with a larger sampling frame. On the contrary, 'The practice of sociology is criticism' as Professor Burns has reminded us, 'It is the business of sociologists to conduct a critical debate with the public about its equipment of social institutions.'[9]

1. EXISTING CONFUSION

It may now be useful to consider some of the taken-for-granted assumptions of the planning situation in South-East England, as these are reflected in two official reports. The first document was published by the Standing Conference on London and South-East Regional Planning (LRP 1180).[10] It represents the views of the local authorities responsible for physical land-use planning in the area. The other document was published by what used to be the Government's Department of Economic Affairs ('The Green Book') which represents the views of the South-East Regional Economic Planning Council (SEEPC).[11] Each of these may be examined in turn. The role of the sociologist may be shown as it were negatively by the confusions which may arise when he is not actively taking part in the process of analysis.

LRP 1180

The document attempts to specify some social goals for the region, which may be listed as follows:
(*a*) Variety and reasonable choice of residential environment and facilities (para. 92)
(*b*) Personal satisfaction in work (para. 97)

(*c*) The provision of what is described as a 'more complex relationship between homes, jobs, leisure and social activities by a wider approach than that embodied in the idea of a single-town, all purpose community' (para. 98)

(*d*) The possibility 'on social grounds', for the individual to retain a sense of identity with his place of residence (para. 98)

These four objectives appear under the heading 'The fulfilment of individual work, leisure and social aspirations' and are described in para. 99 as 'sociological', i.e. not simply social, objectives.

These objectives must not be seen in isolation: they must be considered in relation to other, possibly conflicting, objectives particularly that of economic *efficiency* which is taken as the *prime* purpose of regional planning (para. 103). Economic efficiency includes the fostering of large and compact labour and demand markets, which may be at variance with social objective (*a*) above. These goals may now be considered in greater detail.

(*a*) *Variety and reasonable choice of residential environment and facilities.* This is taken to be a self-evident good and yet, of course, it is clear that to increase the *choice* for the few might also be to increase the *constraints* for the many. Thus, to turn the goal on its head, it might be equally valid to argue for *minimal* standards, so that the least-advantaged in the economic sphere might be compensated, by positive discrimination in access to housing, facilities and other spatial resources. Allowing 'choice' by having, say, greater private mobility for some may lead to greater immobility for others as public transport declines. Of course, it could again be argued that since the affluent will have more 'choice' anyway, one may as well accept and plan for it, but this can be countered by arguing that 'equality of opportunity' is a more worthy good. The Government's Educational Priority Areas programme, following the suggestions of the Plowden Report, is an example of positive discrimination, which aims at minimizing constraints. What tends to happen is that 'choice' (which is a euphemism for the operation of the market) coexists with 'planning' which may or may not be concerned with social justice or equity. This is the basis of the essential ambiguity. The point I am making is that what appears to be a self-evident goal is, in fact, highly value-loaded and could be seen as representing a particular ideological position.

(b) *Personal satisfaction in work*. This goal may appear to be a worthy goal, hardly bearing the need for further comment, and yet it is fraught with difficulties. If it means that the actual work a man does should be satisfying then it is extremely difficult to see how the most efficient production-line technology can provide 'satisfying' work and indeed there are many sociological studies of the workplace which shows that it does not.[12] If, on the other hand, it is being suggested that industrialists should develop more automated productive systems, then the level of structural unemployment might increase. Alternatively, the argument might be that even if the work is unsatisfying if the job is well enough paid men would be 'happier' doing it. This implies a redistribution of wealth in favour of those doing the less-pleasant tasks. A further interpretation might be that men should have the opportunity to choose between a wide range of employment opportunities so that they are more likely to have jobs suited to their ability and aptitudes. In which case the SCLSERP is arguing for a wider range of educational opportunity since it is at present true that job opportunities are very closely related to educational attainments and there has been no increase in the proportion of working-class graduates over the past twenty-five years, during which time it has become increasingly difficult for men to work up into management from the shop-floor without the requisite paper qualifications.[13]

Finally the document could conceivably have been arguing for greater involvement of workers in the day-to-day running and administration of their plants which implies a policy of workers' control. Such goals should be made more explicit so that those whom the report wishes to persuade understand what it is to which they must be persuaded. Whatever the true meaning intended, I doubt whether physical and regional planners are the most appropriate people either to gather the necessary information or to advise those responsible for policy in such fields.

(c) *The provision of 'a more complex relationship by a wider approach'*. This appears to suggest that there is some virtue in mobility for its own sake, which may be a reflection of a current planning fad originating from those over-impressed with parts of the built environment in California. Certainly it is not without controversy, although, as with many such statements on social goals, it is stated as if all men of goodwill must inevitably agree with it. A counter-argument would be that the more facilities are spread about, the more those who are less mobile (the elderly – an increasing proportion of the population – mothers with young children and all those without the use of private cars) are disadvantaged. The proportion of the population that is highly mobile, living in any sense outside a very limited locality, is very small and is likely to remain so. Research for the recent Royal Commission on Local Government[14] suggests that even in the so-called mobile South-East by far the majority of the population work, shop and spend most of their time in an extremely limited local area. Only for leisure and recreation does any sizeable proportion of the population travel long distances. It seems unwise to adopt a major planning goal on the basis of occasional weekend family outings to friends, relatives or 'go-tos'. Similarly it is nonsense to imagine that what the 16–25 age group does today the over-65s will do in the year 2000. Admittedly this is reading a great deal into an apparently innocuous planning goal, but this is the stuff of which myths are made.

(*d*) *The possibility of retaining a sense of identity.* This may again appear a straightforward social goal. However, it is difficult to see this as an objective for *regional* planning. Furthermore, the sense of local identity comes less from *physical* determinants than from *social* factors. Familiar faces in the crowd, a close-knit social network and the social meaning attached to familiar landmarks create feelings of local identity. Clearly high levels of labour mobility would disrupt these local social ties so that economic efficiency might well have the unintended consequences of reducing the sense of local identity. Studies of Hertfordshire commuter villages[15] have shown that the most mobile element in the region's population – the professional/managerial middle class – lay great store upon the importance of the local social situation which they create amongst themselves. They may resent breaking the local social ties if their firm promotes them by moving them elsewhere, just as much as coal-miners may be reluctant to leave Durham mining villages. Local identity based on close-knit social networks is generally gained at the expense of growth and change. The basic conflicts underlying such goals are not acknowledged.

A strategy for the South-East

Turning now to the document produced by the SEEPC, a similar confusion about social goals and social policies emerges. The Green Book accepts the need for a close assessment of 'the social implications of the pattern suggested' (para. 31) but curiously this is to be done after the strategy has been decided. One cannot help concluding that the proposal for future research work on the social implications was envisaged more as providing further material to support an established position, rather than as providing the basis for a serious criticism of the entire strategy. A hint of this is provided in para. 28 where the pattern of development, based on a communication network, is defended on the grounds that this will provide wider job opportunities and greater consumer choice. This represents the same ideological position as I discussed above in relation to LRP 1180.

There is a tension between paragraphs 71 and 74 which the Green Book does not resolve. On the one hand a perfectly legitimate social goal is suggested: positive discrimination in favour of certain categories of the population is said to be 'essential'. By this it is assumed that society will be 'better', more just or whatever. The categories suggested in para. 71 are as follows:

(a) '*In housing need.*' This means, in effect, those who are living in appallingly overcrowded rented accommodation in parts of Central London. *The Report of the Committee on Housing in Greater London* (Cmd. 2605) provides a lucid analysis of the problem. There it was argued that the shortage of good property to rent in the centre of London was partly because of the lack of incentives for private landlords. The urban poor are the product of the low wages provided by the semi- and unskilled employment concentrated in the centre.

(b) '*A cross-section of the population.*' This presumably means everyone from unskilled low-paid workers to the most affluent young professional worker. It is difficult to see why it is essential to aim at this complete cross-section.

(c) '*Other people with or without working relations.*' These poor, old people will be moved out to provide a 'better' age structure in the new communities, although it is not made clear who benefits and how. Moving old people without relations away from familiar places and a circle of friends is a dubious proposition.

Thus the case for positive discrimination in favour of these categories is not convincingly argued. It is apparent that the authors of the Green Book have not themselves been persuaded, since in para. 74 they state it is the 'essential skilled workers' who must be housed promptly, lest any firms get discouraged. These skilled workers, we are assured, are attracted by new shopping centres, hospital services, pubs and community centres. When they hear of all this good social provision they leave their employment in London and move out. It is only after the labour has moved out that the cautious employer will risk moving his firm (para. 100). Perhaps I am reading too much into paragraphs that were not meant to be taken seriously. However, there is an implication that the workers must bear the risk which managers are reluctant to do and that they will be induced to do this on the basis of new social facilities, such as pubs and (of all things) community centres.

Elsewhere in the Green Book there are a number of *implicit* values, many of them in conflict with each other. In para. 188 is a demand for social amelioration and the prevention of slums: there is an implicit architectural determinism here (that old houses *per se* lead to social problems). It thus seems fair to conclude that there has been no attempt to formulate social goals and then to consider the most appropriate policies necessary to achieve those goals.

It seems clear from this analysis that there has been little systematic sociological appraisal of the planning process or situation. The specific social goals, which ought to be the ends for which the planning process is the means, are confused, ambiguous and sometimes conflicting. Since social goals are not clear, it is not surprising that appropriate social indicators are lacking: it is very difficult to understand social problems, which have to be solved by regional planning machinery, if the appropriate indicators to measure the nature and extent of the problem are lacking.

2. AN IDEAL PROGRAMME OF ACTION

Let us in ideal-typical terms set out a programme of activities which a sociologist, working with planners at a regional or national level, might pursue. The programme may be crudely broken down into the following stages:
1. Appraisal of the 'social health' of the region based on broad societal values, by analysing the distribution of appropriate social indicators in the light of the social goals they are designed to measure.
2. Reconsideration of existing goals and the reformulation or designation of new goals in the light of this. Sociologists are not limited by society's designation of a social goal but may also suggest new ones, arising from their understanding of social processes and the unforeseen consequences of existing policies.
3. A review of social 'problems' and social goals in the light of the existing social and economic situation: social problems are the opposite of social goals.
4. The formulation of appropriate policies to achieve the social goals: these policies need not necessarily have a physical component and may be designed to solve a social problem analysed for the first time or to make good existing but inadequate policies. I now comment and enlarge on each of these in turn.

1. Social health

The sociologist will probably acquire data presented in many ways, such as by area and by the socio-economic status of the head of household. He will not assume that shared domestic facilities and a high ratio of persons per room will mean the same thing qualitatively for young, unmarried people of high socio-economic status as it would for married people of low socio-economic status with children. A variety of indicators may be used and the following list provides a sample of the sort of information that may need to be considered.

(a) The distribution and incidence of disease and various symptoms of mental and physical stress. Since such information depends, in turn, on the distribution and effectiveness of those able and qualified to diagnose such disabilities it will be hard to get standardized reliable data. Again, borrowing an example from Horowitz, it is not clear whether the nation's mental health would be assumed to be in a 'better' state as a result of an increase or of a decrease in institutions for the mentally ill.[16] A more useful indicator might be the incidence and distribution of deaths from a variety of causes, relating such data to other physical and social characteristics of the population.

(b) The level of educational achievement or attainment of the population. In particular, there is likely to be a wide variation in the distribution of educational opportunity: the proportions of a given age group which pursues full-time education beyond the statutory school-leaving age, the proportion of the age group which moves on to technical and other further education and, finally, the proportion that moves on to university and other forms of higher education, may all be significant indicators.

(c) Unemployment rates, short-term and long-term, and related to the age, industrial and occupational structure of the population. Time-series data of both unemployment rates in relation to the national situation and also the incidence and distribution of those receiving low pay in relation to the national cost of living index. The relationship of income to expenditure is also of critical importance.

(d) Rates of social and geographical mobility and their correlates. The relationship between different types, distances and rates of social mobility and the occupational structure.

The range of potential indicators is very great – time budgets related to the occupational structure, crime rates, changing household composition, indicators of consumption, e.g. purchase of books and high quality records or various consumer durables, incomes, fluctuations in earning, membership of political parties, and so on.

Enough has been said to show that the indicators will inevitably be chosen in relation to specific goals. Thus, if the goal is to close income differentials to promote equality, or perhaps to increase them in the hope of aiding efficiency, then time-series data on income would be of interest to both sociologists and economists.

The problem is that it may not be clear *which* data most appropriately relates to which goals. If the goal is, for example, to reduce inequality, would constant income differentials but high rates of inter- and intra-generational social mobility both upwards and downwards and including movement in and out of the élite, be deemed as successful as declining income differentials but with very low rates of social mobility? The answer, of course, will depend on one's definition of equality. Similarly if 'assimilation' of minority groups is a goal and we find that, over time, such a minority is physically dispersed but is alienated from the political system, would this be deemed more 'successful' than a situation showing marked social and physical segregation but vigorous political activity by the minority group within the system?

2. Social goals and social processes

Faced with considerable ambiguity and uncertainty, as a result of his critical appraisal of the social indicators, the sociologist is forced to consider which social problems have most chance of being solved at that particular time. Following Merton,[17] we take the basic ingredient of a social problem to be 'a substantial discrepancy between widely shared social standards and actual conditions of social life'. The problem, of course, is to devise acceptable measures of this disjunction between social standards and social reality. The extent of the disparity varies within and between societies. What is intolerable in one situation is simply the acceptable way of doing things in another. Thus, if in one situation houses are little valued, since most social life is conducted outside them, whereas in another situation social life is largely carried on within the house, then it is difficult to devise policies to cover both situations. The sociologist should be able to report on the consequences for those concerned of both maintaining and discarding certain values and practices. In doing this he may disagree with those who wield power and authority, whose appraisal of the situation may differ. The sociologist is not necessarily bound by Cornford's principle of 'the ripeness of time'.[18]

Whatever policies are currently operating, since the social and economic situation is extremely unlikely to be totally static, change of one sort or another will introduce strains, conflicts and diswelfares, which in turn require new or modified policies. In order to understand these changes, the sociologist is obliged to concern himself with the social processes which bring them about. This leads directly to the occupational structure: it is this which is the key to the sociologist's main contribution at regional or national level. This will remain so, as long as the main source of economic reward and social placement comes from the work a man does. Occupation is still the basic indicator of styles of life and life chances generally, and even though recent research by Professor Wilensky points out the need for detailed analysis of the work situation and work history,[19] other factors such as age, sex, life-cycle characteristics or religious faith by and large account for less of the variance in social patterns.

Hence, if we are concerned with styles of life in twenty years' time, the first task is to get some understanding of the changing work experiences reflected by the changing occupational structure. This presents very great problems. Technological change and innovation is leading to changes in the occupational structure of existing industries and the development of new industries with new occupations. Even though the occupational structure has remained relatively stable over the first half of this century,[20] there are signs that there have been more fundamental changes over the past ten or fifteen years.[21] It is difficult to know what the full social and economic consequences of such changes are. If, for example, we consider the rapid expansion of the education industry over the past decade, we do not know how much the recruitment of the necessary manpower comes from intra-generational social mobility (rapid promotion of those from lower status-levels), inter-generational mobility (recruitment of able sons from less-prestigious fathers), horizontal social mobility (movement from another occupational hierarchy, which may or may not be declining), or physical mobility (recruitment from the same level in the same industry but in a different region). Problems in measuring and interpreting the different rates and forms of social mobility are still very great as Professors Duncan and Wilensky, among others, have recently pointed out.[22] We lack the kind of study produced by Professors Blau and Duncan in the United States,[23] but without this information it is not possible to forecast with any accuracy the likely social effects of changes in the industrial and occupational structure. As we saw in Chapter 8, to assume without question that the physical mobility of some workers to new or expanded towns necessarily facilitates social mobility up the occupational hierarchy for those who remain is unwarranted. It may be that much of the physical planning on a regional scale has simply served to draw apart the more skilled workers, who have been able to consolidate and establish their position in the new and expanding industries, from those with low or no skills who have to put up with low pay as well as poor housing and access to other facilities back in the centre of London.

3. Which problem and which goal?

However well social indicators are related to social goals, and however well social goals are arrayed, it is unlikely that an obvious order of priority will emerge. Even in a situation of political consensus (if such a Utopia is truly possible) there may be some doubt about which of a number of equally good goals should be achieved first. Since regional or national planning is concerned with a redistribution of resources some will gain – by benefiting from increased government investment in infrastructure, the location of new jobs or, negatively, for example, by not losing guaranteed peace and quiet – and others will lose. Resources and facilities are necessarily scarce and limited and the decision between sharing more equally what is available or promoting efficiency in an increasingly competitive world situation is not easily made. On the morning when the first man set foot on the moon, the main leader in *The Times* said that some of the main problems facing Britain were racial, constitutional and social and that

None of them can be solved simply by the production of greater wealth. In many cases it will be easier to find solutions when the economy is thriving. In a few instances prosperity brings further hazards – though that is, of course, no argument for a lower economic performance. But all these questions demand a concern for the health of society that cannot be measured in economic terms.

The quality of life has for some time had a respected place in political perorations, but the public of tomorrow seem likely to require as much practical concern for the uses of wealth as for its production.[24]

The larger the scale of operation and the bigger the budget which the planner can influence, the more acute the problem of 'whose good life?' becomes.

This tension between 'efficiency' and 'equality' can also appear at a regional level, where differential investment programmes fundamentally affect the life chances of people in different social and spatial contexts. Since the economists appear to be mainly concerned with growth, development and incentives for the strong, progressive and those with 'choice', the sociologist very often finds himself concerned with softening the unintended consequences of economic policies on the least strong. Put very crudely, a bias in favour of the rich and powerful is concerned with increasing the potential for *choice* (more golf courses, yachting marinas and motorways), whereas a bias in favour of the poor and least powerful would be concerned with *minimizing constraints* (retraining the unskilled, tackling the problems of the 'twilight' areas in cities, providing facilities for the old and immobile, and so on). The regional planner may be inclined to hold two sets of attitudes which have the unintended consequence of disadvantaging the poor. Firstly, a concern with the long term avoids immediate confrontation with the problems of today. Secondly, a concern with physical aspects of urban and regional form may lead planners to a mistaken view that social problems can be cured by physical policies alone. The slum problem is not cured when the houses have been pulled down. As the American experience clearly shows, urban and regional planners can only achieve their social objectives when they link in with other instruments of social policy. This understanding of the systemic nature of planning is slow to develop in Britain.

Decisions are being made every day on hunch (or at best 'common sense') since social cost/benefit analysis is still at a very elementary stage. For example, a new Health Centre policy might be more efficient for the professionals concerned with the service, and the concentration of expensive items of equipment might enable a 'better' service to be provided. However, the centralization and concentration of facilities, which this more efficient plan would involve, may mean that certain sections of the population may be very severely disadvantaged. The old, the poor and the less mobile are likely to find themselves further from the facilities which they, above other more fortunate sections of the population, are likely to need most. This dilemma relates to the spatial distribution of many other services and facilities: the optimal and 'most efficient' pattern or strategy may be one which provides acute disadvantages or diswelfares to certain sections of the population least able to withstand them. Urban redevelopment and renewal provides another very good example of this kind of problem.

A possible role for regional planning could be as a form of intervention into the market to ensure that those who are poorly rewarded in one sector (the job market) should not find themselves further penalized in their access to housing, education, health facilities and so on. This implies a set of priorities which would be concerned first with the problems of the very poorest. This in turn raises two questions: *who* are the very poorest and *when* is their 'problem' to be solved? Only when these are resolved can the policy issue of how to do it arise.

Who the poor are relates to the problem of social indicators, which we have discussed. When something is to be done raises difficulties of a different kind. 'The more distant the time horizon, the fewer are the constraints. The distant future appears to constitute a far greater area of freedom of choice than the immediate present.'[25] The more we know the context in the immediate future the more political pressures and economic constraints make policies 'unrealistic'. Those who believe that 'the market' will solve present problems in the long run are mostly likely to argue against intervention now. On the other hand, those committed to 'the plan' may be equally reluctant to narrow their vision (as they might put it) since the bundle of policies needed to minimize constraints in the present may be messier than the new city on a near-virgin site planned for the year 2000. It is more comforting to be concerned with the expected mobility, second homes and leisure demands of the future affluent than with the present problems of the poor who, irritatingly, appear to be always with us. Problems connected with the poor seem more ambiguous than problems connected with affluence, and planners, by their very nature, may not like to live with such ambiguity. There is a clear need to avoid what Michael Young has called 'the dictatorship of the imagined future over the present'.[26]

4. Policies

The problems posed by finding appropriate social indicators, selecting social goals and determining priorities may have seemed overwhelming, but even if agreement on each of these can be achieved there still remains, finally, the problem of 'which policies?' Even the assumption that all policies will have to bring together a combination of land use, investment and other social and economic decisions, the problem of which combination is likely to be the most effective still remains and it is possible that the most effective solution may not be the most politically acceptable. Furthermore, a policy which is concerned with planning *with* rather than for people, might be democratically more desirable but economically less efficient.

CONCLUSIONS: SOCIAL CONCERN AND SOCIOLOGY

It may be objected that the economist's concern for efficiency, economic growth and affluence has forced the sociologist to champion the underdog. The distinction between maximizing choice and minimizing constraint is somewhat unreal, it could be argued, and there is no reason why sociology, as an academic discipline, should necessarily and inevitably argue for a lessening of compounded inequalities. There may be good prudential grounds for intervening on behalf of those with least power, wealth and prestige, since this may serve to dissipate a potential source of violence. Yet this involves a commitment to the *status quo* and other sociologists might argue for a more fundamental restructuring of society as a solution to what are, in effect, national problems. The very consideration of such problems in the context of regional planning could be seen as a way of avoiding more fundamental redistributive problems.

Since there will always be less-esteemed jobs and some will always be paid less than others, should we not simply learn to live with inequality? We know that the poorest people in England are among the richest in the world and perhaps by stressing poverty and inequality, some sociologists are guilty of creating the poor, in a sociological sense. As Simmel put it:

> The poor, as a sociological category, are not those who suffer specific deficiencies and deprivations, but those who receive assistance or should receive it according to social norms . . . It is only from the moment they are assisted . . . that they become part of a group characterized by poverty. This group does not remain united by interaction among its members, but by the collective attitude which society as a whole adopts towards it.[27]

Furthermore, as Lewis Coser, commenting on Simmel's essay, remarks:

> Social workers, welfare investigators, welfare administrators and local volunteer workers seek out the poor in order to help them, and yet, paradoxically, they are the very agents of their degradation. Subjective intentions and institutional consequences diverge here. The help rendered may be given from the purest and most benevolent of motives, yet the very fact of being helped degrades.[28]

Coser goes on to argue that those who cannot give but only receive are assigned the lowest status in an instrumentally-oriented society. Hence poverty will remain until the poor are offered the opportunity to give. In order to *abolish* poverty the poor have to escape from their despised status position. 'This is why rent strikes, demonstrations, and other political activities by the poor should be seen as avenues of activization which tend to lead to a restructuring of their relationships in the community.'[29]

Such lines of thought may sound thoroughly disagreeable to many planners, who would prefer sociologists to tell them the proportion of managers in industry who will want second homes by the year 2000 or what proportion of the working class want their parents-in-law round the corner. However, it is clear that when concerned with the distribution of resources for a region with a population of 17 million, the distinction between regional and national planning is hard to make. Inevitably a concern with the national distribution or redistribution of resources raises important social, political and moral problems. It is clear from this essay that at least one sociologist finds the opportunity of taking part in a regional planning exercise both challenging and confusing. It is easier to discuss the consequences both unintended and intended of given courses of action proposed by others, than to initiate such policies oneself on the basis of limited social data. It is safer for the sociologist to stick to the former course of action but as an informed individual member of society he may feel obliged to attempt the latter.

REFERENCES

1 See, for example, the reports from the Institute of Community Studies, particularly Townsend, P., *The Family Life of Old People*, Routledge & Kegan Paul, 1957. The middle class are discussed in Willmott, P. and Young, M., *Family and Class in a London Suburb* 1960. More recently see Bell, C. R., *Middle Class Families*, Routledge & Kegan Paul, 1968.

2 Stacey, M., *Tradition and Change: A Study of Banbury*, Oxford University Press, 1960.

3 Frankenberg, R., *Communities in Britain: Social Life in Town and Country*, Penguin Books, Harmondsworth, 1966.

4 Plowman, G., Minchinton, W., and Stacey, M., 'Local social status in England and Wales', *Sociological Review*, Vol. 10, 1962.

5 Research Studies 9, *Community Attitudes Survey: England*, Royal Commission on Local Government in England, 1969.

6 Research Report 3, The Socio-Geographic Enquiry by Mrs

Patricia Ellman in Research Studies 1, *Local Government in South East England*, Royal Commission on Local Government in England, 1968.

7 The two documents which perhaps most helped to lay the foundation of the conventional wisdom in regional planning are the *Royal Commission on the Distribution of the Industrial Population* (*Barlow*) *Report*, Cmd. 6153, 1940, and Abercrombie, P., *The Greater London Plan*, 1944.

8 Orr, S. C., and Cullingworth, J. B. (eds.), *Regional and Urban Studies: A Social Science Approach*, 1969, 12.

9 Burns, T., 'Sociological explanation', *British Journal of Sociology*, Vol. 18, 1967, 367.

10 *The South East: A Framework for Regional Planning* 1968, Standing Conference on London and South-East Regional Planning.

11 South-East Economic Planning Council, *A Strategy for the South-East*, HMSO, 1967.

12 See, for example, Walker, C. R., and Guest, R., *The Man on the Assembly Line*, 1962, or Chinoy, E., *Automobile Workers and the American Dream*, 1955. In general see Touraine, A., *et al.*, *Workers' Attitudes to Technical Change*, OECD, Paris, 1965.

13 Westergaard, J. H., and Little, A. N., 'The trend of class differentials in educational opportunity in England and Wales', *British Journal of Sociology*, Vol. 15, 1964, 301–16. See also Clements, R. V., *Managers: A Study of their Careers in Industry*, 1958.

14 *Community Attitudes Survey: England.*

15 Pahl, R. E., 'Class and community in English commuter villages', *Sociologia Ruralis*, Vol. V, No. 1, 1965. Reprinted here as Chapter 1.

16 Horowitz, I. L., *Professing Sociology*, 'Social indicators and social policies', 1968, 328–39.

17 Merton, R. K., 'Social problems and sociological theory', in *Contemporary Social Problems*, Merton, R. K., and Nisbet, R. A. (eds.), 2nd edn, 1966, 780.

18 Cornford, F. M., *Microcosmografia Academica*, Being a Guide for the Young Academic Politician, 1908.

19 Wilensky, H. L.,
   (a) 'Work, careers and social integration', *International Social Science Journal*, 12, 1960, 543–60.
   (b) 'Orderly careers and social participation', *American Sociological Review*, 1961, 521–39.
   (c) 'The uneven distribution of leisure: The impact of economic growth on "free time"', *Social Problems*, 9, 1961.

20 Routh, G., *Occupation and Pay in Great Britain 1906–60*, 1965.

21 *Occupational Changes 1951–61*, Manpower Studies No. 6, Ministry of Labour, HMSO, 1967.
22 Duncan, O. D., 'Methodological issues in the study of social mobility'. Wilensky, H. L., 'Measures and effects of mobility' in *Social Structure and Mobility in Economic Development*, Smelser, N. J., and Lipset, S. M. (eds.), Routledge & Kegan Paul, 1966.
23 Blau, P. M., and Duncan, O. D., *The American Occupational Structure*, 1967. A comparable British study is now underway at Nuffield College, Oxford.
24 *The Times*, 21 July 1969.
25 Friedman, J., 'A response to Altshuler – comprehensive planning as a process', *Journal of the American Institute of Planners*, August 1965.
26 Young, M., *Forecasting and the Social Sciences*, 1968, vii.
27 Simmel, G., 'The Poor', first published in German in 1908, translated by Jacobson, C., in *Social Problems*, Fall 1965, 118–40.
28 Coser, L. A., 'The sociology of poverty: to the memory of Georg Simmel', *Social Problems*, Fall 1965, 140–48.
29 ibid., 148.

Chapter 12   Urban processes and social structure*

Urban sociology is noted more for the cogency of its internal criticism than for its capacity to generate concepts of wider significance. An area of study has developed whose main discipline and body of knowledge exists to show that those who traditionally argued for a distinctive urban sociology were mistaken.[1] If the health of a field may be judged by the amount of self-criticism it is prepared to indulge in, then, in that view, urban sociology flourishes to the point of indecency. Further shaking of the subject's empty boxes is hardly needed and has already been done many times with various degrees of vigour and effectiveness. My aim in this chapter is to reformulate the goals of the sub-field so that they are more outward-looking than inward-looking.

My central thesis is really very simple. I shall argue that the main reason for the confusion, aridity and lack of development in the field for so long is that sociologists had as their main objective the sociological understanding of the city *per se*. Paradoxically, the fundamental error of urban sociology was to look to the city for an understanding of the city. Rather the city

* The first version of this paper was read as an Open Lecture at the Technical University of Berlin, 13 July 1972, at a seminar of the Research Committee on Urban and Regional Development of the International Sociological Association. In its second, slightly modified, version it was read to the British Sociological Association's Teachers' Section Conference at Leeds on 18 September 1972. I would like to acknowledge the many helpful and valuable comments I received on those occasions and also a very thorough critical analysis by my colleague Jack Winkler. This paper does not reflect the help I have received in clarifying and expanding the last section. I have decided that I must start afresh.

should be seen as an arena, an understanding of which helps in the understanding of the overall society which creates it. Thus our questions should not be framed in terms of specifically 'urban' problems or 'urban' processes, as if these could be understood separately and independently of the host society, but rather in terms of what we can learn about the nature of feudal, market or command economies from the interrelationships of their social and spatial arrangements. *The sociological study of the city then becomes a means to the end of a broader understanding of society and not simply an end in itself.* The central focus becomes the distribution of power and the organization of the productive processes, as exemplified in the control and organization of urban social and spatial arrangements.

A consideration of the urban sociology of Max Weber illustrates my point admirably. According to Martindale, Max Weber's theory of the city was directly related to the independence of the city as a political and legal entity: when the city loses its autonomy, by definition a specific urban sociology must cease to exist. Hence, as Martindale puts it, 'The modern city is losing its external and formal structure. Internally it is in a state of decay while the new community represented by the nation everywhere grows at its expense. The age of the city seems to be at an end.'[2]

That may indeed be one interpretation of Weber's urban sociology. An alternative, and to my mind equally plausible, interpretation is that Weber was stressing the political autonomy of the medieval occidental city not in order to generate an urban sociology *sui generis* but rather in contrast to the oriental city. To emphasize the legal and political autonomy of the medieval occidental city without recognizing the essential *comparative* point Weber was making is to misunderstand Weber's whole concern with the sociology of the city. He was primarily concerned with the development of rationalization and the capitalist economic system, and he looked to the distinctive economic, legal, political and military arrangements of the Western medieval city as an essential seed-bed for the development of the larger system he was seeking to describe and understand. Weber's sociology of the city was a means to an end, and the fact that, for his purposes, he stressed the autonomy of a specific type of city in a specific time and place does not mean that he would not have viewed the capitalist city of early-twentieth-century America or the socialist city of late-twentieth-century Eastern Europe quite differently. Indeed, it would be consistent with Weber's methodology for those who are concerned about so-called 'post-capitalist society' or the differences between command and market economies to focus on the city as a basis for exploring these differences.[3]

I am begging the question of what it is in the 'city' that the sociologist would now consider. Evidently at one extreme the city does not have political autonomy *vis-à-vis* the state but, equally, at the other extreme even in centrally planned economies some decisions must be taken outside the central bureaucracy. It is logically virtually impossible for matters such as the allocation of housing to be completely centralized at a national level even though the rules may give the impression that this is the case. Cities, then, are bits of a society on the ground. They occupy a distinctive spatial configuration and resources are allocated in a distinctive pattern as a result of particular historical, economic, political or, indeed, social circumstances. They present distinctive problems which the society as a whole has to resolve and they generate forms of conflict which are relatively distinct from the conflicts arising from the productive process.

Whether my interpretation of Weber's urban sociology is legitimate or not my main thesis need not stand or fall on the strength of this alone. One way to test my argument is to take an approach to urban sociology as an end in itself, which may be the most widely known outside the field, and to consider the degree to which *that* sociology is indeed truly comparative and independent of the political and economic order which generated it. The obvious candidate would seem to be the Chicago School of urban ecology. In a recent text Thomlinson states, 'The only unique integrant of urban sociology is urban ecology,'[4] and Schnore claims that 'within sociology, one school of thought – human ecology – has been traditionally concerned with the analysis of spatial structure'.[5] Even such a critical commentator as Reissman concluded:

The ecological period in the history of urban sociology was as valuable as it was necessary. Its value derived from the quantity of information gained about the city. It was necessary because, as in the development of any science, the more apparent clues have to be evaluated before more abstractions are possible.[6]

Frequently in textbooks on urban sociology the chapter on the ecological approach or, taken as synonymous, the spatial structure of the city are assumed to have universal validity, differences between societies being due to idiosyncratic differences in 'values'.[7] The assumption is that this ecological or spatial–structural analysis can help in an understanding of the city no matter what the distribution of power or political system.[8] Recent textbooks published in Czechoslovakia, Hungary and Poland adopt the same concepts with only minor modifications, assuming that the models apply to cities *per se* rather than to a specific economic and political order.[9]

There is no doubt that Park and his followers at the University of Chicago in the early decades of this century imagined that they were developing a *sociological* theory of the city.[10] There is no need to rehearse the main arguments which have been adduced to refute the ecological approach: ecological analysis has moved from sociology to become a descriptive tool for geographers.[11] What is of interest is that the critics in general failed to see that whilst urban ecology had serious weaknesses in its power to generate concepts which would have universal applicability to an understanding and explanation of the city as a specific entity, it nevertheless did much to illuminate the workings of capitalism as a system. R. E. Park's unashamedly uncritical acceptance of capitalism appears in many of his writings and it is curious that, for example, in societies without a capitalist land market sociologists should endorse theories based on statements such as the following:

The area of dominance in any community is usually the area of highest land values. Ordinarily there are in every large city two such positions of highest land value – one in the central shopping district, the other in the central banking area ... it is these land values that determine the location of social institutions and business enterprises.[12]

Park viewed the city in an evolutionary perspective: drawing on the thought of Darwin and Spencer and relating this to works such as that by Clements on *Plant Succession*,[13] he saw the city caught in an implacable logic: 'Economic competition, as one meets it in human society, is the struggle for existence, as Darwin conceived it, modified and limited by custom and convention. In other respects, however, it is not different from competition as it exists in plant and animal communities.'[14] Thus Park assumes that the capitalist order is the right, 'natural' and most highly evolved system to which people must accommodate. For him evolution and the development of capitalism come to the same thing. Thus under what he calls *Hochkapitalismus*

stability and security have come to be more important than expansion and speculative profits ... Changes such as these are the characteristic symptoms of an approaching maturity not merely in the capitalistic system but in the society of which that system is so essentially a part.[15]

The Chicago of the second and third decades of this century displayed the capitalist order 'on the ground' with startling clarity but there is little discussion of inequality or class conflict by the Chicago urban sociologists. McKenzie, one of the most explicit theoreticians of the Chicago School, described the inhabitants of the decaying area adjoining the central business district in the following terms:

It is a common observation that foreign races and other undesirable [*sic*] invaders, with few exceptions, take up residence near the business centre of the community ...

The commencement of an invasion tends to be reflected in changes in land value. If the invasion is one of change in use, the value of the land advances and the value of the building declines. This condition furnishes the basis for disorganization. The normal improvements and repairs are, as a rule, omitted, and the owner is placed under the economic urge of renting his property to parasitic and transitory services which may be economically strong but socially disreputable, and is therefore able and obliged to pay higher rentals than the legitimate utilities can afford.[16]

Comment seems superfluous. Perhaps more strikingly, later in the same article, McKenzie is analysing segregation in Seattle and he contrasts 'the conservative, law-abiding, civic-minded population elements' of the suburbs with the downtown areas which 'are populated by a class of people who are not only more mobile but whose mores and attitudes, as tested by voting habits, are more vagrant and radical'.[17]

Further quotation would be to labour the point. The Chicago School may have produced some brilliant urban ethnography but its theoretical underpinnings – such as they were – were based on a consensual view of society later to be paralleled in the writing of those who proposed a functional theory of stratification in the 1940s. Typically comments on slums were less in terms of poverty and inequality and more in terms of 'fascinatingly combining old-world heritages and American adaptations'.[18] Again, it is more frequently the individual or the newcomer who gets sifted and sorted into the appropriate part of the city for him. Only if some ethnic or religious 'communal organization' existed could individuals get protection from the harsh realities of *Hochkapitalismus*.

Even when the social ecologists did turn to problems of poverty or planning there was little indication that these were matters which involved any radical changes in social structure. Social problems were seen essentially as individual problems. Despite the precedents of Charles Booth and Rowntree, who saw the need for broader social policies, although perhaps nothing more radical, Park observed in 1929, 'It is, however, within comparatively recent years that poverty and delinquency have come to be reckoned along with insanity as personality and behaviour problems.'[19] Similarly Zorbaugh, in 1926, asserted that 'city planning and zoning, which attempt to control the growth of the city, can only be economical and successful where they recognize the natural organization of the city, the natural groupings of the city's population, the natural processes of the city's growth.'[20] Thus, if we are looking at the city as a means of understanding the tensions and contradictions of capitalist society, the Chicago sociologists are of interest more for their assumptions and values than their sociology.

The recent paper by Vance[21] provides a valuable introduction to a distinctive analysis of land assignment practices in capitalist cities as compared with pre-capitalist and socialist cities. In particular he draws attention to capitalism's failure to cope with the urban housing problem in Britain which led to a fundamental retreat from market principles in the nineteenth century. When the offering of employment ceased to carry with it a guarantee of housing then rent-paying ability became the chief determinant of the quality and location of housing. The Royal Commission on the Housing of the Working Classes reported in 1884–5 that over 85 per cent of the working classes paid over one-fifth of their income in rent and almost one half paid between a quarter and a half. Wohl notes that after 1885 rents rose even more steeply than before, holding back any gains in real wages which might have accrued from falling prices generally. 'Taking 1900 as the base year of 100, working-class rents rose in the following manner: 1880 (87), 1885 (92), 1890 (90), 1895 (96).'[22] Even though the development of the capitalist system did not lead to the relative decline in industrial wages which Marx predicted, it did lead to a severe housing crisis. As Wohl remarks, 'Land in central London became so expensive as to make the building of working-class housing there an impossible task ... Suburbs or subsidized housing appeared to be the only solutions to an overwhelmingly difficult housing situation.'[23]

The development of working-class suburbs was made possible by the development of the rail network and cheap fares. However, the lower suburban rents were offset by the appalling standard of jerry-built housing which was hardly an answer to the working-class housing problem. As *The Lancet* put it in 1874:

It is difficult to understand the argument of those who contend that the labouring classes ought to live in the suburbs – i.e. in unhealthy, cheap undrained districts, often beyond the pale of sanitary legislation, and in adulterated houses whose foundations were rotten, whose walls were scarcely weatherproof, and whose owners but too often belong to the most unscrupulously dishonest class to be found amongst us.[24]

The problem of working-class housing forced commentators to consider the fundamental workings of their society. In the words of Sir J. P. Dickson-Poynter, the Chairman of the LCC's Housing of the Working Class Committee in 1883, 'It provokes the vexed question of the relation between rent and wages, which easily slides into that of capital and labour.'[25]

Analyses of the contradictions of capitalism, seen through the failure to cope with working-class housing and other aspects of the operation of the urban system, are now slowly emerging, largely from historians working on nineteenth-century material. Gareth Stedman Jones's work on London housing and employment is a particularly good example.[26] Such work does not appear to be so heavily obsessed with the need to understand the city *per se* but is more ready to draw from the detailed empirical studies of specific cities more general statements about the strains and tensions in the society as a whole.[27]

It is this direct movement from an analysis of a specific product of urban development to the encapsulating social structure and its relations to the means of production which is of the essence of a vigorous urban sociology. However, I am in danger here of reifying the social structure. It would be wrong, I think, to see 'the city' as simply an example of the social structure in action–whatever that may mean. The city *is* society and to view it as peripheral to the centre is misleading. Certain problems can only appear at the city level, others must be analysed with an equal attention to both levels. Housing is a good example where to divorce the city from society or society from the city would both, I suggest, lead to misunderstanding. The failure of capitalism to provide adequate working-class housing helped in large measure to generate new forms of interventionism in the early twentieth century.

I now want to return to Weberian analysis, this time to consider whether it is possible to develop a systematic urban theory out of his conceptual thinking on stratification. In particular I want to explore the possibility of understanding the nature of what has been described as a 'Welfare State' type of society[28] where public intervention, particularly in such fields as municipal housing, severely disturbs the more naked manifestations of capitalism and clearly is not so amenable to ecological analysis. In particular I shall consider the recent work by Rex and Moore, when they attempt to formulate a new approach to the city as a social system using the concept of 'housing classes'. Again my central concern is to consider how far their approach serves to highlight problems and tensions in the wider society. In passing one must observe that Rex and Moore also fail to develop an independent focus for urban sociology, since they, too, make the mistake of focusing on the city as a sociological entity in itself.

Rex and Moore see the central process of the city as a social unit as a class struggle over the use of houses.[29] This struggle or conflict is not simply a reflection of inequalities in the labour market since, as Donnison has shown,[30] intervention by the Government is now so great that it is no longer appropriate to refer to a housing market in Britain. Thus, the housing classes are defined, according to Rex and Moore, not solely by their capital or income but by their *degrees of access* to housing 'and it is this which immediately determines the class conflicts of the city as distinct from the workplace.'[31] There are as many classes as there are kinds of access and being a member of one of them 'is of first importance in determining a man's associations, his interests, his life style, and his position in the urban social structure'.[32]

This formulation contains many difficulties. First, it is clear that Rex and Moore have rejected both the job market and a unified housing market as the main allocative mechanism for determining position in the urban structure. They are obliged to emphasize the bureaucratic rules and procedures which determine access to private finance and public allocation. Thus, for example, if a local authority has a rule which requires a minimum period of residence before being eligible for the allocation of a dwelling in the public sector and also has made a decision in the past to build dwellings for a 'normal' family of two parents and two offspring, then, inevitably, new arrivals to the area and large families will, amongst others, find themselves similarly disadvantaged with regard to that means of housing.

The second difficulty is that by defining members of a housing class by the kinds of access to housing, insufficient attention is given to the resources of the individual actors concerned. Quite clearly, newly arrived migrants with capital are hardly constrained by the local authority rules in the same way as those without such resources.

Thirdly, there is no place in the model for the local authority: is it a class? It controls the allocation of housing – indeed it owns most of the houses in some northern cities. Yet presumably if those living in these dwellings wished to change the rules of allocation they could do so by electing their candidates to the Council. In addition, there is no place in Rex's and Moore's model for the large property-owners who still own so much in some British cities. A map of the great estates of central London,[33] for example, indicates the enormous holdings of, say, the Duke of Westminster and the smaller, but by no means insignificant, holdings of certain Oxford and Cambridge colleges.

Fourthly, who is in conflict with whom? Rex and Moore are obliged to posit a *common value system* which generates some agreement on what constitutes desirable housing. But detailed surveys, such as that of the Centre for Urban Studies[34] for the London Borough of Camden, demonstrate that alternative value systems are held by those in the same objective situation. Whilst some may feel frustrated that they are not able to move to a more desirable suburban location and others may wish to become owner–occupiers, equally others prefer different housing situations by physical situation and tenure. Thus it is not clear that, for example, all renters are in potential conflict with all owner–occupiers. Yet it is also clear that tenants are not in conflict with landlords as a class whether public or private. Similarly, there appears to be no basis for conflict between those specific individuals who act as agents of the controllers of the means of housing – such as housing visitors, housing managers, representatives of building societies and the like – and those who are controlled. Indeed the conflict would seem to be more likely *within* one of these 'classes' rather than between it and another. This would more appropriately be termed market competition: thus those on local authority waiting-lists, for example, are competing with each other and not with those seeking with limited capital to own their own houses who may be in competition with those having more capital.

Rex and Moore argue that a common market position produces common market interests and hence housing 'classes'. Under their formulation, married offspring of local authority tenants, living in privately rented accommodation but on the waiting-list for a local authority dwelling, appear in a different housing class from their parents. In a later formulation Rex is quite specific:

> ... Among those who share the same relation to the means of production there may be considerable differences in ease of access to housing. This is part of the 'superstructure' which manifestly takes on a life of its own. A class struggle between groups differentially placed with regard to the means of housing develops, which may at local level be as acute as the class struggle in industry. Moreover the independence of this process is emphasized the more home and industry become separated.[35]

To exemplify the main difficulties with this thesis, the above argument implies that those with different degrees of access to housing (by being newly arrived or having a large family) will tend to struggle with those better placed in the struggle for the same housing (longer-established people or those with small families?). Clearly if this occurred then there would be a process different from the class conflict which takes place at work.

Rex and Moore have been criticized for assuming a unitary value system and for assuming that there is a class of landlords which is obliged to take tenants because of their economic position, rather than doing it by choice for the substantial profits it affords.[36] These are important criticisms but they can be accommodated within the model as Rex in his most recent statement acknowledges.[37] The most telling criticism is, however, that put forward by Haddon;[38] he argues that Rex and Moore have confused categories of the *population* and types of *housing*.

I would suggest that it is not groups or categories of the urban population which are defined by their relationship to the means of access but simply *types of housing* which the controllers allocate according to their rules and procedures. The *present* housing condition need not necessarily be any guide to an indicator of 'class' conflict. Many categories know that they are simply temporarily in their present accommodation and may, for example, be in furnished rooms for a time before moving on to owner–occupation. However, if a category is condemned to remain in such a housing situation because there are no alternatives open to it, and if this blockage is not primarily due to that category's position in the productive process, then, indeed, there is an independent basis for conflict. The conflict will not be directed against those in another housing situation but rather on the means and criteria of access and those who determine and control them. If the *means of access* become central to the model rather than housing situations then presumably the following housing classes emerge:

1. Large property-owners, public or private.
2. Smaller landlords (e.g. charitable trusts).
3a. Owners of capital sufficient to own their own homes and owning.
3b. Owners of capital sufficient to own their own homes and renting.
4. Those who *must* rent.

With this model there is very little mobility between classes and the crucial differentiating factor is capital. Those in class 1 are able to turn their rental income into capital for further investment and speculation; those in class 2 can live off the profits on their rents; those in class 3 can enjoy capital appreciation and can use that part of their income which would otherwise go on rent in other ways; finally, those who must rent have no alternative but to pay what they are asked to a public or private landlord.

It is in the determination of the level of rent and interest rates that there is considerable scope for political interventionism. Where the principles of the market are the dominant dogma attempts will be made to raise rents to a 'fair', that is profitable, level as occurred in Britain in the early 1970s. A scheme of rent allowances will permit landlords to raise rents to a fair (return on investment) level and rents in the public sector are also raised in parallel with all profit on the housing revenue account after the payment of rent rebates accruing to the central Government.[39] Such a policy could be seen as a punitive measure against the rent-paying class by those who stand to benefit from the increases.

On the other hand where the prevailing dogma is that of the plan and the housing is allocated according to criteria determined by the central bureaucracy with an ideological bias against the market, rents may be reduced to a token level. Under these circumstances those who own their dwellings will be disadvantaged, as they will probably be living in older dwellings with worn or inadequate facilities and they will be responsible for the repair and maintenance of their property in a situation where private services may be at a premium and public services favour the publicly rented sector. Some rent-payers will also suffer some disadvantage under such a system: since rents are at a token level the bureaucratic allocators will be unable to differentiate between property which is more desirable to prospective tenants on account of its position, level of facilities, space, modernity and so forth and that which is less desirable. Those who allocate tenancies in a non-market system may either distribute privilege and advantage randomly or they may, as appears to be the case in Hungary,[40] reward differentially and systematically by allocating a greater proportion of the modern tenancies to the highest socio-economic levels. Housing classes in Hungary appear, then, to include the following categories.

1. Tenants of new and desirable state housing.
2. Tenants of old state housing.
3. Owner–occupiers.

Szelényi and Konrád's scheme is somewhat more elaborated but the main point remains: the state has the power to reflect, to reinforce or to compensate for inequalities created by the differential wage and salary structure of a society. A policy to compensate may have the unintended consequence of reflecting or even reinforcing existing differentials. I return to this theme later.

Returning to Rex and Moore's thesis, it is clear that the rules and criteria of access are crucial and reflect the ideology and values of the dominant class in market or command economies. In Weberian terms, as Haddon again reminds us,[41] class as an analytical category is determined by having more or less power to *dispose* of goods and skills for the sake of income in a given economic order. Thus, Haddon claims that Rex and Moore have confused *disposal* with *use*. *The use of housing is an index of achieved life chances not a cause*. The ability to dispose of property or skill in the market depends on the existence and strength of a market. Hence, in Hungary, owners of property are in the lowest housing class. In a capitalist society those who own substantial urban estates are the strongest housing class. Individually they could all live in hotels but they would still be members of the dominant class.

My purpose in discussing the work of Rex and Moore is not intended to be destructive: on the contrary it is only on the basis of such analyses that it is possible to build further. The main focus of an urban sociology, as I have previously stated, is to lead from the city to the broader society and to highlight the strains and tensions of particular kinds or types of society attempting to solve similar problems. Rex and Moore have helped us to see more clearly the crucial importance of *means of access* to housing and the way a differentiated population negotiates the institutions and the various rules of eligibility. Paradoxically they stimulated Szelényi and Konrád to formulate a structure of housing situations in Hungary but, like them, they did not distinguish between people's housing situation at a particular time and their long-term position in relation to the means and criteria of access to housing. Paradoxically it seems as though the allocation of state housing in Hungary was more regressive than the allocation of local authority housing in Britain, although, of course, tax relief to owner–occupiers offsets to a large degree public interventionism of a progressive kind. Finally, Rex and Moore fail to demonstrate that there is a common value system which would provide the nexus for an urban system based on the allocation of housing. Despite all the criticisms that have been made of this study, the authors' focus on the patterned distribution of an urban resource which appeared to generate structures of inequality distinct from the field of employment was a major step forward at the time. It is now time to turn to my own formulation of the urban problematic. In doing so I am glad to acknowledge the stimulation I myself have gained from a consideration of Rex and Moore's discussion of housing classes and locality-based conflict groups.

TOWARDS A NEW URBAN SOCIOLOGY*

The interrelationship between the social and the spatial has not been adequately conceptualized in sociological analysis: any such analysis which attempts to ignore matters such as the friction of space as expressed in time/cost distance or the spatial distribution of the material artifacts of a previous economic and political order is also ignoring part of the *social* situation.[42] Spatial structures both reflect and determine economic and political processes. The most difficult problem, which has eluded both Chicago ecologists and contemporary Marxists, is to encompass the dialectic of the spatial and the social in a coherent analytical framework. Classical economics and the theory of rents deriving from Ricardo have an elegant clarity which did much to describe and to provide an understanding of capitalism on the ground. Since the taken-for-granted values supported the spatio-economic theory the ecologists could virtually dismiss the cultural super-structure as epiphenomenal. Hence Zorbaugh could emphasize the dominance of the '*natural* organization of the city, the *natural* groupings of the city's population and the *natural* processes of the city's growth'[43] (my italics). Even those critics such as Firey[44] who emphasized the cultural values, which they claimed the ecologists neglected, did little to undermine the *basic* assumption of the spatially oriented school. In some respects they strengthened the position of those they attacked by implying

*Undoubtedly the most powerful approach to the urban question is a form of Marxist analysis which developed primarily in France in the early 1970s. Those working with this approach would not necessarily see themselves as urban sociologists at all. I recognize that I am being old-fashioned in continuing to use the term and yet I am prepared to justify my position. First, I think that the sociology of urban sociology should include the sociology of Marxist urban analysis too; secondly, I consider that the problems of urban and regional development in 'State Socialist' or centrally planned economies are appropriately considered as topics in urban sociology; and thirdly, questions such as whether the public provision of urban services and facilities 'serves' capitalism or is a burdensome drain on profits can become more metaphysical than empirical. Finally, I find the Marxist theory of the state inadequate and the Weberian analysis of bureaucracy more compelling.

that the exceptions, such as Beacon Hill Boston, proved the rule.

The development of a coherent spatial logic has been advanced substantially in recent years from the early formulations of Lösch[45] and Christaller.[46] The extensive research of Berry and his colleagues[47] and the new-found elegance of certain modelling techniques developed and modified by recent authors[48] have helped to bring spatial analysis firmly back into the field of geography. The development of threshold analysis for various goods and services has been applied not only for shopping models[49] in a traditionally capitalist context but also for the provision of various public services and facilities.[50] Given that under any economic and political system there are some limitations on resources and, given further, that within these limitations the most efficient use and distribution of those resources is held to be desirable, the search for a spatial logic to help in the 'rational' allocation of such resources will continue. Thus, for example, in the provision of highly specialized medical facilities regard is generally taken of the size of catchment area to ensure that the facilities will be used up to some minimum level and hence justify that expenditure as against the expenditure on more general medical facilities which might be required by the population as a whole.[51] It is central to my argument that these spatial constraints on the distribution of resources operate to a greater or lesser degree independently of the economic and political order. This is a point which seems to me to follow from much of the recent work in mathematical or theoretical geography. As Bunge[52] put it, there is an optimum way to rake a lawn clear of leaves by raking them into little piles on a hierarchical system. It is, of course, possible to invent a machine that will suck all the leaves off in a trice or one could have a slave class pick up each leaf by hand. However, at a given level of technology and with limitations on the use of manpower the spatial logic will put similar constraints on those responsible for clearing the lawn. To assume that policies operate aspatially is inequitable. These constraints can be ameliorated by political intervention but such intervention cannot totally negate their effects and, indeed, without a full understanding of the spatial logics, political intervention can frequently lead to the reverse of the intended consequences. This clearly is a matter of deep concern in centrally planned economies, where the effects of intervention are intended to be considerable and therefore unintended consequences can be equally substantial. Hruska's work in Czechoslovakia[53] indicates the difficulties of combining an efficient distribution of industry with equality of accessibility and Zaslavska's work in Siberia[54] shows similarly that the inadequacies of accessibilities led to unintended migrations.

These advances in spatial analysis have not, as I have indicated, been undertaken by sociologists and it is perhaps because of this that they have not figured in recent sociological analysis. It also perhaps explains why it is the most primitive spatial analysis of half a century ago which still appears in contemporary sociological textbooks. Not that I am arguing here for sociologists to become geographers, rather I am arguing that in the same way that industrial sociologists have regard to techniques and technology in their studies of industrialism and industrial man, so, too, must the urban sociologist understand the equivalent constraints in the spatial sphere. No one expects the industrial sociologist to invent automated productive processes for a particular product but he must understand the logics of such a process as it may affect social relationships. However, I am uncertain about the aptness of this analogy since industrial techniques and technologies appear to be more dependent on economic and political decisions than do spatial logics.

Sociologists quite rightly stress the social nature of the process of *allocation* of urban resources and facilities, whether or not these have a direct spatial manifestation. Thus, in matters such as the location of industry, the location and allocation of housing, the distribution and allocation of educational, health and cultural facilities, conscious decisions and policies are adopted and gatekeepers or managers of the urban system, on their own account or as agents, control the *access* to such facilities. Such *allocative structures* are based on their own reward distributing mechanisms and these could operate independently of the reward distributing mechanisms which allocate differential wages and salaries. This latter need not necessarily be the dominant allocative structure. Thus, distinct from the allocative structure based upon the division of labour, there may be firstly, *compensatory* allocative structures, based on rules of eligibility, which ensure that, say, those with the least income get the best housing, or those over a certain age get free or priority travel on public transport. In this way urban allocative structures could provide the main driving force towards equity in a society with a range of wages and salaries based on paid employment. This evidently would not be an equity based on an equal or even equitable distribution of wages and salaries yet nor would it be based on absolute equality of accessibility to resources and facilities but, rather, on the assumption that different needs of differentially categorized populations (both socially and spatially) have to be met differentially and that these needs vary over time. Thus, for example, young unmarried people may have high incomes but less good housing, married people with large families might have lower incomes but better housing in relation to the average situation and older people might be spatially dispersed in a declining rural area but have a high level of access to transport and communication (with, say, free telephones).

Secondly, in an ideal-typical market-dominated society all these allocative structures would be based entirely on the capacity to buy housing, education, health facilities and so forth and hence the differentials provided by wages and salaries would simply be *reflected* by these structures. There is yet a third way in which the urban allocative structures could operate and that is by *widening* the differentials already generated by the distribution of wages and salaries. This compounding of inequality can be achieved intentionally or unintentionally. In capitalist societies, where private investment depends on the expectation of appropriate profitable returns on the capital invested, those responsible for the allocation of a specific resource – for example planners determining the use of a site with high accessibility to other services and facilities – may be obliged to allocate this resource to a speculative office-developer, since the 'market rent' puts it beyond the range of, say, a public authority wishing to purchase it for low-rent accommodation for low earners. Under these circumstances if the public authority had the power to acquire compulsorily such sites at less than market value, the powerful private economic interests thus displaced would describe such activity as 'unfair'. Thus compounding inequalities may be considered to be more 'fair' than reducing inequalities. A congruence between the system of differentials generated by the division of labour and all other accessibility structures is assumed. Yet the compounding of inequalities can also occur unintentionally. Thus, a particular resource, for example housing, could be allocated according to need or some equitable principle, the working-out of which in practice may create new inequalities.[55] This is partly because the operation of a first principle may be very difficult to apply in certain practical circumstances; the national rules may not be applicable in a specific social, economic and spatial configuration. Partly, also, this may be because there is considerable difficulty in determining whether, in specific instances, a policy is progressive or regressive in its effects – road pricing may be one such example.[56] Thus, in these spheres, it cannot be easily determined whether the 'managers of the urban system'[57] are the agents of the national or local political system, advocates of the poor in their locality or operators of some abstract professional principles, the distributional effects of which are not known in detail, if at all. And they may not know themselves. A fundamental difficulty, of course, is that those who are, as it were, 'entering' an allocative structure do so already differentially rewarded by incomes and salaries. If such inequalities are disregarded by the controllers of the given urban resource then that itself is inequitable. Treating the unequal as equal creates a new inequality if those with stronger economic resources use them to operate 'hidden markets' or to develop to their own advantage public resources intended for those with fewest economic resources. Thus, in Hungary, Szelényi and Konrád have suggested that newer, better equipped or better situated accommodation goes to those who can either manipulate the allocative structure by their greater knowledge and pattern of social contacts or by offering 'key rent' to poorer tenants who exchange their state-allocated advantage in one sphere – housing – for the economic resources which they can choose to deploy in another sphere.[58] In Britain the more affluent, similarly, are able to use publicly provided grants for the improvement and conversion of older property to raise the capital value of such property and hence to acquire substantial capital gains.

A further way in which allocative structures can reinforce inequalities is by the combination of structures which, whilst being severally designed to decrease inequality, in combination serve to cancel each other or even to reinforce the pattern of disadvantages.[59]

So far, I have discussed spatial logics and allocative structures. There is a further aspect of the dynamics of socio-spatial inter-action which must be considered and that is the set of linkages or the specific configuration of resources and facilities in specific localities, whether these be cities or regions. The interconnections between homes, jobs, consumption facilities and so forth creates a unique pattern of constraints within particular regions so that a common national policy will have differential effects in specific contexts. The legacy of the past dominates to a greater or lesser degree, creating regional inequalities which persist long after the forces and factors creating such differences have ceased to exist. Thus, it is extremely difficult to devise allocative structures which have equal validity and force in, say declining industrial areas, areas of intensive agriculture and areas of rapid metropolitan growth. In the same way that Britain has to cope with the physical residue of early-nineteenth century capitalism when devising contemporary policies for the North-West of England, so also must the command economies of Hungary and Czechoslovakia deal with the physical legacy of the Austro-Hungarian empire and the spatial inequalities that continue to constrain contemporary policy-makers. The pattern of land use and the physical configura-tion and condition of the built environment constrain policy in certain areas and, no matter what the economic and political system, force those in power to allocate resources differentially.

To break down the perpetuation of continued spatial inequali-ties can present a post-revolutionary regime with greater prob-lems and difficulties than those connected with the redistribution of wealth and income in the field of employment. In China the compulsory drafting of urban-based populations to remote rural areas has met with considerable resistance.[60] There are similar resistances to the planned limitation of the growth of Warsaw or

Budapest[61] and to the restriction of migration from Siberia.[62] The reluctance of those in *spatially* privileged positions to be moved or to be redeployed in the name of equality and, conversely, the widespread desire for populations to improve their accessibilities by migration introduce a new element into our conceptual scheme.

The interrelations of spatial logics, allocative structures and contextual configurations of land use and the built environment are not sufficient in themselves to generate the dialectical pattern of forces I am describing. The product of an allocative structure is an *accessibility structure*. Specific populations have distinctive positions in regard to the social and spatial allocation and distribution of resources and are able to express their satisfaction or dissatisfaction in different ways in different types of societies – thus rising or falling property values, rates of migration and more direct political action can all be used to express dissatisfaction. The generation of conflict and the articulation of political interests in the urban context has only recently received serious scholarly attention.[63] Approaches to the dynamics of the socio-spatial dialectic are rudimentary and reflect the differences of approach in the study of power generally. In the USA Williams, for example, argues that the power structures of urbanism are those which manipulate space and place for the allocation of social access. He sees location as a resource distinct from wealth, status and power and less liquid in terms of its interchangeability. Like the classical ecologists, Williams sees competition rather than conflict as the basis for urban politics. 'The rush to the suburbs, crowded highways, ghettoes and slums, decaying empty factories and stores, declining core city populations, urban renewal, riots, and air pollution are a few of the indications that the allocation process does not operate to the satisfaction of all and that the distribution has inequalities.'[64] In order to get better access, Williams argues, people can either move or change the characteristics of the place they at present occupy. Fundamentally Williams is a pluralist and an individualist. He does not analyse urban problems in terms of structured conflict, but in terms of individuals improving their market position. Where a collectivity gains more from communal action than from voting with its feet a situation may arise where a radical community 'counters the American individualistic way' or 'assumes an anti-social stance *vis-à-vis* the larger society'.[65] He argues that 'most urban dwellers vote by moving van' yet he acknowledges that 'it is possible to aggregate urban access interests explicitly but we rarely do'.[66] Williams himself seems uncertain how far, as a political scientist, he is prepared to analyse geographical mobility as the expression of political activity and how far he is prepared to make conscious the accessibility structures of those suffering from urban false consciousness. Further, he assumes that 'the basic nature of the urban process is the achievement of goals through access gained by *persons* deploying themselves in space in relationship to other *persons*' (author's emphasis).[67] The crucial importance of information as a means of access and the systematic or structural basis of urban inequalities are both neglected in his discussion. Despite his acknowledgement that the urban benefits are unequally and inequitably distributed, and his admission that the least mobile suffer in a system which emphasizes individual responses to location as the key political act, Williams stops short of a socio-logical analysis on a level of that proposed, say, by Rex and Moore in their study of conflict over housing in Birmingham.

In an earlier study Williams and Adrian were concerned with the material circumstances which led to different patterns of decision-making in four cities and this approach has been developed by others in later studies.[68] However, the American commentators seem unwilling to extend their work to a more thoroughgoing materialistic analysis. The development of an active 'urban consciousness' and political actions based on the relationships to the 'urban' situation would seem to be a crucial and necessary ingredient of the approach I am outlining. Castells makes a brave attempt to articulate a materialist approach to the urban question but, on his own admission, he is venturing more on a voyage of faith than synthesizing a body of solidly based research. He considers it 'a good bet' that the fecundity of historical materialism will be sufficient to discover laws in the urban field too.[69] He has, as he puts it, 'a certain faith in the analytical force of Marxist concept'.[70] Even in his short study of urban social movements Castells does little more than bring together 'recent examples of popular mobilizations'.[71] In a recent contribution Lojkine and Preteceille[72] claim that so-called 'urban' problems are simply the manifestation of the contradictions of monopoly capitalism and that urban and regional planning can be best analysed in terms of the nature and role of the state's power. This comes out very clearly in Castells' review of the urban renewal programme in the United States.[73] Similarly Bleitrach and Chenu[74] pick up a similar theme from their work on the ideology of planners operating in the Marseilles metropolitan region. Conventionally urban problems resulting from what the planners describe as spontaneous or natural tendencies or disequilibria were said to require a technical solution. The general position of this new school of Marxist-inspired French urban sociologists is that these problems are the reflection of a certain type of society which is now showing its internal contradictions most clearly in the urban sphere. However refreshing it is to have a new and vigorous development in urban sociology the contributors to *Espaces et Sociétés* have relatively little empirical substantiation for their assertions. The literature is growing and, although one might share Castells' faith in the future development of Marxist analysis, it is hard to evaluate it until more is published and is available to an English readership (but see Lefebvre[75] for a different Marxist interpretation).

CONCLUSION

I have assumed that as sociologists we agree that although Calcutta, Budapest, Paris and London all may have severe housing problems, we are less interested in that common element than in the ways a consideration of such problems leads us back to the different power structures of the societies of which those cities are a reflection. My concern has been to express something of the complexities of the dialectic between social allocative processes and spatial logics, acknowledging that each of these has within itself its own dialectic. Thus the allocative structures themselves logically must have a spatial element embodied in them: resources cannot be allocated aspatially and the right to a facility does not imply that that facility is adjacent to one's dwelling or to other facilities that one needs. The spatial logic is a logic of inequality and without compensatory interventionist policies by the central administration even a society with an egalitarian wage structure would engender its distinctive spatial inequalities. Similarly, although the overall system of dynamics contains within itself the accessibility structures which flow from the dialectic of allocative structures and spatial logics, the societal dialectic creates its own allocative structure which at a different level creates, in turn, its own societal accessibility structure, which again has its own feedback to urban social–spatial dynamics. Thus the whole system of dynamics is a finely balanced pattern of dialectics between the social and the spatial and between allocative structures and accessibility structures.

It is this delicate balance of interventions and of constraints, of power and of the limitations of knowledge, that I understand by the city or the region. The complexities of this system of dynamics are enormous and the amount of conceptualization on the subject is limited. Each society both determines and is determined by its internal spatial structure. I am not certain whether a distinctive class struggle over the means of access to scarce urban resources and facilities could emerge. Implicitly I am postulating a massive false consciousness now, since the assumptions of radical parties, trades unions and many students of stratification[76] are that differentials in wages and salaries are the most sensitive indicators of patterns of inequality within societies. Perhaps this is a more open question. As the middle levels of advanced industrial societies gain wages or salaries which enable them to lead a life free from the fear of material want and poverty they are likely to get more concerned about the provision of resources and facilities. Conditions at work may still be very bad in many areas and industries but increasingly political pressure may be less to reduce inequalities at the work place than to reduce inequalities at the place of residence.

Perhaps the first manifestations of this increasing concern with the *use* of income and the means of access to urban resources and facilities is seen in the migration of young wage-earners out of the city. A concern with the physical surroundings, with lower density, with open space and so forth need not necessarily imply reintroducing *embourgeoisement* through the garden gate. Nor need it imply the acceptance of Rex and Moore's unitary value system of the suburban ideal for everyone. Vague generalizations about 'middle-class' pressure groups for amenity or grass-roots activists, rent strikers and squatters need to be sharpened-up with specific sociological analysis. The growth of locality-based journals and newspapers seems to me to be a significant straw in the wind.*

In Britain we can perhaps more readily dismiss the 'urban' as epiphenomenal and turn back through the factory or dockyard gates for the basic confrontations. In Italy the contradictions of a different form of capitalism express themselves more dramatically outside the industrial context. As Mingione[77] has recently shown in his work in Milan

> The industrial social forces are interested in goals other than that of increasing productivity; above all they are interested in exercising a close control of the social and political activities of the lower classes. In socio-ecological terms this means segregation, differentiation and a hierarchic organization of space utilization, the organization of social consumption and a high commuting rate.

As a result of various policies discussed by Mingione in his paper 'the resistance of immigrants and workers living in the working-class zones in the centre of Milan already has the character of a political struggle against the present utilization of space'. The spread of a rent strike to a wide section of the manual working class and junior non-manual workers heightened consciousness and led to new conflicts 'on account of the lack of schools, transport, hospitals, parks and leisure facilities'.[78] Realizing that their reduced hours of work were offset by increased commuting time and that the peripheral estates were in some respects inferior to their previous inner-city residences, they turned more and more to the urban context as a focus for their grievances. Mainly as a result of working-class resentment of their

* See, for example, the new journals such as *West Midlands Grass Roots* produced by Community Planning Associates, Handsworth, Birmingham B19 1JD, or *Community Action* which aims at a national coverage. 9 Pattison Road, London, NW2. Both of these were founded in 1972.

urban situation the trade unions called a general strike in 1970. It is too early to say whether the accounts which Castells or, indeed, all of us can recount on urban conflict indicate the early stirrings of a movement which will become a force for change in modern societies. It seems to me to be certainly worth watching carefully.

Urban sociology has suffered from more than its share of pedestrian empiricism and little work has been cumulative in the problem area I am describing. I have argued that the outstanding weakness of urban sociology has been its incapacity to recognize that any attempt to provide a sociological theory of the city, independent of the economic and political system in which it exists, is singularly unsociological. Yet if, instead, we are to focus on the city as a means to an end rather than an end in itself the problem of what we as sociologists mean by the city becomes acute. This paper represents a stage in my attempt to come to grips with this problem and others are now beginning to recognize the difficulties.

Under these circumstances any attempt to turn the urban sociologist into the human relations officer of the city would be extremely misguided. Others may use their judgement as best they can: as sociologists our job is to try to understand and the fact of the matter is that we do not yet know *what it is* that we are trying to understand. The articulation of power in society is hardly a new field of study: we would be in good company returning to it.

REFERENCES

1 Castells, M., *La Question urbaine*, Maspero, Paris, 1972; Glass, R., 'Urban sociology', in *Society: Problems and Methods of Study*, Welford, A. T., *et al.* (eds.), Routledge, 1962; Manheim, E., 'Theoretical prospects of urban sociology in an urbanized society', *American Journal of Sociology*, 66(3), 1960, 226–9; Martindale, D., 'Prefatory remarks: The theory of the city', in Weber, M., *The City*, Martindale, D., and Neuwirth, G. (trans.), Heinemann, 1960; Pahl, R. E., 'A perspective on urban sociology', editor's introduction to *Readings in Urban Sociology*, Pergamon Press,

Oxford, 1968; Reissman, L., *The Urban Process*, Free Press, Glencoe, 1964.

2 Martindale, op. cit., 62.

3 Bell, D., 'Post-industrial Society', *Survey* 17(2), 1971, 102–68; Parkin, F., *Class Inequality and Political Order*, MacGibbon & Kee, 1971.

4 Thomlinson, R., *Urban Structure: The Social and Spatial Character of Cities*, Random House, New York, 1969, vii.

5 Hauser, P. M., and Schnore, L. F. (eds.), *The Study of Urbanization*, John Wiley, London, 1965, 348.

6 Reissman, op. cit., 120.

7 Schnore, L. F., 'On the spatial structure of cities in the two Americas', in Hauser and Schnore, op. cit.; Theodorson, G. A., *Studies in Human Ecology*, Row, Peterson, Evanston, Ill., 1961, Part III.

8 Pahl, R. E., 'Urban social theory and research', *Environment and Planning*, 1, 1969, 143–53. Reprinted here as Chapter 10.

9 Musil, J., *Sociologie Soudobého Města*, Nakladatelství svoboda, Prague, 1967; Pioro, Z., *Ekologia spoteczna w urbanistyce*, Wydawnictwo 'Arkady', Warsaw, 1962; Szelényi, I., *Urban Sociology*, Közgazdasagi és Jogi Könyvkinadó, Budapest, 1973.

10 Park, R. E., Burgess, E. W., and McKenzie, R. D., *The City*, Chicago University Press, 1925, reprinted 1967.

11 Carter, H., *The Study of Urban Geography*, Arnold, 1972; Johnston, R. J., *Urban Residential Patterns*, Bell, 1971; Robson, B. T., *Urban Analysis*, Cambridge University Press, 1969.

12 Park, R. E., *Human Communities*, Free Press, Glencoe, 1952.

13 Clements, F. C., *Plant Succession*, Carnegie Institution, Washington, DC, 1916.

14 Park, op. cit., 228.

15 ibid., 238.

16 McKenzie, R. D., 'The ecological approach to the study of the human community', *American Journal of Sociology*, 30, reprinted in Short, James F., Jr (ed.), *The Social Fabric of the Metropolis: Contribution of the Chicago School of Urban Sociology*, Chicago University Press, 1971, 29–30.

17 ibid., 32.

18 Burgess, E. W., *The Growth of the City*, in Park, Burgess and McKenzie, op. cit., reprinted in Theodorson, op. cit., 41.

19 Park, op. cit., 81.

20 Zorbaugh, H. W., 'The natural areas of the city', publication of the American Sociological Society, 20, 188–97, reprinted in Theodorson, op. cit., 49.

21 Vance, J. E., Jr, 'Land assignment practices in the precapitalist, capitalist and postcapitalist city', *Economic Geography*, 47(2) 1971, 99–120.

22 Wohl, A. S., 'The housing of the working class in London 1815–1914', in *The History of Working Class Housing*, Chapman, S. D. (ed.), David & Charles, Newton Abbot, 1971, 26.

23 ibid., 28–9.

24 Quoted in ibid., 34.

25 ibid., 38.

26 Jones, G. Stedman, *Outcast London*, Clarendon Press, Oxford, 1971, esp. Ch. 11.

27 See also Anderson, M., *Family Structure in Nineteenth Century Lancashire*, Cambridge University Press, 1971, and Foster, J., 'Nineteenth-century towns: a class dimension', in *The Study of Urban History*, Dyos, H. J. (ed.), Arnold, 1968.

28 Goldthorpe, J. H., 'The development of social policy in England 1800–1914', in *Transactions, 5th World Congress of Sociology*, International Sociological Association, 1964; Marshall, T. H.' The Welfare State: A sociological interpretation', *European Journal of Sociology*, 1961, 284–300; Titmuss, R., *Essays on 'The Welfare State'*, Allen & Unwin, 1958.

29 Rex, J., and Moore, R., *Race, Community and Conflict*, Oxford University Press, 1967, 273.

30 Donnison, D. V., *The Government of Housing*, Penguin Books, Harmondsworth, 1967, 97.

31 Rex and Moore, op. cit., 274.

32 ibid., 36.

33 Greater London Council, *Report of Studies*, 1969, 258.

34 Centre for Urban Studies, *Housing in Camden*, London Borough of Camden, 1969.

35 Rex, J., 'The sociology of a zone of transition', in *Readings in Urban Sociology*, Pahl, R. E. (ed.), Pergamon Press, 1968, 214–15.

36 Davies, J. G., and Taylor, J., 'Race, community and no conflict', *New Society*, 406 (9 July 1970); Lambert, J. R., and Filkin, C., 'Race relations research: Some issues of approach and application', *Race*, 12(3), 1971.

37 Rex, J., 'The concept of housing class and the sociology of race relations', *Race*, 12(3), 1971, 293–301.

38 Haddon, R. F., 'A minority in a Welfare State society: Location of West Indians in the London housing market', *The New Atlantis*, Milan, 1(2), 1970, 80–133.

39 HMSO, *Housing Finance: A Bill*, 1971.

40 Szelényi, I., and Konrád, G., 'Sociological aspects of the allocation

of housing' in *Industrialization, Urbanization and Ways of Life*, Institute of Sociology, Hungarian Academy of Sciences, Budapest, 1971.

41 Haddon, op. cit., 131–2.

42 Pahl, R. E., 'Poverty and the urban system', in *Spatial Policy Problems of the British Economy*, Chisholm, M., and Manners, G. (eds.), Cambridge University Press, 1971. Reprinted here as Ch. 8.

43 Zorbaugh, op. cit.

44 Firey, W., *Land Use in Central Boston*, Harvard University Press, Cambridge, Mass., 1947.

45 Lösch, A., *The Economics of Location*, New Haven, Conn., 1954.

46 Christaller, W., *Die zentralen Orte in Süddeutschland*, Jena, 1933, translated by C. W. Baskin, *Central Places in Southern Germany*, Prentice-Hall, Englewood Cliffs, N.J., 1966.

47 Berry, B. J. L., *Central Place Studies: A Bibliography of Theory and Application*, Regional Science Institute, Philadelphia, 1965, and *Spatial Analysis: A Reader in Statistical Geography*, Prentice-Hall, Englewood Cliffs, N.J., 1968.

48 Garner, B., 'Models of urban geography and settlement location' in *Models in Geography*, Chorley, R. J. and Haggett, P. (eds.), Methuen, 1967; Haggett, P., *Locational Analysis in Human Geography*, Arnold, 1965.

49 Models Working Party, *Urban Models in Shopping Studies*, National Economic Development Office, 1970.

50 Royal Commission on Local Government in England, *Report*, Research Studies 1–10, HMSO, 1969; Davies, B., *Social Needs and Resources in Local Services*, Michael Joseph, 1968.

51 Hart, J. T., 'The inverse care law', *The Lancet*, 27 February 1971, 405–12.

52 Bunge, W., *Theoretical Geography*, Lund Studies in Geography, Series C, 1962.

53 Hruska, E., 'Bemuhungen um eine neue Siedlungsstruktur in der Tschechoslowakei', *Archiv für kommunalwissenschaften*, 3(1), 1964, 57–80.

54 Zaslavska, T., 'Objectives and methods in planning rural urban migration', *The New Atlantis*, 2(2), Milan, 1971, 123–36.

55 Szelényi and Konrád, op. cit.

56 Foster, C. D., *Evidence to the Greater London Development Plan Inquiry on the Regressiveness of Road Pricing*, Background Paper B654. Response by the GLC Support Paper S30/136. Discussion by H. W. Richardson, 'A note on the distributional effects of road pricing', mimeo, University of Kent, 1972.

57 Pahl, 'Urban social theory and research'.

58 Szelényi and Konrád, op. cit.

59 Pahl, 'Poverty in the urban system'.

60 Lewis, J. W. (ed.), *The City in Communist China*, Stanford University Press, Cal., 1971; Luccioni, M., 'Processus révolutionnaire et organisation de l'espace en Chine – vers la fin des séparations entre villes et campagne', *Espaces et Sociétés*, 5, 1972, 63–104.

61 Konrád, G., and Szelényi, I., *Social Conflicts of Under Urbanization*, paper presented to the ISA Research Committee on Urban and Regional Development Seminar, Berlin, July 1972. First published in *Valóság*, 12, 1971.

62 Osipov, G. V. (ed.), *Town, Country and People*, Tavistock Publications, 1969.

63 Castells, op. cit.; Foster, J., op. cit.; Hobsbawm, E., 'La ville et l'insurrection', *Espaces et Sociétés*, 1, 137–47; Horowitz, I. L. (ed.), *Masses in Latin America*, Oxford University Press, New York, 1970; Rude, G., *Paris and London in the Eighteenth Century: Studies in Popular Protest*, Fontana, 1970; Tilly, C., 'A travers le chaos des vivantes cités' in *Urbanism, Urbanization and Change*, Meadows, P., and Mizruchi, E. H. (eds.), Addison-Wesley, 1969.

64 Williams, O. P., *Metropolitan Political Analysis*, Collier-Macmillan, 1971, 29.

65 ibid., 34.

66 ibid., 46.

67 ibid., 48.

68 Williams, O. P., and Adrian, C. R., *Four Cities*, University of Pennsylvania Press, Philadelphia, 1963; Clark, T. (ed.), *Community Structure and Decision Making: Comparative Analyses*, Chandler, San Francisco, 1968, and 'Comparative research on community decision-making', *The New Atlantis*, 2, Milan, 1970; Eyestone, R., *The Threads of Public Policy*, Bobbs-Merrill, Indianapolis, 1971.

69 Castells, M., 'Y a-t-il une sociologie urbaine?', *Sociologie du Travail*, 1, 72–90.

70 ibid., 399.

71 Castells, M., *Luttes urbaines et pouvoir politique*, Maspero, Paris, 1973.

72 Lojkine, J., and Preteceille, E., 'Politique urbaine et stratégie de classe', *Espaces et Sociétés*, 1, 1970, 79–84.

73 Castells, *La Question urbaine*.

74 Bleitrach, D., and Chenu, A., 'Le rôle idéologique des actions régionales d'aménagement du territoire: l'exemple de l'Aire métropolitaine marseillaise', *Espaces et Sociétés*, 4, 1971, 43–55.

75 Lefebvre, H., *La Pensée marxiste et le ville*, Casterman, Paris, 1972.
76 Parkin, op cit.
77 Mingione, *Urban Development and Social Conflict: The Case of Milan*, paper presented to the ISA Research Committee on Urban and Regional Development Seminar, July 1972, 15.
78 ibid., 19.

Chapter 13   'Urban managerialism' reconsidered*

The previous two chapters have raised issues of allocation and accessibility which deserve further discussion. The notion that there is a redistribution of real income as a result of the allocation of public resources and facilities is becoming understood.[1] At the same time many cling to allocation according to need, as part of the trappings of 'the Welfare State' as a type of society, and professional groups claiming special expertise in the determination of and provision for such needs have grown in power as the resources they allocate increase.

RESEARCH ON URBAN MANAGERS IN THEORY AND PRACTICE

Whilst, as I have argued in Chapter 11 in particular, a focus on these urban managers or gatekeepers is a useful research strategy, and whilst an exploration of their implicit goals, values, assumptions and ideologies may provide a valuable approach for students exploring the role of professionals in bureaucracies, such an approach lacks both practical policy implications and theoretical substance. Practically, the implication is so often that there is need for more sensitivity and more resources: basically, the planners, social workers, housing managers and so forth are very

*I have received very generous, pertinent and detailed comments on an earlier draft of this chapter from Michael Harloe, John Lambert, David McCrone, Rosemary Mellor and Chris Pickvance. Some of their criticisms were so fundamental that they must be faced in later work. Hopefully, the open sharing of ideas amongst us may enable some advance in sociological analysis of the urban question to be achieved collectively.

often trying to turn the taps of their resources to favour the most disadvantaged; but either through a mistaken belief in the validity of their data, a lack of awareness of the unintended consequences of their actions or simply through human error, the results of their activity fail to improve, and possibly add to, the plight of the poor. Sometimes, it is true, they are carrying out basically inequitable government policies, often with reluctance, and knowing that this is against their own values, if not their professional training. Generally a lack of resources inhibits the full development of their programme, plan or provision and the central government is accused of having the wrong order of priorities, or private employers and entrepreneurs are accused of putting private gain above public interest. Thus, in practical terms, the implications turn out to be remarkably similar: researchers show that the area of operation of the professional allocator is far more complicated than his training and policies suggest.[2] Wiser, more sensitive and better-trained urban managers, supported with more resources, is inevitably the policy conclusion. As with industrial relations there is a permanent plea for 'better communications'. Since that is an inherent problem in large-scale bureaucratically organized societies, there is no reason why every research worker should not discover the point for himself.

I consider that this emphasis on the local gatekeepers is perfectly valid and I consider further that it is part of the sociologist's general responsibility to explore, expose and to demystify the workings of our institutions, which must not become 'iron cages' or reified structures which dominate us. We should not be surprised to find that within local government structures there are conflicts, feuds, factions, cliques, cabals and all the strains and tensions common in bureaucracies.[3] In particular, we should not be surprised that individuals and professional groups often dress up their plans for personal and collective career advancement with altruistic and professional ideologies, emphasizing the needs of their clients as a basis for their own expansion. Some may believe that with different relationships to the means of production different motivations and a different 'human nature' may emerge. Until such time comes, it would be unwise for us to expect that local government bureaucracies would operate very differently from other types of bureaucracies.

That there may be some differences between urban managers and, say, industrial managers would be hard to deny. Despite the attempts, no doubt well-intentioned, of those who seek to make local government 'more efficient' by introducing management consultants, operational research and other aids from the world of profit-maximizing, not all those in local government are concerned with providing efficient services at least cost to the rates. Those who believe in public service, who believe that the library service, for example, has always too little money and too few clients, would claim that more money spent is not profligate but rather a form of community investment in the good life. Similarly, those responsible for education, health services, the personal social services and the like would rarely consider their task solely in terms of efficiency, but would also be concerned with equity or even equality. Local government's search for a collective managerial ideology and identity is certainly an interesting research field, but it needs to be related to a broader intellectual context.

This brings me to the second weakness in the approach – that of theoretical substance. The focus on urban managers or gate-keepers 'allocating' indirect wages and controlling access to scarce urban resources and facilities in 'an urban system' is useful, but too much should not be built upon it. Certainly the danger of reifying concepts such as 'allocative structures' should be avoided. Recent research in Britain has focused on the urban gatekeepers, largely because the researcher has been heavily on the side of the lower participants who may have suffered at the hands of insensitive local officials. It is understandably very easy for the researcher to view the situation through the eyes of disadvantaged local populations and to attribute more control and responsibility to the local official than, say, local employers or the national government. Following Gouldner's scathing discussion of this issue, it does seem likely that it is easier for sociologists receiving their research funds from government departments or national research councils to combine with, as it were, the bottom and the top in blaming the middle. As Gouldner remarks, such 'a criticism of local managers of the Caretaking Establishment' and 'of the vested interest and archaic methods of these middle dogs' may lead to an uncritical accommodation to the national élite and to the society's master institutions.[4] Such is the danger, and it does seem to be the case from recent British studies that the middle dogs have been the chief target for champions of the underdog.[5]

These local studies, focusing mainly on local government officials, are admirable in enabling us to understand the workings of bureaucracies and organizations. The detailed accounts of the use and misuse of rules, the internal struggles, the confusions, decisions and non-decisions are all useful accounts of the workings of large-scale organizations and, in particular, of their relationships with those outside the organization. More of such studies are needed since they certainly add much to our understanding of the city in capitalist society. However, we must be careful lest they confuse and mystify us by suggesting that research on the sociology of the urban manager implies an understanding of an *independent* variable in the creation of the urban system. Such is the position I have adopted above in Chapter 11 and which I am now terming 'urban managerialism'. It involves *systematic* control of the *same* urban resources and facilities in *different* localities; it further implies the ineffectiveness of the elected councillors. It ignores the constraints of capitalism.

SOME PARALLELS WITH THE MANAGERIALIST THESIS IN THE INDUSTRIAL CONTEXT

Turning to the industrial sphere in order to clarify the point about the inadequacy of the thesis of urban managerialism, the crucial point industrial managerialists put forward is that ownership and control have become separated.[6] Thus, even in such matters as forward planning and investment decisions it is the managers and not the shareholders, or their representatives the directors, who take the crucial decisions. Clearly, this argument applies most strongly when investment is drawn mostly from retained earnings and, in the case of public companies, assets are

appropriately reflected in the quoted share price. Without the
former the managers would be dependent on external sources of
finance and the control that might follow from that; without the
latter the company would be in danger of being taken over.[7]
Managers maintain control largely because of their technical
expertise in industries operating with the more advanced technologies; the logic of science and technology is said to determine
the way such industries must develop. Managers thus form part
of the technostructure, in Galbraith's term.[8]

Further discussion of managerialism in the industrial context
would be misplaced here. Even those who would hold to a thesis
of industrial managerialism – and this is hard to sustain in the
light of Nichols's attack – would be even more pressed to develop
a thesis of urban managerialism.[9] Certainly the professional
officers of a local authority can manipulate their elected councillors by withholding information or presenting it selectively and
by other means. Also, to some degree and in some cases, they
have control over income from rates. Further, they can influence
the scope and range of central government legislation by informal
pressure exerted by their most senior professionals and also
through their various associations and institutes. However, at
best, they only have slight, negative, influence over the deploy-
ment of private capital, and their powers of bargaining with central
government for more resources from public funds are limited.

Indeed, it is evident that far from there being a clear-cut
relationship (as I argue on pages 201–11) between the managers
and the managed in an urban system – taken to mean a local
configuration of social, economic and political power structures –
the whole notion must be seen as extremely problematic. Unless
one assumes a relative amount of autonomy within local configurations, life chances would be solely determined by national
decisions and there would be no variation in access to resources
such as housing or education, from one part of the country to
another (holding position in the occupational structure constant).[10] It is well documented that there is, however, considerable
variation in the level of services and accessibility to resources
between localities.[11] This must imply variations in real income
in different milieux or spatial configurations. It may appear in a

specific context that those controlling the local 'taps' – whether planners, housing managers or medical officers of health – are the true 'gatekeepers' and the way that they use and interpret their rules and procedures influences life chances in a fundamental way. There are recent case studies which support this argument.[12] However, if it is the case that in one area of provision the 'managers' can operate according to one set of criteria, it is equally plausible for 'managers' in a different area of provision to control their local taps according to different principles such as 'positive discrimination' or 'least charge on the rates'. Indeed, this must be partly the cause of the empirical variation in the provision of facilities which has been demonstrated.

If it is the case, then, that the existing state legislation in the fields of planning, housing, social welfare and so on permits wide discretion on the part of the local controllers, it is more difficult to see how organized, systematic and structured opposition, implying the linking and coordination of many different groups in different localities over some length of time, can emerge. If the local gatekeepers of public resources and facilities do not *systematically* work together to reinforce, reflect or recompense inequalities engendered through the productive process, then a 'pure' urban managerialist thesis could hardly be sustained.

ALTERNATIVE MODELS OF RESOURCE CONTROL AND ALLOCATION

In an attempt to clarify the distinctions I am making, I now set out four alternative ideal types.

(a) The 'pure' managerialist model

This assumes that control of access to local resources and facilities is held by the professional officers of the authority concerned. Such 'gatekeepers' share a common ideology (which it is the job of sociologists to uncover), manipulate their elected representatives so that the political composition of the council makes little difference to the policies pursued and, hence, there is a common impact on real incomes of the population as a whole.

(b) The statist model

This assumes that control over local resources and facilities is primarily a matter for the national government and that local professionals or managers have very little room for manoeuvre. National legislation in the fields of housing, planning, education and so forth, effectively determines the indirect wages or real income of the population as a whole. While there may be *marginal* differences between one local configuration and another, these do not substantially affect the consumption capacities of different social classes.

(c) The control-by-capitalists model

This assumes that at either national or local levels resources are allocated primarily to service the interests of private capitalists. These may be taken to be the reproduction of a docile, well-trained and healthy labour force. If housing affects the supply of labour then resources must be allocated to ensure that the supply is adequately maintained. If growth and profits depend to some extent upon investment in education, then, again, minimal resources must be allocated accordingly. Public services and facilities are always seen as a 'luxury' according to this model. At a local level private profit is a more legitimate basis for the allocation of, say, central locations than public good.

(d) The pluralist model

This assumes a permanent tension between national bureaucracies, committed to obtaining and distributing larger resources (following partly their own internal logic of growth), and the interests of private capital manifested through the economic pressures of 'the City', private industry and the political party representing the dominant class. Cuts and increases in public expenditure ebb and flow between different sectors as the lines of conflict shift. Similarly, local authorities are in competition with each other to get larger shares of central funds and, once funds are obtained, there is the same tension between public and private interests at a local level.

Each of these ideal-typical models produces different explanatory frameworks for answering the question 'Who gets what?' in given spatial contexts. Leaving aside for the present the difficult questions of political economy, which would have to be resolved to determine which model is most appropriate for any given society (for example, is Sweden more like model (*b*) or model (*d*)?), there remains the problem that local configurations have neither equal demands nor equal needs for national resources. Since in Britain the physical and demographic variation is considerable between one locality and another, the opportunities for *ad hoc* special pleading in the claiming of national resources are very great. Given, too, that territorial justice is an elusive concept,[13] implying an ability to come to a satisfactory definition of social need by the benevolent dictator or benevolent bureaucracy at the centre, some kind of negotiating or bargaining between the centre and the periphery is likely to be an inevitable element in any system. That being so the problem of ultimate allocative control remains.

LOCAL VARIATIONS, ORGANIZED COLLECTIVE ACTION AND URBAN CLASS-CONSCIOUSNESS

The very differences in local configurations, which give rise to different cases and therefore the allocation of different amounts of national resources, inhibit the establishment of organized collective responses to the allocative process across a wider area. While one local bureaucracy may have made an effective claim for more resources for local schools in the light of its demographic structure, a neighbouring authority might have less good schools but better health provision. Since peoples' conceptions of the provision of these services are likely to be heavily influenced by their local subjective experiences, a sense of common deprivation or 'urban class-consciousness' may not easily develop. Further, since different groups benefit at different times from different services, common urban consciousness is undermined. Sporadic protests may, indeed, develop: the mobile and the affluent may protest by moving their location; the poor may take part in rent strikes or squatting.

Taking direct action may lead to a local authority amending its housing policy or providing more pre-school playgroups but, once the particular goal has been achieved, there seems little evidence that such groups continue, aiming at broader political goals. In one recent account of a successful attempt to change a local government decision it was claimed that 'there is a chance that community power can begin to turn the scales of social justice'. The author, who led the local campaign, claimed, 'We can now regard ourselves as part of a new social and political force at the local level. In time, it will have national significance.'[14] These are large claims; if they are substantiated they will confirm the urban managerialist thesis by action from below. Ironically such claims could also be held to support a model of central state control, by showing how reformist demands are being met in order to preserve the system. However, it is the thesis of this paper that such sentiments must be wrong. Since different groups benefit at different times in different parts of the same city, common city or nationwide situations of deprivation rarely occur. Those who claim that they can see the development of 'urban social movements' leading to radical changes in the nature of urban society would find difficulty in getting empirical support from British experience, although there may be more valid reasons for using the term elsewhere.[15] Very rarely would situations arise in the British context where workers were *systematically* deprived of indirect wages through the administration and distribution of what is most aptly termed in France collective consumption. One example of a collective response to a widespread threat was the coordination of a whole cluster of local organizations set up to oppose the concentric system of urban motorways proposed by the Greater London Development Plan. The London Motorway Action Group appeared to be more concerned with preserving 'amenity' and protecting property values and gained its support from home owners more than from local authority or private tenants. An attempt to put forward separate candidates to oppose the two main political parties in an election, held at a time when feeling was running high, was singularly unsuccessful.

With so many local authorities, and with services provided at different levels in different historical and geographical contexts, it is hard for the academic researcher to find a clear pattern. Unlike the situation in France, with its very rapid postwar urbanization and massive suburbanization of the working class, Britain had a rather slower and more piecemeal urban development. Local authority building was more evenly balanced between the inner city and the periphery and the quality of the dwellings and level of public provision, while not exactly lavish, nevertheless maintained a modest standard. Indeed, the quality of working-class dwellings in some areas produced a sort of housing aristocracy within the working class in comparison with those in the privately rented sector. It is hard to see an aggressively exploitative capitalism at work, if one considers simply the national standard and the distribution of local authority dwellings. Tenants' associations did not organize collectively to produce a national rent strike during the period when the Conservative government introduced a system of 'fair rents' for local authority housing, essentially tying them to a local free-market rent structure. Many local authorities made it clear that they were introducing this measure reluctantly and the transparency of the power situation was clear enough for the opposition to be focused at a national level where the measure was vigorously attacked clause by clause through the committee stage of the Bill by the Opposition.[16]

Similarly the activities of property speculators, whilst generating sporadic local squatting in unoccupied office blocks, did not stimulate working-class collective action against the private ownership of urban land. Controlling the excess profits of property speculators became a national political issue at the end of 1973 when, amongst others, Lord Plowden, Chairman of Tube Investments, one of the largest of British industrial enterprises, wrote to *The Times* urging government action. It is significant that this presssure to take action seemed to come at least as much from the controllers of industry as from trade unionists, and was directed, evidently, against the capitalist system in housing and land and not at the capitalist system in industry. 'The City' was seen as serving 'finance capital' at the expense of industrial capitalism.

Now whether Britain has a more divided ruling class than France, whether we have adopted a 'softer' form of capitalism and whether a French Prime Minister would own up to the 'unacceptable face of capitalism' (in Mr Heath's phrase) is in each case hard to say. One conclusion does, however, seem clear, and that is that *urban conflicts relate directly to the specific nature of the particular type of capitalist society concerned.* It is clear to me that it is *not* possible to generalize about cities in capitalist societies without making many serious qualifications. The 'urban question' will be very different in France, Australia, the United States, Germany and Britain.

Finally, it is worth remembering that by focusing attention on indirect wages and excluding the generation and distribution of direct wages the sociologist may create the very mystifications I am at pains to describe. By focusing on urban resources and facilities and by alerting urban populations to their relative deprivations in the field of consumption, attention is shifted from the main *source* of inequality in society, namely, the field of production. The work by Hindess in Liverpool shows that the extreme salience of housing opportunities for workers' life chances has made this a central feature of working-class political discussion. As Hindness puts it, 'local government is experienced not simply as providing a background but also as an external constraining and coercive organization'.[17] In many northern cities the Labour party in control is seen as being as constraining and as coercive as the alternative. If workers are made to think that their *main interests* are in the field of consumption, and if sociologists adopt a form of urban managerialism to explain the allocation of resources within an urban system, then clearly basic inequalities arising from the productive process may remain hidden.

TERRITORIAL INEQUALITY, POLITICAL IDEOLOGY AND THE POWER OF OVERT AND HIDDEN MARKETS

Up to now we have noticed the tension between the national and the local and hinted at the inevitability of territorial injustice. It is now necessary to make certain points explicit: *no economy can develop in a 'spatially neutral' way.* Inevitably certain areas will have certain advantages for the production of certain goods and services. As technology develops or (but not necessarily) as markets change, certain areas grow more rapidly, while others decline. This unbalanced development follows as much from the logic of technological development as from the logic of profit associated with capitalist ownership of the means of production. As the division of labour becomes more fine, differentiation and concentration of the workforce inevitably creates a spatial form to an economy, which seems to acquire a relative autonomy of its own.

In the same way that a certain *scale* of production leads to the creation of a resource – the economies of scale – so too does the physical concentration of the workforce in cities create a resource, namely *accessibility*. As long as facilities are concentrated so that some locations are more favoured than others, then inequalities of accessibility will occur, which again are inevitably reflected in hidden or overt market structures.

There are only two ways of overcoming such inequalities: the first would be to allocate centrality according to need. Since need changes over the life cycle (being close to a primary school when under 11 is an advantage, being close when over 65 can be a disadvantage) and since the facilities are more spatially fixed than the users, then a high level of individual mobility would be necessary. However much this might disrupt social relationships and draw families apart, it would have to be insisted upon in the interests of territorial justice. The second alternative would be to 'abolish centrality'. Cities are inherently inegalitarian structures and ultimately the only way to eradicate spatial injustice is to eradicate the city. This would seem to imply a regression to a simpler mode of production and a less fine division of labour. So far I am arguing that *technology and the division of labour create inequality independently of that engendered by the capitalist mode of production*. If cities are predominantly privately owned then a *second* source of inequality, over and above that connected with accessibility will emerge, namely differential rent. And the two aspects of inequality are interrelated. High accessibility is generally equated with high rents. But areas of very high rent are in turn created by the existence of the mass of the population that surrounds these areas. If, overnight, the city was totally depopulated, apart from those living in the area of the very highest rentable value, such high rents could not be sustained. Thus, the owners of central locations get a 'surplus rent' over and above what is required for their personal needs and the maintenance of their property. They further gain an increase in *capital* value which can be used for other purposes. I am arguing for a position which recognizes that centrality cannot be analysed as simply the basis for another commodity market.

The fundamental difference between a 'capitalist city' and a 'socialist city' appears, therefore, to be in terms of the *ownership of land and rent structures*. Hence, it is possible to postulate a 'socialist city' in a capitalist society. This would be the case if the state owned all urban land, despite the ownership of the forces of production still remaining in private hands. Apart from paying rent (however determined) to the state, private capitalist enterprises could presumably carry on much as before. Such a situation raises in acute form the relationship between the political economy and the territorial structure of the society. How would a city owned on a socialist basis interrelate with a privately owned system of production?

Under these circumstances the strong urban managerialist thesis I have discussed above would have force. Possibilities for genuine redistributive policies would emerge so that indirect wages could compensate for low direct wages. Tension would then arise between the polity and the economy as capitalists found that their control over local labour markets was thereby diminished. Indeed it is through the construction of such a scenario that the realities of power in a truly 'mixed' economy emerge. The city then becomes a short-hand term for the public allocation of all services and facilities (including accessibility), apart from position in labour markets. Such a situation would create enormous strain, as firms' competitive position was under-mined by state action. In such a situation the urban managers would not necessarily have any more power than at present to get information on incomes from local employers, to change the structure of local labour markets by introducing new and more flexible types of employment, to prevent closures or to affect earned incomes, hours of employment or anything else. The recent *Report of the Panel of Inquiry into the Greater London*

Development Plan summarizes the situation as it exists at the present time:

We are driven, therefore, to the view that the local planning authority can, within its area, over the long term influence only marginally the tendency of employment to contract or alter, or retain its nature. It can somewhat more effectively exercise, or fail to exercise, its power to inhibit expansion, but even here the power of the market renders less than perfect the ability of an authority to check it consistently in the long term.[18]

Yet even in an area where the local authority *does* have the power to intervene directly in the market, as in the case of allocating land for private residential development, there is no clear evidence that there is redistribution towards the poor. Indeed the best evidence suggests the reverse. The massive study evaluating land-use planning in England since the 1947 Act concluded:

The objectives of the planning system result in various economic and social costs being created and borne by different sectors of society. At the present time, the lower end of the private housing market (both the groups who succeed in purchasing and those who fail) seems to be bearing a high burden of real or opportunity costs. In effect, this is indirect *redistribution of income*. Unfortunately, this is in the wrong direction; in this case from the relatively less well-off house purchaser to the rural landowner . . . Rather than contribute and be instrumental in achieving an egalitarian society, the current planning of land development has made matters worse.[19]

Similar general points can be made in relation to the urban low-paid workers.[20]

In the light of this kind of evidence, it is hard to sustain the more extreme urban managerialist thesis which I advanced in Chapter 10. Even when the state does make attempts to 'solve' the housing problem or to restructure the declining regions by introducing new employment through the Regional Employment Premium, it does not seem to have much success. Indeed, examples of government decisions leading to unintended consequences are unhappily only too common:

In London the siting of the GPO Tower in an area that has long been a traditional centre for a tightly-knit community of small tailors, working largely for West-End stores, has affected the trade. Here was an area occupied by rather seedy buildings, which were perfectly adequate from the viewpoint of their occupiers, who were sometimes their owners. Some were demolished in order to make room for the Tower. Now that the Tower exists there is a large tourist interest in the area. Higher rents can be obtained from souvenir shops and cafes. As short-term leases expire, tailors are asked for higher rents, and often they cannot afford them. They move to other places, in a way that disrupts this trading community and leads to a decline in its efficiency.[21]

Such examples indicate that it would be by no means certain who would lose in a genuinely mixed economy, so long as the main productive forces were outside the control of the state. Evidence from the command economies of Eastern Europe indicates that even with state control of all investment and allocations to urban resources and facilities, there still exists in such societies:

(a) Hidden market mechanisms favouring those with higher incomes over those with lower;
(b) territorial injustice in access to resources and facilities;
(c) inequitable tax redistribution between one locality and another;
(d) all the informal operations within bureaucracies that favour those who know how to work systems and probably implying further redistribution of real wages;
(e) conflicts over the 'needs' of one socio-economic category in relation to another.

Indeed, paradoxically, if urban managerialism applies anywhere it is most likely to have relevance in societies operating systems of state socialism where the power of central bureaucracies is increased.

THE NEED FOR COMPARATIVE AND HISTORICAL ANALYSIS

It is now becoming more widely accepted by sociologists that Marx's unitary model of capitalist society is misleading, particularly in so far as it relates to the European societies of his time. By taking Britain as 'the most typical form' of capitalist society and then developing a typology which could be applied to other European societies Marx, in Giddens's view, committed the error of 'misplaced concreteness'.[22]

The point is, that rather than being the 'type case' of either capitalist or industrial evolution, Britain is the exception; or, more accurately, it represents only one among various identifiable patterns of development in the emergency of the advanced societies. In Britain – no doubt as the overall result of a complicated (and still highly controversial) set of specific historical antecedents – the way was paved in the nineteenth century for the mutual accommodation of capitalism and industrialism within a general framework of bourgeois democratic order. Consequently the process of industrialisation took place in an 'undirected' fashion, through the agency of a multiplicity of entrepreneurial activities in a relatively stabilised 'bourgeois society'. France in the nineteenth century, and arguably ever since, was dominated by the legacy of the 1789 revolution.[23]

It would be ironic if contemporary sociologists adopted the same error in reverse and derived a new abstract model from an analysis of the urban question in France or Italy which they then applied to the situation in Britain. Comparative analysis can do much to illustrate the *differences* between capitalist societies and the distinctive nature of British urbanism.

Giddens discusses some of the differences in the infrastructure and space economy between Britain, France and Germany in the nineteenth century. It is curious that Marxist geographers such as Harvey have not, apparently, recognized the relevance of the historical geography of the nineteenth century and its relationships to the political economy of early capitalism and developing urbanization in Britain.[24] As Briggs points out, 'the first effect of early industrialization was to differentiate English communities rather than to standardize them'.[25] Briggs goes on to emphasize how far Manchester and Birmingham 'diverged very strongly in their economic life, their social structure and their politics' and

Sheffield had much in common with Birmingham in its economic system, but the shape of its society and the chronology and trend of the municipal history were quite different. A full study of social structure must take account of property relations as well as income, of religion as well as economics, and not least of demography, which provides a quantitative basis for much subsequent generalization . . .

In the fundamental study of comparative property relations obvious points to note are the pattern of ownership of urban land, the extent of aristocratic interest (including absentee interest), the volume of industrial investment, the amount of corporate wealth and the total rateable value.[26]

Different types of corporation and sources of finance meant that 'the early- and mid-Victorian cities would confront urban problems with differing degrees of imagination and efficiency . . . Some Victorian cities quite deliberately embarked upon large-scale programmes; others lagged behind'.[27] Professor Briggs does not make it clear who is confronting and who is embarking.

It is certain that the industrial and occupational structure of cities varied greatly and that the life chances of the urban working class varied according to social, economic and political factors in the different cities. Foster's comparative analysis of Oldham, Northampton and Shields provides clear evidence of the variation in pattern and style of exploitation between towns as industrialism advanced.[28]

The growth in the scale and volume of grants-in-aid from the state during the nineteenth century was gradually to lead to a decline in provincial autonomy and the increasing dominance of the power of the state in determining appropriate levels of education, health, housing and so forth. However – and this is the point of this brief excursion into nineteenth-century history – the development of national standards of public provision during the twentieth century was grafted on to a wide variation in local infrastructure. Thus, Norwich, Bristol, Sheffield and Manchester, to take four cities at random, not only had different local economic structures but also, consequently, had different levels of indirect wages.

Then, in the twentieth century, in the same way that some cities had acquired greater growth and greater wealth in the previous century, so differential industrial and urban decay produced a pattern which increasingly has come to be seen as a national and not a local problem. Further, as Britain's competi-

tive position in the world declined, as it lost its overseas investments, its Empire, its supply of cheap raw materials and its
captive markets for manufactured goods, so that political power
of its productive industry increased, forming, as it does, the
foundation of our economic base. Unlike France, Britain has
to import about half its food and this means that the production
of goods and services for export occupy a particularly key role in
our political economy. The competitive arena of international
capitalism puts very severe constraints on Britain's room for
manoeuvre. The pursuit of what are seen by international
financiers as 'too radical' measures could lead to a massive flight
of capital from the City of London to money markets elsewhere
and, possibly, a similar flight of skilled managerial and professional workers. If Britain cut itself off from trading partnerships
with western capitalist societies it would be likely to enter acute
balance-of-payments crises if food imports were to be maintained.
In this context, with continuing inflation, aided by the inevitable
increase in world primary-product prices (especially oil), expenditure on urban infrastructure is inevitably seen as a 'cost' restrict-
ing our overall competitiveness in world markets.

In the light of this, it is surprising that the level of our public
provision is as high as it is in comparison with, say, France.
Partly this can be accounted for by the incorporation of the
working class into the political process, the extension of the
rights of citizenship and the reform of social security in the 1940s.
However, it would also be reasonable to attribute some measure
of credit to the forces of bourgeois, liberal, humanitarian reform-
ism in the Fabian tradition for ameliorating the harsh logic of
capitalist enterprise. The lower-middle-class values of decency,
orderliness and 'balance', enshrined in such ameliorist pressure
groups as the Town and Country Planning Association,[29] have
done much to create a climate of opinion in which the small
scale of our urban scene, epitomized in the New Towns, has been
preserved and maintained. The fact that a unitary capitalist
ruling class did not exist in nineteenth-century Britain and that
while the aristocracy 'ruled officially', the bourgeoisie ruled 'over
all the various spheres of civil society in reality' as Marx noted,
has led Giddens to conceive of a system of 'leadership groups' to

describe the situation today.[30] This pattern may serve to soften and moderate more aggressive capitalist tendencies.

There has been remarkably little research on the ideology which has produced British urbanism and on the relationship between urban allocation and the political economy of the state. Ruth Glass's survey of the nineteenth-century literature[31] and Raymond Williams's masterly work on the literary images of *The Country and the City*[32] provide valuable starting points, and detailed case studies such as that by Stedman Jones[33] or Wohl[34] are also notable. For recent years we have to rely on journalistic analyses, such as *The Property Boom*,[35] and somewhat garbled attempts to link the activities of property speculators with the housing crisis in London.[36] What is needed is a systematic socio-economic analysis of the implications of the rapid movement of capital into land and property markets.[37] The recent operations of capitalism are sucking resources out of local spatial economies in a way previous industrial investment did not. (At least it provided local employment.) Such shifting patterns of investment have led Eisenschitz to conclude that 'now the city as a physical artifact is being used in order to absorb the economic surplus and promote the welfare of the capitalist system'.[38] Eisenschitz's emphasis on the flows of investment capital is correct. As he puts it:

> To understand the relation of the city to the world and in particular the relations of areas within the city one needs to know where the surplus is generated and absorbed, and the magnitude, generation and destination of wages, rent, profits and output. Areas and land uses should be examined with regard to their relative production and consumption, and their generation and absorption of profits, relating land use patterns to economic forces. Each pattern of flows has an associated pattern of social relationships.[39]

This must be done in the context of *British* political economy, based on our distinctive infrastructure and distinctive position in the pattern of world trade in capitalist markets. Hopefully, we may be able to explicate the constraints within which the urban managers must operate and to show the relationship between access and allocation in urban and regional systems. Unless we have a clearer notion of the nature of *British* capitalist society it will not be possible to come to a sound theoretical understanding of 'the city' and the space economy. Certainly in terms of practical policies in connection with 'the urban crisis' (variously defined) it is clear that attacks at the level of urban management may be misdirected. It is rather like the workers stoning the house of the chief personnel manager when their industry faces widespread redundancies through the collapse of world markets.

CONCLUSIONS

'Urbanism', as Harvey reminds us, 'entails the geographic concentration of a socially designated surplus product.'[40] Cities are essentially unfair. A distinctive focus for urban sociology in capitalist society is to explore the system by which that society allocates its urban resources and facilities. I am arguing, somewhat elliptically perhaps, that British urbanism and the indirect wages generated and distributed, are a product of *the tensions between competitive international capitalism and ameliorist Welfare-State-type ideologies*. Since the urban managers are the central mediators between urban populations and the capitalist economy and since they also serve to generate and maintain the ideology of Welfare-Statism, their role remains crucial in the urban problematic.[41] This *may* mean that the British urban working class suffers less naked exploitation in the area of collective consumption, and that the central government is less *dirigiste*, than *may* be the case in France. However, in making these analyses of the distinct nature of various forms of capitalist urbanism there is an urgent need to remember – as Marx and Engels first saw – that 'the housing question', and much else that is wrong in our cities, can *never* be solved while 'modern big cities' survive. Even if we had the social control and ownership of the means of production, so long as such 'modern big cities' exist, so also, if in a different form, will the inequitable generation of indirect wages continue. The search for a just city is self-defeating. As long as there are 'modern big cities' there will be a need for ameliorism and the allocation of resources by managers and gatekeepers. And, to return to Harvey, 'the reputation and significance of individual cities rest to a large degree upon their location with respect to the geographic circulation of the surplus. The qualitative attributes of urbanism will likewise be affected by the rise and fall in the total quantity of surplus as well as the degree to which the surplus is produced in concentratable form.'[42] The urban managers remain the allocators of this surplus; they must remain, therefore, as central to the urban problematic.

REFERENCES

1 Harvey, D., 'Social processes, spatial form and the redistribution of real income in an urban system', in Chisholm, M., Frey, A. E., and Haggett, P., *Regional Forecasting*, Butterworth, 1971.
2 See for example the work by Norman Dennis, *People and Planning*, Faber & Faber, 1970, and *Public Participation and Planners' Blight*, Faber & Faber, 1972; and Davis, J. G., *The Evangelistic Bureaucrat*, Tavistock, 1972.
3 A good instance of this is given by D. M. Muchnick, in *Urban Renewal in Liverpool*, Bell, 1970.
4 Gouldner, A. W., 'The sociologist as partisan: Sociology and the Welfare State', in *For Sociology*, Allen Lane The Penguin Press, 1973, 51.
5 In addition to the work by Dennis and Davis cited above there are the Birmingham studies by Rex, J., and Moore, R., *Race, Community and Conflict*, Oxford University Press, 1967, and by Lambert, J. R., and Filkin, C. J., *Ethnic Choice and Preference in Housing*, Report to the Social Sciences Research Council, 1971, and in Glasgow by Damer, Seán, 'Wine Alley: The sociology of the dreadful enclosure', *Sociological Review*, 22, 1974, 221–48.
6 These arguments are admirably summarized in Nichols, Theo, *Ownership, Control and Ideology*, Allen & Unwin, 1969.
7 See Pahl, R. E., and Winkler, J. T., 'The economic élite: Theory and practice', in Stanworth, P., and Giddens, A. (eds.), *Élites and Power in British Society*, Cambridge University Press, 1974.
8 Galbraith, J. K., *The New Industrial State*, Hamish Hamilton, 1967.
9 It is only fair to note that I have come probably as close as anyone to adopting this position in my previous work. See also Lambert,

J. R., 'The management of minorities', in *The New Atlantis*, 2(1), Milan, 1970.

10 See Pickvance, C. G., 'On a materialist critique of urban sociology', in *Sociological Review*, N.S., 22(2), 1974, 203–20.

11 Taylor, G., and Ayres, N., *Born and Bred Unequal*, Longman, 1969; Davies, B., *Social Needs and Resources in Local Services*, Michael Joseph, 1968; and Harvey, op. cit.

12 See above, the works cited in references 2 and 5.

13 See Harvey, op. cit., Chapter 3.

14 Clark, G. 'The lesson of Acklam Road', in Butterworth, E., and Weir, D. (eds.), *Social Problems of Modern Britain*, Fontana, 1972, 186.

15 See *Espaces et Sociétés*, 1, 1972, 6–7, particularly the introduction by M. Castells. See also Castells's books, *La Question urbaine*, Maspero, Paris, 1972, and *Luttes urbaines et pouvoir politique*, Maspero, Paris, 1973.

For a discussion of the French work in relation to British examples, see Pickvance, C. G., 'From "social base" to "social force"': Some analytical issues in the study of urban protest', paper prepared for the session on Social Conflicts in Urban and Regional Development at the Eighth World Congress of Sociology, Toronto, 1974.

16 See, for example, *Hansard*, Vol. 826, No. 10, Cols. 32–160.

17 Hindess, B., *The Decline of Working Class Politics*, Paladin and MacGibbon & Kee, 1971, 77.

18 *Report of the Panel of Inquiry into the Greater London Development Plan*, HMSO, Vol. I, 79.

19 Hall, P., *et al.*, *The Containment of Urban England*, Allen & Unwin, 1973, Vol. II, 402.

20 See Chapter 9 above.

21 Medhurst, D. Franklin, and Lewis, J. Parry, *Urban Decay*, Macmillan, 1969, 75–6.

22 Giddens, A., *The Class Structure of the Advanced Societies*, Hutchinson, 1973, 146.

23 ibid., 144–5.

24 Harvey, D., *Social Justice and the City*, Arnold, 1973.

25 Briggs, A., *Victorian Cities*, Penguin Books, Harmondsworth, 1968, 33.

26 ibid., 35–6, 38.

27 ibid., 42–3. See also Hennock, E. P., *Fit and Proper Persons: Ideal and Reality in Nineteenth Century Urban Government*, Arnold, 1973.

28 Foster, J., 'Nineteenth-century towns: A class dimension', in Dyos, H. J. (ed.), *The Study of Urban History*, Arnold, 1968.

29 Foley, D., 'Idea and influence: The Town and Country Planning Association', in *Journal of the American Institute of Planners*, 28, 1962, 10–17.

30 Giddens, A., 'Élites in the British class structure', in *Sociological Review*, 20(3), 1972, 345–72.

31 Glass, R., 'Urban sociology: A trend report', in *Current Sociology*, 4(4), 1955.

32 Williams, R., *The Country and the City*, Chatto & Windus, 1973.

33 Jones, G. Stedman, *Outcast London*, Clarendon Press, Oxford, 1971.

34 Wohl, A. S., 'The housing of the working class in London 1815–1914', in Chapman, S. D. (ed.), *The History of Working Class Housing*, David & Charles, 1971; also the forthcoming book by Professor Wohl.

35 Marriott, O., *The Property Boom*, Hamish Hamilton, 1967.

36 Counter Information Services, *The Recurrent Crisis of London*, 1973.

37 Gibbs, R., and Harrison, A., *Land Ownership by Public and Semi-Public Bodies in Great Britain*, University of Reading, Department of Agricultural Economics and Management, 1973.

38 Eisenschitz, A., 'Planning and inequality', mimeo, Architectural Association, 1973.

39 ibid., 73.

40 Harvey, *Social Justice and the City*, op. cit., 246.

41 I am grateful to Michael Harloe for pointing this out to me.

42 Harvey, *Social Justice and the City*, op. cit.

Chapter 14   Social processes and urban change

WHAT IS URBAN CHANGE?

Sometimes we speak as if urban change is a novelty. I am doubtful whether the contemporary city is changing at a greater speed than did cities in the past. In terms of *political* change, I do not see the reorganization of local government as necessarily leading to dramatic changes. Certainly, the level of political change is small today in comparison with, say, the battles between medieval cities and the monarchy and Parliament. Very few new powers are currently under discussion. Even cities like London are not arguing for new legal powers – repeatedly the professional witnesses assured the recent Layfield Inquiry into the Greater London Development Plan (GLDP) that they had sufficient powers. Nor is the current electoral debate centred on the imposition of new taxes or the means of creating more municipal wealth and power. The issues of noise, disturbance, housing, communication, jobs and so forth are the perennial concern of urban government and there is little new in the way they are currently being presented and discussed.[1]

Turning to *economic* change and, in particular, the shift from manufacturing to service industries, and the decentralization of growth industries, it again seems to me that the level of change is relatively small. Not all British cities are primarily concerned with manufacturing and I doubt whether the great cities such as Norwich, York and Bristol of our historic past or Manchester, Leeds and Newcastle of the more recent industrial development in the nineteenth century are in a particularly parlous economic state at the present time. Again, I suspect that the rate of change in this sphere was probably much greater in the past – for example at the time of rapid industrialization or when insurance and banking expanded from the end of the nineteenth century.[2]

The same point can be made for *physical* change – the destruction of the urban fabric for new homes, factories or lines of communication is said to be without precedent. Yet the coming of the railways and the creation of dwellings for vast new urban populations in the period from 1840 to 1870 would have created far greater physical changes. The noise, disturbance and displacement were appalling.[3] Now we are more concerned with conserving the historic fabric, which clearly does create unprecedented tasks of rehabilitation and refurbishing of existing stock, but that creates problems more of management and administration than simply physical disruption. Certainly our cities are wearing out at great speed and at much the same time. This applies particularly to those built during the heyday of industrial expansion between 100 and 120 years ago.[4] However, our technical and managerial skills are now much greater for coping with these problems so that, given the political will, they should not be seen as overwhelming.

Any suggestion that we are not on the verge of an imminent urban crisis is a very unfashionable point of view to adopt. So many people earn their living as advisers, consultants, managers, technicians and researchers within the urban system that it is understandable that there should be strong incentives for them to portray things in alarming terms. When there is overall competition for resources, and industry is demanding substantial Government support and subsidy, the 'urban interest group' has to struggle to get its share. With large national companies being saved from bankruptcy by government intervention it is not surprising that some should want to use the argument of urban bankruptcy in the hope of getting more resources. Again that argument is not without its historical precedents.

I am not, of course, suggesting that our cities are without their problems. I am simply suggesting that our current urban pundits seem to lack a historical perspective when making their contemporary diagnoses. I suspect that the economic, physical and political dimensions of urban change are quite plausibly less today than they have been at previous times. In *social* terms cities are also probably as stable as they have ever been. This is largely because it is only within the last 150 years or so that cities have been self-recruiting. Before then, the scale of immigration required to maintain them led to permanent social currents flowing through the city, similar to those found in rapidly urbanizing cities in the Third World today.[5] Secondly, the dominant cities are no longer the only source of social mobility. Whilst it may be true that all those aspiring to the heights of, say, the legal profession have to pass some part of their careers in London, this would not be the case for engineers, university teachers or clergymen. Thus, I suspect that the migration flows for recruitment and social mobility are proportionately much less now than in medieval times. Most young people born in Bristol, Nottingham or London are likely to spend their whole lives in and around these places, keeping in touch with friends and relatives by public or private transport and the services of the Post Office.

THE SOCIO-ECONOMIC CHARACTERISTICS OF
CONTEMPORARY CITIES

Whilst I do not think that it is very helpful to characterize the contemporary city as necessarily having unusual or novel significance I would like to make some suggestions on why the problem may seem to be different. I list these summarily:

(a) *Physical separation of homes and work*
Whilst the average time of the journey to work may not have changed very much over the past fifty years, the combined effect of decentralization, the growth of municipal and large-scale speculative building and the development of land use planning has produced a more segregated urban spatial structure. The socio-economic characteristics of areas of cities show a uniformity which is reflected in stable voting patterns.[6] The break-up of this segregation is resisted by both political parties.[7] Working-class expansion into middle-class areas is resisted by the Conservative party and middle-class movement into working-class areas (or

gentrification as it has been called) is resisted by the Labour party. Change in patterns of segregation is universally resented by those with a vested interest in the political *status quo*.[8]

(b) The growth of owner-occupation

For the first time in our history the majority of our domestic properties are owner-occupied. The maintenance of property values and the possibility of making appreciable capital gains has become a dominant value. A family may gain more from the housing market in a few years than would be possible in savings from a lifetime of earnings. Thus any attempt by the state to reduce these values by public works detrimental to amenity meet with vigorous disapproval. Whilst Dr Arnold of Rugby might have hailed the coming of the railways as marking the end of feudalism, most see the coming of the motorways as the end of capital appreciation. The majority of the population thus has a vested interest in stability and non-change. This also has important implications for the status of publicly rented housing.

(c) The arrangement of urban land use

Town and Country Planning legislation developed through a series of acts, particularly in the last thirty years, largely to control the use of land in the interests of the property-owners. Peripheral expansion and central area development and redevelopment were limited and controlled. This preserved the amenity of those in the traditional upper-class commuter areas and forced the new army of white-collar commuters to travel in across the sterilized Green Belts in overcrowded trains from speculatively built private estates beyond. Restrictions on central area redevelopment in the immediate postwar years and then on office development in the 1960s created vast fortunes for property-developers, held central land values at a very high rate, maintained office rents well above those in other Western European countries and made it even more difficult for the ordinary wage-earner to live near the centre.[9] Visitors to Britain are generally impressed by the tidiness and neatness which our land use planning has created. This *noblesse oblige* element in property-defending capitalist land use planning has its echoes in the well-laid-out villages of semi-feudal England. (In the village in which

I live the squire put Gothic eaves and doors on cottages of a
variety of different periods in order to tidy it all up about a
century or so ago. The whole effect is so tidy we have all been
made a Conservation Area. Neatness and uniformity is similarly
rewarded in urban areas.) Perhaps I should add that I, too, would
wish to preserve the Regency terraces of Bath and so forth. The
point I am making is that the rest of society pays a high price for
its system of estate-management, or land use planning as it is
called.

(d) Aspirations for social planning

The development of the social sciences from the late 1950s and
the parallel expansion of higher education led to much teaching
and research of a mildly reformist hue, concerned with such
matters as 'equality of opportunity'. Starting with education in
the early 1950s and moving on to health services, children's
services, public housing, open space and physical accessibility
generally, the conclusions of these and many other research
studies were both similar and unsurprising. Those whose abilities
and income were least got least from the public services and
facilities that were said to be provided universally. This combination of lack of knowledge and lack of market power created a
problem for interventionists who wished to develop schemes of
'positive discrimination' in education, housing, welfare services
and so on. These schemes were generally unsuccessful and self-
defeating. Thus, for example, the more state schools were
improved, the more the middle class used them, their children
often profiting from fee-paying nursery schools before arrival
at age five. State schools used the successes of their middle-class
pupils who went on to higher education to justify the quality of
what they were doing. The proportion of working-class students
in universities has hardly changed over the past forty years.[10]
What is novel is not that *plus ça change plus c'est la même chose*,
but rather that change was expected in the first place. None of the
legislation which backs the activities of town planners is in any
way concerned with equality or positive discrimination. The
disjunction between the unrealistic aspirations based on reformist
social science training and the realities of a property-owning

capitalist society has led some to proclaim new versions of 'the crisis' and new versions of ameliorative measures.[11]

(e) *Urban planning and capital growth*

As mentioned in (c) above the public restriction on the supply of land has provided the basis for enormous capital gains. With restrictions on the *supply* of land and no restriction of its *price* the private gains have been greater than could be obtained in any other way. It was recently calculated in the *Sunday Times* (25 March 1973, p. 15) that one company – Land Securities – has probably made more than £500 million in the past seven years through capital appreciation and rent, which is equivalent to Britain's entire contribution to the Concorde project. Yet Land Securities will have paid tax of barely 2 per cent, as compared with the 40 per cent corporation tax, which would have been paid by a similarly placed industrial company over the same period. It is not my purpose here to expand on the importance of these developments for the development of British capitalism generally. It is sufficient to note that cities are providing the basic capital for a new generation of financial controllers and entrepreneurs whose activities have dominated the financial pages of our newspapers over the past decade. We need to know what the long-term economic impact of controlling office rents and nationalizing the development rights of land might be on our economy as a whole and on our competitive position in the EEC. The indications are that more national control will make us more competitive, not less.[12]

To summarize: much of what I am saying is not new, but simply emphasizes that the majority of the population has a vested interest in stability and non-change; planning legislation is largely concerned with buttressing property values, preserving 'amenity' and creating a tidy environment; urban managers and their supporting researchers have both over-estimated their powers of intervention and indulged in shrill polemics about the nature of the problem; British cities have provided enormous capital gains to property-developers and financial entrepreneurs and smaller but still appreciable capital gains to home-owners; it is uncertain whether this situation would be inevitable in any capitalist society; certainly a comparison with German cities would be extremely interesting.[13]

POLITICAL INFLUENCE

Research in the last two or three years has broken the pattern which had developed during the 1960s. During that period the urban research industry was mobilized towards an understanding of 'the urban system' so that 'planners' could intervene to push the system in the chosen direction of efficiency, equality or equity. Now, however, the limits of interventionism in social democracies have been well documented and discussed by Marris, Miller, Parkin, Rein and Scase, to name but a few, and it is becoming more clearly understood that rhetoric is little substitute for reality.[14] A burst of highly original research by Manuel Castells and his colleagues in Paris has helped us to see that the relationships of people to the means of production–distribution–consumption–communication and its overall administration (or the capitalist mode of *aménagement territoire*) is a more subtle basis for the exploitation of the workforce. The collective basis of the reproduction of the workforce is the focus of what he calls 'the urban question'. This focus on collective consumption and the coercive element of regional planning in capitalist society is refreshing.[15] David Harvey has provided a similar impetus to a growing school of radical geographers in Britain and the United States.[16] The generation of inequality in capitalist cities cannot be avoided by a few piecemeal reforms and this is not a point made only by the Left. Similar points have been made in more official and right-wing publications. President Nixon's advisers Banfield and Moynihan have published extensively showing the failures of interventionism.[17] The Layfield Report on the GLDP shows conclusively how inadequate and inept recent attempts at planning the employment structure of London have been.[18]

Faced with the fact that there is neither the political will nor the knowledge to intervene in order to avoid those with least skills and resources from getting a smaller share of urban facilities or 'goodies', baffled radicals turn to slogans about 'changing the system'. It is my view that in the next few years this bafflement will spread to other groups. This, perhaps, is the main element in urban change which is new and which is likely to have political consequences. At present the political activists are a long way behind the analysts I mentioned, but as an increasing proportion of the population is brought to see the symptoms of urban problems they may gradually come to see the causes. Putting it bluntly, the urban false consciousness which perceives a divorce between the control of the supply of land and other resources from the capitalist system is very unlikely to be maintained. This is what I see as the key social process. I am arguing not for a new definition of the problem but for a new awareness of the problem.

Earlier programmes of urban renewal or physical change affected the working class more than the middle class. Now with the suggestion that motorways should go through outer suburbia and with vaguely liberal middle-class groups getting drawn into inner-city problems an understanding of the redistributive elements in urban planning and management is developing. In London I think the Layfield Inquiry has led more people to see the limitations of and assumptions in planners' models and tools. Economists are seen to be right-wing or left-wing, transportation experts are seen to be supporters of public transport or supporters of private transport and so on. The professionals are seen, like the Emperor, to have no clothes. Some fear and deplore such a situation. If it helps to bring the politics back in then I think it should be welcomed. However, it is evident that when dealing at the level of symptoms it is very difficult for a clear political response to be articulated. There is a danger that a motorway scheme that involves knocking down working-class homes will be fought by the Labour party and one which affects middle-class amenity will be fought by the Conservative party. Yet now the Labour party has control of the GLC and has cancelled the motorway proposals it is not clear what it should do instead. There is no clear acceptance amongst economists that road pricing, as an alternative, would be progressive or regressive in its effects. The latent functions of free public transport have hardly been canvassed and so on. An obsession with symptoms has led political parties to avoid working on policies which might deal with causes.

My point is that the political philosophy of urban governance has failed. The only coherent philosophy is that of those who oppose change and uphold the capitalist values of property and markets. Planning has effectively served this value system together with most of those in the urban research industry and, indeed, perhaps most urban sociologists. At present there is no radical alternative. The basic political issues of urban development have got lost and discussion centres round *ad hoc* issues or symptoms of the problem more related to expediency than fundamental political differences. However, as the limits of interventionism become more widely understood and as a dissatisfaction with a political process that deals with symptoms and not causes grows, I would expect a more radical alternative to emerge. We may then have a return to genuine urban politics.

POLICY ALTERNATIVES

The urban political process is basically concerned with allocation, access, rent and property. At present the systems of allocation and accessibility reinforce the inequalities engendered by the division of labour or, at best, reflect them. The outstanding element of the urban process, as seen in London and other British cities over the past twenty years, is its ability to create massive fortunes for some property speculators.[19] A radical alternative would have to face the fundamental question of land values, development rights and rents. Now that noise and pollution in urban centres are declining and time is gaining in value for the middle and upper classes, centrality is gaining the value for residence which it lost during the earlier stages of industrialization. The classical Ricardian theories of capitalism on the ground are as relevant as they ever have been. There is little profit to be had from the poor so they must retreat from the centre to areas of lower land-values and commute back to their low-paid jobs in the centre. This familiar double penalty which gets compounded in so may ways is the inevitable consequence of the capitalist system.

Before retreating to our slogans about the inadequacy of our 'system' it would be as well to consider some of the dilemmas and difficulties that any urban administration must consider. Again I set these out in summary form:

(a) Allocation according to need

Various attempts have been made to measure 'need' without success. Self-defined need may not be the same as so-called objective need. We have no knowledge of any society which is sufficiently wealthy to allocate all urban resources according to need, even if it had thought it desirable. Experience from Eastern Europe has pointed up the difficulties. In housing, for example, which category has most 'need' to live near the centre – old people, lower-paid people or professional people? Similarly who has the greatest 'need' for dwellings with the best views or in areas of historic character?

If 'need' is not to be the sole basis for allocation who is to decide priorities? If certain 'key workers' are to be given privileged access who is to decide who these are and how are the more-informed and better-connected people prevented from using their social networks and informal contact to get priority in allocation?

Given scarce urban resources – and it is a reasonable assumption that that will always be the case – and given a sufficiently common value system for similar resources to be equally highly prized, allocation according to need is probably an impossibility, although, of course that does not prevent us from working towards it. Those most privileged in income and knowledge will always impede plans for positive discrimination.

(b) Spatial accessibility

Quite evidently, not everyone can live in an equally advantageous physical position in relation to all urban resources and facilities. Planners attempt to make spatial arrangements more convenient by bringing primary schools to areas where children of that age-group at present live or by encouraging industry to move where there are workers with the appropriate skills. But people age, and new skills are needed. One either accepts that the population will move house sufficiently readily to sift and sort themselves into an optimal pattern or the system of allocating urban facilities and the infrastructure is made more flexible. It is generally safer to assume that spatial inequality (in terms of accessibility) is inherent in society and that planners can do little about it. Attempts to minimize spatial inequality very often have latent consequences the reverse of those expected. The British New Town policy may provide a good example. The channelling of resources to skilled-manual-worker and green-field sites took away capital and professional expertises from inner city environments and the less-skilled workers.

(c) The problem of ownership

As long as it is possible to accumulate substantial capital gains through housing careers, and as long as this possibility is denied to a large proportion of manual workers the major inequality in our urban system will remain. Given different rewards from the division of labour there will always be opportunities for some to spend their resources on housing rather than holidays, other consumer goods or what have you. This is not, of course, a bad thing. It is when the capital gains derived from housing advantage a whole class in society at the expense of another that it has socially divisive consequences. One solution to the problem of ownership would be to reduce the scarcity value by producing a very high vacancy reserve in all labour market areas. However, since job opportunities vary differentially this might produce undesirable migration streams, since marginal gains in incomes would not necessarily be offset by housing costs. An alternative policy would be to make renting as attractive as owning. By providing cheap or free maintenance and services some might prefer the lack of responsibility of this type of tenure. The time saved and convenience offered might offset the more modest advantages of saving and investment in ownership. Certainly I see this tension between ownership and non-ownership increasing in the years ahead.

Equally problematic is the problem of capital gains and high rents which accrue from the urban centrality created by the community. Central city employers and property-developers do not pay the social costs they incur and gain disproportionate income and capital advantage. If the state nationalized inner-city land, the problem of allocation would still remain. On what criteria would sites be allocated and rents fixed? A theory of market rents has to be imputed if it is not there. There is no socialist theory of the city which would help us to solve this practical problem. Alternative principles of allocation are lacking. What land uses 'need' to have central sites? In the same way that ownership would have to lose some of its attractiveness relative to renting, so, too, would centrality have to be devalued. Yet attempts in Eastern Europe to devalue centrality have singularly failed. A very heavy rent and asset tax, assessed annually, would probably work more equitably than state ownership of the land. I consider that the taxing of resources gained through the manipulation of the urban system could be considerably developed. Yet such fiscal measures hardly figure in current urban political debates.

Quite evidently, we are in no position to shout slogans about the present system or to assert what obvious principles we would apply if our present pattern of constraints were removed. The constraints of large-scale bureaucratic allocation would be equally great. Even if income differentials are reduced, knowledge differentials and spatial inequalities remain. It is curious how little the urban inequalities figure in any systematic way in political debate. Partly I attribute this to the vested interests of the majority category of owner–occupiers and partly I suggest that people are simply not aware of the systematic redistribution of real income, which the management of the urban system entails. It is also curious that the conventional wisdom should continue to associate interventionism – and planning in particular – as redistributive or concerned with 'social' ends. Perhaps I should explain a British euphemism: in the nineteenth century the exploitation of the poor was referred to as 'the social question'. Now the Department of the Environment, local authorities and consultants refer to 'social aspects' of structure planning, which most frequently means inner-city poverty. This need not, of course, necessarily be the case.[20] Planning is an essential tool of the capitalist order; planning lawyers see this most clearly; young activist planners say it is but do not really believe it.

CONCLUSION

If urban problems are partly a product of capitalist modes of production and partly created by 'modern big cities', then ameliorism must fail. I have argued that political debate is more concerned with stability and non-change and that this is due to the massive commitment to the ownership of property and its appreciation and the lack of knowledge about the systematic distributional effects of urban allocative structures. I see statutory land use planning as basically concerned with the allocation of use of land and as having created vast fortunes for capitalist entrepreneurs. Planners have tidied up the physical urban scene so that one might see them as the estate handymen of the major property-owners. Those who have been able to be genuinely discriminatory in favour of the disadvantage have done this, in spite of, not because of, their enabling legislation. Planners should make clear the distributional effects of what they propose, but very few do. Perhaps there is a case for a revision in professional conventions and codes of practice so that no matter what the specific Acts demand, planners would have a professional obligation to make public the distributional effects of alternative plans.

The basis of a political sociology of urban life is emerging in France and urban social movements are emerging which are articulating the injustices of the oppressed urban populations. Yet no clear radical alternative to the capitalist city has emerged. Recent publications describing the situation in China provide enthusiasts with little comfort.[21] Cities seem to be tied more closely to capitalism than is the productive system. By their very scale and complexity they give every support for Michels' thesis on the iron law of oligarchy.[22] If there has been an 'urban managerial revolution' aided and abetted by the Institute for Local Government Studies, the Centre for Environmental Studies and so forth, then I suspect the new urban corporate managers will serve capitalism more efficiently and effectively than ever. The Labour party and the trades unions have no concept of the complexity of the issues and their energies are largely focused on earned income, not on real income. We are a long way from urban collective bargaining. Hence there is no real debate on *urban* politics. The question 'Whose City?' is more often posed than answered. I very much hope that by international discussions and comparisons some clearer conception of a radical or alternative city may emerge.

REFERENCES

1 For London in the fourteenth and fifteenth centuries see Thrupp, Sylvia L., *The Merchant Class of Medieval London*, University of Michigan Press, Chicago, 1948, and for the eighteenth century George, M. Dorothy, *London Life in the Eighteenth Century*, 1925, reissued by Penguin Books, Harmondsworth, 1966.

2 Nineteenth-century examples may be found in Dyos, H. J. (ed.), *The Study of Urban History*, Arnold, 1968. See also Jones, G. Stedman, *Outcast London*, Clarendon Press, Oxford, 1971.

3 See, in particular, Kellett, John R., *The Impact of Railways on Victorian Cities*, Routledge & Kegan Paul, 1969. For a vivid account of different social effects see Coleman, T., *The Railway Navvies*, Hutchinson, 1965, and Penguin Books, Harmondsworth, 1968.

4 See Dyos, H. J., 'The speculative builders and developers of Victorian London', in *Victorian Studies*, 1968, Vol. XI, Supplement pp. 641–90, and the references therein. In general see Chapman, S. D. (ed.), *The History of Working Class Housing*, David & Charles, Newton Abbot, 1971.

5 For a very striking exemplification of this point see Wrigley, E. A., 'A simple model of London's importance in changing English society and economy 1650–1750', in *Past and Present*, No. 37, 1967, 44–70. For the early nineteenth century see the very interesting and detailed account in Anderson, M., *Family Structure in Nineteenth Century Lancashire*, Cambridge University Press, 1971.

6 For an account of segregation in London see the chapter by J. H. Westergaard in *London Aspects of Change*, Centre for Urban Studies (ed.), MacGibbon & Kee, 1964, and more recently the GLC paper for the GLDP Inquiry S11/113, 'Some aspects of the polarization issue', and Norman, P., 'Third survey of London life and labour: a new typology of London districts', in *Quantitative*

Ecological Analysis in the Social Sciences, Doggan, M., and Rokkan, S. (eds.), MIT Press, Cambridge, Mass., 1969.

7 There is a large literature on urban voting behaviour. For an extremely interesting and provocative account see Hindess, B., *The Decline of Working Class Politics*, Paladin Books and Mac-Gibbon & Kee, 1971.

8 A good account of the Labour party's defence of the *status quo* in London is given in Smallwood, Frank, *Greater London: The Politics of Metropolitan Reform*, Bobbs-Merrill, Indianapolis, Ind., 1965.

9 See Marriott, O., *The Property Boom*, Hamish Hamilton, 1967; Pahl, R. E., 'Poverty and the urban system', in *Spatial Policy Problems of the British Economy*, Chisholm, M., and Manners, G. (eds.), Cambridge University Press, 1971, and *The Recurrent Crisis of London*, Counter Information Service, London, 1973.

10 See the brief comments and statistical tables in the Annual Reports of the Universities Central Council for Admissions (UCCA).

11 For a general review of the inadequacy of reform in the late 1960s see the collection of essays, *Labour and Inequality*, Townsend, P., and Bosanquet, N. (eds.), Fabian Society, London, 1972.

12 The growth of monopolistic national companies is forecast with great confidence by G. D. Newbould and A. S. Jackson in *The Receding Ideal*, Guthstead, Liverpool, 1972. The political implications are enormous.

13 See the German contributions to Rose, R. (ed), *The Management of Urban Change in Britain and Germany*, Sage Publications, London, 1974.

14 This material is still largely in unpublished drafts which have been circulated from the Centre for Environmental Studies. However, Frank Parkin's *Class Inequality and Political Order*, MacGibbon & Kee, 1971, opens up the argument boldly.

15 Castells, M., *La Question urbaine*, Maspero, Paris, 1972. See also the journal *Espaces et Sociétés*.

16 Harvey, D., 'Society, the city and the space economy of urbanism', American Association of Geographers' Commission on College Geography, Paper No. 18, 1972. See also the journal *Antipode* and Harvey's forthcoming volume of essays.

17 Banfield, E., *The Unheavenly City*, Little, Brown, Boston, 1970. Moyniham, D. P., *Maximum Feasible Misunderstanding*, Collier-Macmillan, 1969.

18 Greater London Development Plan, *Report of the Panel of Inquiry*, Vol. I, Ch. 5, HMSO, 1973.

19 See *The Recurrent Crisis of London*.
20 Few people make any attempt to teach planners anything further than to associate 'problem' with 'poverty'. It would be more accurate to assert that the problems of our big cities are a product of affluence and inequitable concentrations of wealth. A worthy attempt to remedy this situation has been made by J. B. Cullingworth in two recent books: *Problems of an Urban Society*, Vols. I and II, Allen & Unwin, 1973. However these volumes are not radical and do not directly address themselves to the issues raised in this paper.
21 Lewis, J. W. (ed.), *The City in Communist China*, chapter by Salaff, Stanford University Press, Cal., 1971; Luccioni, M., 'Processus revolutionnaire et organisation de l'espace en Chine – vers la fin des séparations entre villes et campagne', in *Espaces et Sociétés*, 5, 1972, 63–104.
22 Michels, R., *Political Parties*, Collier, 1962.

Epilogue

'On the distributional systems of ice cream on a uniform sandy beach'

Let us assume in all cases a warm sunny day, a sandy beach and people of all ages scattered fairly regularly along it. The problem is to provide them with ice cream under capitalist, socialist and Maoist principles. What distributive system would serve each power structure most appropriately and how would the spatial forms vary?

In the capitalist system the state has passed legislation preventing a monopoly. Thus two ice-cream-sellers are on the beach. There may have been more smaller operators offering ice cream of various sorts and qualities in the past. Over time, however, as a result of mergers, takeovers and bankruptcies only the two remain. Each is unwilling to allow the other to have access to any market in which the one might gain at the expense of the other. Hence, whilst it might be more convenient for the customer to have an ice-cream-seller closer than half a beach-length away, neither capitalist operator is prepared to move away from the centre point of the beach. To do so would risk losing more than half the market. The consequences of such an arrangement would probably be tacit price-fixing agreements. The state would tend to support the spatial pattern by directing the access road and by concentrating other beach facilities to the centre point. The effect of this would be to attract a higher concentration of population, especially those with young children, towards the centre of the beach. This, in turn, would encourage vendors of other commodities eagerly seeking the opportunities for making profits.

Under socialism such territorial injustice would not be countenanced. Given that no extra resources can be devoted to the distribution of ice cream in the early years, it nevertheless seems necessary to decentralize in order to improve the accessibility structure for those on the ends of the beach. The socialist planners conclude that each ice cream outlet should be two-thirds of the way along the beach. In this way no one will be more than a third of a beach-length away from ice cream, as opposed to the possibility of half a beach-length under capitalism. In order to be sure that each ice-cream-seller has exactly the same quality of product, the state would probably employ a quality-checker to make sure that the fixed price-level guaranteed a standard quality. Since the wages of the ice-cream-sellers would not be related to the amount of ice cream sold there would be a danger that some sellers would prefer to go swimming than to stay in the stuffy ice-cream-dispensing hut. There might therefore be temptations to reduce stock or price in order to sell out more quickly and thus gain more leisure time. The fertile minds of the two vendors might devise more ingenious ways of working the system to their advantage by various forms of collusion. The state system of checking might have to be increased in the absence of genuine socialist consciousness amongst the state ice-cream-vendors. This might increase the cost of ice cream. In order to economize it might be necessary to have but one ice-cream-seller who would obviously move to the centre of the beach. The young people would say that the old territorial injustices of capitalism had reappeared.

Under Maoist Communism the whole notion of state-controlled ice cream manufacture and distribution is open to question. The people can make their own ice cream: let a hundred flavours freeze! By contriving ingenious methods of insulation with old newspapers, a simple mass-produced thermos container is devised and each family is able to have its own supply of ice cream on the beach. All take their turn at making ice cream – but some unhappy families with incompetent ice-cream-makers rarely taste anything resembling the commodity it is understood once existed under other political systems. Nevertheless, despite a wide variation in the quality of the homely ice cream, the people believe that there is no inequality of the *distribution* of ice cream and they are content with their system of territorial justice for a time. However, some of the younger people, who taste the various sorts of home-made ice cream as they make comradely contact with their fellows, begin to consider it unfair that some families should provide themselves with privileged taste-sensations. Clearly injustice does exist: some ice cream is better than others.

There is no alternative but to forbid the consumption of ice cream on the beach in the interests of egalitarian principles and for the good of all. Water quenches thirst better and is also better for health. Unfortunately, there is only one water tap on the beach and it is exactly in the middle. The people wisely decide to erect a public convenience close to the tap. Other facilities, such as a store for beach shades, are put at the central location. In time, as the people become more prosperous they start to complain ... The young people want ice cream ... An old woman who remembers the recipe sets up a stall ...

More about Penguins and Pelicans

Penguinews, which appears every month, contains details of all the new books issued by Penguins as they are published. From time to time it is supplemented by *Penguins in Print*, which is a complete list of all titles available. (There are some five thousand of these.)

A specimen copy of *Penguinews* will be sent to you free on request. For a year's issues (including the complete lists) please send 50p if you live in the British Isles, or 75p if you live elsewhere. Just write to Dept EP, Penguin Books Ltd, Harmondsworth, Middlesex, enclosing a cheque or postal order, and your name will be added to the mailing list.

In the U.S.A.: For a complete list of books available from Penguin in the United States write to Dept CS, Penguin Books Inc., 7110 Ambassador Road, Baltimore, Maryland 21207.

In Canada: For a complete list of books available from Penguin in Canada write to Penguin Books Canada Ltd, 41 Steelcase Road West, Markham, Ontario.